GWYNNE DYER

CRAWLING FROM THE WRECKAGE

RANDOM HOUSE CANADA

www.randomhouse.ca

Random House Canada and colophon are registered trademarks.

Library and Archives Canada Cataloguing in Publication

Dyer, Gwynne
    Crawling from the wreckage / Gwynne Dyer.

Also available in electronic format.

ISBN 978-0-307-35891-2

        1. History, Modern—21st century—Miscellanea. 2. World politics—2005–2015—Miscellanea. I. Title.

D862.D93 2010   909.83   C2010-901386-7

Design by Andrew Roberts

Printed in the United States of America

10 9 8 7 6 5 4 3 2 1

CONTENTS

If I could be a fictional character, I think I would choose to be Hari Seldon, the "psychohistorian" in Isaac Asimov's Foundation series who devised a scientific method to predict the future of human civilization, and to steer it onto better courses. Since that does not appear to be an available option, I make do with being a newspaper columnist, and plod on with my highly unscientific analyses of where our collective actions are leading us. It keeps me busy and it feeds my family, so I shouldn't complain.

I did spend a lot of time complaining during the past decade, however, because it seemed to me that just about everything was going wrong. Stupid wars, obsessions about terrorism, denial about climate change, rapacious turbo-capitalism and lies, lies, lies: from 2001 to 2005, it just got worse and worse. When I published a collection of my columns from that time, I called it *With Every Mistake* [We Must Surely Be Learning]. The lawyers made us drop the latter part of the quote for fear of infringing on George Harrison's copyright, but the truth is that I didn't really think we were learning at all. Just making more and more mistakes, and putting the future more and more at risk. It was a bad time.

So, here we are in 2010, and I must admit that I feel a lot better. The world is not a perfect place, nor even a safe and happy one, but that sense of sliding out of control towards ten different kinds of disaster has gone. This book is called *Crawling from the Wreckage*, not "The Broad and Sunlit Uplands," because we still have a long way to go, but I think Hari Seldon would agree that the prospects have improved considerably. We must be doing something right. What is it?

That is the theme of this book, to the extent that a collection of columns can really be said to have a theme. I have ransacked the five hundred or so articles I wrote during the past five years for clues to how and why we turned the corner, just as in the previous book I looked for the reasons why things had gotten so bad. This time it has been a much more pleasant task.

So you will find that inquisitive strand running through this book, but don't expect miracles. Causation in history is the slipperiest of commodities, and identifying the causes of good outcomes is much harder than determining the causes of disasters.

Most disasters are clearly delineated events that are finite in time and space, and the proximate causes are generally choices made by a relatively small number of decision makers. You can actually put names to the people, policies and organizations that were responsible for the incompetent response to the inundation of New Orleans in 2005 or the financial meltdown of 2008. Whereas positive outcomes are more diffuse and less dramatic, and we in the media rarely launch a hunt for those who were responsible.

Suppose all of our current worries go away: climate change is contained before it causes really big catastrophes; China and India take their places as the world's biggest and third-biggest powers without violent resistance from the other powers being demoted (like the United States), and they behave responsibly in their new roles; Iran doesn't build a bomb; the Israelis and Palestinians make a peace deal that sticks; and post-occupation Iraq lives happily ever after. It could all happen, although the odds are long against it. Still, some of it probably will happen: not everything that we worry about in today's world will actually come to pass in tomorrow's. As they say in the financial world, "goldbugs" (pessimistic investors who flee to gold for safety) have successfully predicted eleven of the last three recessions. So the present moment, which seems rife with possibilities for good and evil, may not actually be the hinge of fate on which all of the future hangs. In which case, what we do now shouldn't matter much—or does it?

Good outcomes get less attention than bad ones and their parentage is harder to discern, but they do have causes. Somebody, or some large number of people, made the right decisions and not the wrong ones, which is why we are here and not in a much worse place. But on the positive side of the ledger it is hard to pin down who and when and where, and, to make things more difficult, we do not know what will happen in the near future.

If I were writing this introduction exactly a century ago, for a hypothetical collection of my columns written from 1905 to 1910, I would be completely ignorant of the fact that the worst war in history was going to break out in 1914. I would not look for the remote causes of that war in the events of my own time because I would not know where the tide of those events was taking us.

I am therefore engaged in an essentially futile pursuit, because what I try to do in these columns is draw connections between a present that I only half understand and a future that I do not know. But I was trained as an historian, and I still think like one. I believe that actions have consequences, and I cannot help trying to trace the threads of causation that reach out from current events into the future. I go on doing it even though I know how capricious history can be. Welcome to my obsession.

NOWHERE TO GO BUT UP

History doesn't really have a plot, and even the patterns that we imagine we see depend mainly upon our own standpoint. The arc of the past five years would seem very different from a Chinese perspective than from a Western one, and different again from a Middle Eastern one. But from my Western perspective, our recent history is about a painfully slow re-covery from a very bad time.

So, here are some articles about the United States, because that country still sets the tone. I've been going to the U.S. fairly frequently for most of my life, but it never felt as alien as it did in 2004. They were even going to re-elect George Bush. How could they possibly have failed to notice?

I was starting to lose patience — and then my son Owen (aka "Nameless") put me back on track.

October 21, 2004
ANOTHER ENDORSEMENT FOR BUSH

Russian President Vladimir Putin wants George W. Bush to be re-elected, Osama bin Laden undoubtedly wants him to be re-elected, and the head of Iran's Supreme National Security Council has just endorsed him for re-election, so it's hardly surprising that one of my sons has done the same. He must remain nameless, of course, but he has given me permission to quote his exact words on the subject of Mr. Bush's candidacy: "He has sown the wind; let him reap the whirlwind."

This nameless offspring of mine has never worked for the KGB, planned terrorist attacks or been nominated as a member of the "Axis of Evil," but he does share with the three gentlemen above a rather Machiavellian turn of mind. His point is that Iraq will go to hell and the U.S. economy will run into heavy weather in the next four years no matter who is president. Those things are already practically set in stone—so let the man who actually caused them carry the can.

There is no way that Iraqi hostility to the American occupation can be turned around at this point, and the current outbreak of fiscal irresponsibility in the U.S.—a huge budget deficit and a huge trade deficit, amounting to almost half a trillion dollars each—will certainly result in a great deal of economic pain and misery for ordinary Americans in the coming years. We all know who got the U.S. into Iraq and who created the budget deficit, but the man who is president when military defeat and economic crisis can no longer be denied will bear the political blame.

The main concern of Nameless was that a Kerry election victory, followed by a humiliating scuttle from Iraq and a crash in the U.S. dollar at home, would generate a "Dolchstoss" myth on the American right. He was referring to the alleged "stab in the back" by the German left that was used to explain Germany's defeat in the First World War. (In fact, the German left had loyally supported the war, but had little say in its conduct—until, after Germany's generals admitted irretrievable military defeat on the Western Front, the government was swiftly handed over to the Social Democrats, so that they could surrender and take the blame.)

The Dolchstoss myth, which denied that it had been a mistake to start the war and instead blamed Germany's defeat on a failure of will, poisoned all subsequent efforts to create a healthy democratic republic on German soil. No analogy is perfect, but similar myths exist in U.S. politics.

Many on the American right still believe that the Vietnam War could have been won if only the spineless traitors on the left had not weakened American "resolve"—and they say this even though President Richard Nixon, who was elected on a promise to end the Vietnam War and presided over the whole latter phase of it, was a Republican. What could they do with a lost war on a Democratic president's watch?

My son's point was that the mess created by the last administration cannot be fixed and forgotten before the 2008 election, no matter who wins next month—so why not vote for George W. Bush to ensure that the blame is pinned on the right man? That way, there can be no "stab-in-the-back" legend that haunts the Democratic Party in years to come, or that fuels a drive by hard-right radicals flying the Republican banner to regain the White House in 2008.

The downside of this, from a Democratic point of view, is four more years out of executive power, a Supreme Court packed with Bush appointees, and significant damage to both America's reputation and the U.S. economy. The negative consequences from Iraq's point of view are even bigger: years more of violence and death.

It is Hobson's choice, and I am almost glad I do not have a vote in this election: it saves me from the responsibility of choice. If I were an American, however, I would probably abandon all these "tactical" voting calculations: one look at Vice-President Dick Cheney and you know that it's just not worth the risk.

Sin comentario.

November 3, 2004
THE DIVIDED STATES: A MODEST PROPOSAL

Looking at that extraordinary electoral map of the United States with all the liberal, quiche-eating, Kerry-supporting states of the northeast and the west coast coloured Democratic blue, while the "heartland" and the south are solid Republican red, the solution to the problem suddenly occurred to me: "Blueland" should join Canada.

It is getting harder for the two tribes of Americans to understand or even tolerate each other. Once again, as in 2000, the country is divided with almost mathematical precision into two halves, one of which adores President George W. Bush while the other loathes him. And it goes far deeper than mere personalities or even the old left-right split; the clash now is about social norms and fundamental values, about which few are willing to compromise.

Opinions on the foreign issues that seemed to dominate the election — the war in Iraq and the "war on terror" — just mapped onto that existing cultural division. People who go to church regularly and oppose abortion and gay marriage were also far more likely to believe that U.S. troops had found weapons of mass destruction in Iraq and that Saddam Hussein had sponsored the terrorists of 9/11, so they voted for Mr. Bush. People who don't hold such beliefs, didn't.

"Irreconcilable" is the word that springs to mind. Two separate populations have evolved in the U.S., and they are increasingly unhappy living together.

One subspecies, *Homo canadiensis*, thinks universal health care is a good idea, would rather send peacekeepers than bombers, and longs for the wimpy, wispy liberalism enjoyed by their neighbours to the north. The other breed, *Homo iraniensis*, prefers the full-blooded religious certainties and the militant political slogans — "Death to [fill in the blank]" — that play such a large and fulfilling part in Iranian public life.

It is cruel to force these two populations to go on living together, especially since American political life has lost its centre and now pits these two irreconcilable opposites directly against each other in a winner-takes-all election every four years. Since the pseudo-Iranians slightly out-number the proto-Canadians, the obvious solution is for the latter group actually to go to Canada — and indeed, I have lost count of the number of American friends who have told me that if George W. Bush wins again, they are going to move to Canada.

There are problems with this solution, however. A mass migration northwards would leave large chunks of the U.S. virtually empty, and the parts of Canada where people can live in any comfort are pretty full already. Besides, the winters in Canada really are severe, and Californians might not be up to the challenge. Then, looking at the two-colour map of the electoral outcome, the solution hit me. You don't have to move the people; just move the border.

It would all join up just fine: the parts of the U.S. inhabited by *Homo canadiensis* all lie along the Canadian border or next to other states that do (although the blue bit dangles down a long, long way in the case of the Washington-Oregon-California strip fondly known as the Left Coast). True, the U.S. would lose its whole Pacific coast, but we could arrange for an American free port in, say, Tijuana. Plus, lots of Canadians could move to a warmer clime without actually having to leave their country.

At the global level, everybody else would be quite happy with a bigger Canada and a smaller United States. That smaller U.S. would have to pull in its horns a bit, as it would no longer have the money to maintain military bases in every country on the planet, but it would retain enough resources to invade someone every year or so. And the new Canadians would be free to have abortions, enter into gay marriages, do stem-cell research and engage in all the other wickednesses that flourish in Canada. They could even speak French if they wanted to.

No solution is perfect: there would be limp-wristed liberals trapped in the U.S. and God-fearing rednecks who suddenly found themselves in Canada, so some degree of population exchange would be necessary. It's even possible that a few right-wing bits of Canada—parts of Alberta, for example—might prefer to join the U.S. But you can't make an omelette without breaking some eggs, and think how happy everybody will be when they are living exclusively among like-minded people.

Fast-forward four years, and the Bush era is finally stumbling to a close. A man we had barely heard of four years ago is heading for the White House, and we are all trying to figure out whether he can really make a difference. How much of the disaster has been the personal fault of Bush and his friends, and how much is implicit in the system?

May 7, 2008
PRESIDENT OBAMA

It is now a near certainty that Obama will be the next American president. The media will try to maintain the illusion of a race for the Democratic nomination until Senator Hillary Clinton finally retires from the race—which may not be until the convention in August—because such an illusion helps to fill the awful gap between the twenty-four-hour news cycle and the actual amount of news available. But, as leading independent pollster John Zogby put it on Wednesday, "To all intents and purposes the race for the Democratic nomination is over."

Having seen off the Hard Man of the Democratic Party, Obama must now defeat the Hard Man of the Republican Party in November. (Senator Hillary Clinton promised to "obliterate" Iran if it attacks Israel; Senator John McCain has threatened North Korea with "extinction.") But it will be hard for Obama to lose while the United States is plunging into a deep recession and the Republican candidate is still shackled to the Bush administration's wars in Iraq and Afghanistan.

So Obama gets the presidency—and then what? He will probably be able to depend on solid Democratic majorities in both houses of Congress but he will inherit a ravaged economy and two lost wars, so he has little room for expensive domestic reforms or dramatic initiatives abroad. Also, he will not be able to cut bloated U.S. military spending, so there is no early "peace bonus" waiting for him on the fiscal front.

Like Bill Clinton before him, Obama will ultimately have the job of repairing the huge budget deficit bequeathed to him by his Republican predecessor, but the only step he can take in the short run is to roll back the huge Bush tax cuts for the rich. So what else can the Democrats do in the meantime that doesn't cost too much?

Obama has said very little about this during his campaign (and Hillary Clinton, haunted by her failure to reform health care in her husband's first term as president, has said even less). But the fact that one-sixth of the American population has no access to high-quality medical care is an astonishing failure in a rich democracy, and Obama has travelled enough to see it for the scandal that it is. He may be unconvincing as a gun-loving, truck-driving, fast-food-addicted son of toil, but he is the candidate of the American poor, even if many of the white poor don't recognize him as such. No single reform would do as much to improve the lives of poor Americans as a fully comprehensive health-care system that is free at the point of delivery. Obama has given us few clues about his intentions but my money says that this will be his first priority in domestic affairs. He might even succeed.

Well, I got that right. I just never imagined that it would take up a full year of congressional time, while everything else had to wait. Neither did he. But I'm a much happier camper now. Let nobody tell you that the United States doesn't matter anymore.

2

AFGHANISTAN: VIETNAM FOR SLOW LEARNERS

As expected, I found lots of pieces on Afghanistan when I surveyed the five years' worth of articles for this book. But there weren't many I could use, because they all said essentially the same few things. You can do endless colour pieces full of human stories: as a private soldier wrote home from another war half a century ago, "Men are never so loving or so lovable as they are in action." But that doesn't change from one war or one army to the next, and it doesn't change the fact that the war will kill or maim many of those soldiers in the end, so we owe it to them to talk about the politics and strategy of the conflict they find themselves in. Unfortunately, there just isn't a lot to say about the war in Afghanistan at the political and strategic level, except that it is unwinnable and unnecessary.

July 10, 2006
SAME WAR, DIFFERENT PLAYERS

1839, 1878, 1979, 2001: four foreign invasions of Afghanistan in less than two hundred years. The first two were British, and unashamedly imperialist. The third was Soviet, and the invaders said they were there to defend socialism and help Afghanistan become a modern, prosperous state. The last was American, and the invaders said they were there to bring democracy and help Afghanistan become a modern, prosperous state. But all four invasions were doomed to fail (although the last one still has some time to run).

When Britain deployed 3,300 troops to Helmand province early last month, then defence secretary John Reid said: "We hope we will leave Afghanistan without firing a single shot." But six British soldiers have been killed in combat since then, and the new defence secretary, Des Browne, announced on Monday that the British force is being increased by another nine hundred soldiers to cope with "unexpected" resistance.

The story is the same across southern Afghanistan. The Canadian army has lost six soldiers killed in action in Kandahar province since late April, and may soon face the same choice between reinforcing its troops or pulling them back.

A country that has been invaded four times in less than two centuries is bound to know a couple of things about dealing with foreign conquerors, and the first thing Afghans have learned is never to trust foreigners, no matter how pure they say their intentions are. There are probably no people in the world more xenophobic than the Afghans, and they have earned the right to be so. If there was ever a window of opportunity for the current crop of invaders to convince Afghans that this time is different it closed some time ago.

The other thing Afghans know is how to deal with invaders. Invaders will always be richer and better armed, so let them occupy the country. Don't try to hold the cities; instead, fade back into the mountains. Take a couple of years to regroup and set up your supply lines (this time around, mostly across the border from Pakistan), and then start the guerrilla war in earnest. Ambush, harass and bleed the foreigners for as long as it takes. Eventually they will cut their losses and go home.

It has worked every time, and it will work again. Des Browne remarked plaintively last week that "the very act of [British] deployment into the south has energized opposition." But the reality is that the rural areas of Helmand province, like most of the Pashto-speaking provinces of the south and southeast, have been under the effective control of the resistance for several years. The arrival of foreign troops in these areas simply gives the insurgents more targets to attack.

The endgame is beginning, even in Kabul. Hamid Karzai, the West's chosen leader for Afghanistan, is now starting to make deals with the forces that will hold his life in their hands once the foreigners leave: the warlords and drug barons. In April, he dropped many candidates who had been approved by the "coalition" powers from a list of new provincial police chiefs, and replaced their names with those of known gangsters and criminals who work for the local warlords. He will also have to talk to the Taliban before long.

The "Taliban" that Western troops are now fighting in Afghanistan is more inclusive than the narrow band of fanatics who imposed order on the country in 1996, after seven years of civil war. The current Afghan resistance movement includes farmers trying to protect their poppy fields, nationalists furious at the foreign presence and young men who just want to show that they are as brave as previous generations of Afghans. In other words, the Afghan fighters have the usual grab bag of motives that fuels any national resistance movement.

Nor should we assume that the regime that eventually emerges in Kabul after the foreigners have gone home will resemble the old Taliban, a Pakistani-backed and almost entirely Pashto-speaking organization. The foreign invasion overthrew the long domination of the Pashto-speakers in Afghanistan (about 40 percent of the population), and it is most unlikely that Tajiks, Hazaras, Uzbeks and Turkmen will accept that domination again. Their own warlords will have to have a share of the power, too, and even Karzai might find a role.

Post-occupation Afghanistan will certainly live under strict Islamic law, but there is no reason to believe that it would export Islamist revolution of the al-Qaeda brand. Even the old Taliban regime never did that; it gave hospitality to Osama bin Laden and his gang, but it almost certainly had no knowledge of his plans for 9/11, and on other issues it was often open to Western pressure. In early 2001, for example, the former Taliban regime shut down the whole heroin industry in Afghanistan, simply by shooting enough poppy farmers to frighten the rest into obedience.

Afghanistan will not be left to its own devices until after the people who ordered the invasion leave office: presumably next year for Tony Blair, and January 2009 for George W. Bush. There is time for lots of killing yet, but Afghanistan stands a reasonable chance of sorting itself out once the Western armies leave.

I would stand by everything in that article, except that it's clearly going to take more time for the Western armies to pull out of Afghanistan.

October 5, 2007
A WAR WON AND LOST

This week is the sixth anniversary of the start of U.S. air strikes against al-Qaeda and its Taliban hosts in Afghanistan. It was a very clever politico-military operation, and by December 2001 all of Afghanistan was under the control of the United States and its local allies for a total cost of twelve American dead.

In the days just after 9/11, George Tenet, the Central Intelligence Agency's chief, came up with a bold proposal. Why invade Afghanistan with a large American army, deploying massive firepower that kills large numbers of locals and alienates the population? Why give Osama bin Laden the long anti-American guerrilla war that he was undoubtedly counting on?

Instead, Tenet proposed sending teams of CIA agents and special forces into the country to win the support of the various ethnic militias, loosely linked as the Northern Alliance, that still dominated Afghanistan's northern regions. Although the Taliban had controlled most of the country since 1996, they had never decisively won the civil war. So why not intervene in that war, shower the opponents of the Taliban with money and weapons, and tip the balance against the regime?

It worked like a charm. Pakistan, whose intelligence services had originally created the Taliban, withdrew its support. The Northern Alliance's forces advanced, the US Air Force bombed wherever they met resistance, the regime fled Kabul, and most of the Taliban troops melted back into their villages. The government of a country of twenty-seven million people was taken down for a death toll that probably did not exceed four thousand on all sides.

By mid-December 2001, the United States effectively controlled Afghanistan through its local allies, all drawn from the northern minority groups: the Tajiks, Uzbeks and Hazara. There had not been the mass killing of innocent bystanders that would inevitably have accompanied a conventional U.S. invasion, so there was no guerrilla war. The traditional ruling group and biggest minority, the Pashtuns, who had put their money on the Taliban and lost, would have to be brought back into the game somehow, but the usual Afghan deal-making should take care of that.

Washington had the wit to make Hamid Karzai, a Pashtun from a clan that had never had much to do with the Taliban, its puppet president in Kabul, but it didn't follow the same logic in its broader policy towards the Pashtuns. It froze out all the prominent Pashtun political and religious leaders who had had dealings with the Taliban—which was, of course, almost all of them.

The Taliban had been the government of Afghanistan for almost five years, and were at the time the political vehicle of the Pashtun ascendancy in the country. If you were a traditional Pashtun leader, how could you not have had dealings with them? An amnesty that turned a blind eye to the past, plus pressure by the United States on its recent allies to grant the Pashtuns a fair share of the national pie, would have created a regime in Kabul to which Pashtuns could give their loyalty, even if they were less dominant at the centre than usual. But that never happened.

The United States confused the Taliban with al-Qaeda and would not talk to Pashtun leaders who had been linked to the Taliban. Six years after the invasion that wasn't, the Pashtuns are still largely frozen out. That is why the Taliban are coming back.

Afghanistan has generally been run by regional and tribal warlords with little central control: nothing new there. But now it is also a country where the biggest minority has been largely excluded from power by foreign invaders who sided with the smaller minorities, and then blocked the process of accommodation by which the various Afghan ethnic groups normally make power-sharing deals.

The current fighting in the south, the Pashtun heartland, which is causing a steady dribble of American, British and Canadian casualties, will continue until these Western countries pull out. (Most other NATO [North Atlantic Treaty Organization] members sent their troops to various parts of northern Afghanistan, where non-Pashtun warlords rule non-Pashtun populations and nobody wants to attack the foreigners.) When the foreigners have finally pulled out of the south, the Afghans will make the traditional inter-ethnic deals and something like peace will return.

Will Karzai still be the president after that? Yes, if he can convince the Pashtuns that he is open to such a deal once the foreigners leave.

Will the Taliban come back to power? No, only to a share of power, and only to the extent that they can still command the loyalty of the Pashtuns. Their hold on Pashtun loyalties may dwindle once they are no longer leading a resistance movement against foreign occupation.

Will Osama bin Laden return and recreate a "nest of terrorists" in Afghanistan? Very unlikely. The Afghans paid too high a price for their hospitality the first time round.

By the time I wrote the next article, in 2009, there was something new in the equation: Barack Obama was the president of the United States, and there were deeply worrisome signs that he was buying into the Washington orthodoxy about the war in Afghanistan. His appointment of a new general and the latter's declaration of a "new" strategy in Afghanistan seemed to indicate that Obama had drunk the Kool-Aid.

May 11, 2009
CHANGING GENERALS IN MIDSTREAM

There is always a high turnover of generals in wartime. Some get replaced because they turn out to be no good at the job, but many others are changed because they have failed at a task that was beyond anybody's ability to accomplish.

They are fired, in other words, because the alternative would be to blame the person who gave them the impossible task in the first place. That certainly seems to be the case with General David McKiernan, the American commander in Afghanistan, who was appointed by Defense Secretary Robert Gates less than a year ago, when President Bush was still in power.

The specific event that caused McKiernan's dismissal may have been his recent admission that there is a "stalemate" in Afghanistan. But his removal was probably inevitable anyway because Gates, who was retained from the Bush administration by President Obama, needed somebody to blame for the fact that the military situation in Afghanistan is now worse than ever. What's needed is "fresh thinking, fresh eyes on the problem," said Secretary Gates, explaining why he was appointing General Stanley McChrystal to the job instead. So what should General McChrystal's fresh eyes see?

He could start by understanding that the United States is not just fighting the Taliban in Afghanistan. It is fighting the entire Pashtun nation, some thirty million people, two-thirds of whom live across the border in Pakistan. That border has never really existed for the Pashtuns, who move freely across it in peace and in war.

It is warlords from the other Afghan ethnic groups, the Tajik, Hazara and Uzbek, who have controlled the Afghan government ever since the U.S. take-over. "The political, religious and economic mafia are all Northern Alliance people," says Daoud Sultanzoy, a member of parliament from Ghazni province, exaggerating only slightly. "Nobody outside the Northern Alliance is in the government." Except, of course, President Hamid Karzai, the token Pashtun, who is mockingly known as "the mayor of Kabul."

This is not a war about ideology, even if all the American and Taliban commanders insist that it is. The Pashtuns are fighting to regain at least a major share of power in Afghanistan, while the U.S. and other foreign troops are for all practical purposes allied to the other ethnic groups. That is why *all* the fighting is in the Pashtun-majority provinces.

Hamid Karzai has ensured his re-election as president in August by bribing or bullying his most serious challenger into withdrawing from the race. And his second term will be a reprise of his first: the same ethnic imbalance; the same rampant corruption and warlordism; the same toadying to the foreigners who provide the cash flow; and the same outbursts of nationalist resentment when U.S. air strikes kill too many innocent civilians.

On top of everything else, the U.S. still insists on eradicating the poppy-growing that provides over half of the country's national income. Opium use is obviously a problem in Afghanistan — as one observer said,

"If you applied a drug test to the Afghan army, three-quarters of them would be kicked out"—but burning farmers' fields leaves them no alternative source of cash income except fighting for the Taliban, who pay $200 CAD a month.

The final thing McChrystal should understand is that "winning" or "losing" in Afghanistan makes almost no difference to U.S. security. The Taliban are not "outriders for al-Qaeda," in the lazy formula used by State Department special envoy Richard Holbrooke. They are an Afghan phenomenon with almost exclusively Afghan goals, and even if the Taliban should win absolute power after the U.S. leaves (which is unlikely), there is no reason to believe that they would send terrorists to attack the United States. Indeed, Osama bin Laden probably didn't even let the Taliban's leaders know in advance about his plans for the 9/11 attacks.

This war is not only unwinnable but unnecessary, and if Stanley McChrystal understood all these things he wouldn't have taken the job. But he did take it, so he doesn't understand.

Then we had an election so spectacularly corrupt that Karzai's Western supporters insisted on a rerun. Afghans were less shocked, since they already understood the name of the game. And in the end, there was no rerun.

August 13, 2009
"ELECTION" IN AFGHANISTAN

"They have the watches, but we have the time," say the Taliban commanders in Afghanistan, and it's perfectly true. The election on August 20 is not going to change that.

The foreign forces, U.S., Canadian and European, are well-trained, well-equipped troops who can inflict casualties on amateur Taliban fighters at a ratio of at least ten-to-one, but the Taliban have an endless flow of fresh fighters, and much popular support among the Pashtuns of the south and southeast. Not to mention all the time in the world.

Now we are asked to believe that an election will restore confidence in the Afghan government. It is nonsense: this election has no more relevance than the ones that the United States staged in Vietnam.

Colonel David Haight, commanding the Third Brigade Combat Team of the U.S. Tenth Mountain Division in Logar and Wardak provinces near Kabul, was helpfully indiscreet about it in a recent interview. "I think that apathy is going to turn into some anger when the administration doesn't change, and I don't think that anybody believes that Karzai is going to lose," Haight told an embedded reporter from the *Guardian*. "There is going to be frustration from people who realize there is not going to be a change. The bottom line is they are going to be thinking: 'Four more years of this crap?'"

Unless bribery, blackmail and threats no longer work in Afghanistan, Karzai is going to win. Karzai isn't even bothering to run a conventional campaign: he bailed out of a televised debate with the other presidential candidates at the last moment, and leaves it to them to hold election rallies in provincial towns. Karzai has made his deals with the warlords and the traditional ethnic and tribal power-brokers, and is counting on them to deliver victory.

The West's government in Kabul is not going to get any better. It cannot, given its origins. There will be "four more years of crap," and by the end of that, the American, Canadian and European voters whose governments sent their troops to Afghanistan will be ready to bring them home. What will happen then?

Nothing particularly dramatic. Afghanistan was invaded in revenge for 9/11, but the U.S. could have played it differently from the start. Right after 9/11, a thousand-strong *shura* (congress) of Muslim clerics in Kabul declared its sympathy with the dead Americans and voted to expel Osama bin Laden and al-Qaeda from the country.

The Taliban regime had just made a lucrative deal with the United States to eradicate poppy-growing in the country, and after 9/11 most younger Taliban commanders wanted to maintain the deal and expel the Arab crazies. Mullah Omar, the Taliban leader, barely managed to overrule them. If the U.S. had shown more patience and spread some serious money around, the regime might well have decided to hand over the al-Qaeda leaders peacefully rather than face overthrow.

Washington wasn't interested in that outcome because, after 9/11, the American public wanted blood. American analyst Edward Luttwak even told me once that he thought a major reason why the U.S. public supported the invasion of Iraq in 2003 was that the invasion of Afghanistan had not involved *enough* blood. But although invading Afghanistan is always temptingly easy at first, it always ends in tears.

There's enough blood flowing in Afghanistan now, certainly, but the exit door for the Western armies remains permanently open—and once the invaders have left, the Afghans never follow them home. It won't happen this time either.

Western government rhetoric insists that the hills of Afghanistan are directly connected to the streets of Manhattan, London and Toronto. But no Afghan, not even any member of the Taliban, was involved in the planning or execution of 9/11, nor in the later, lesser attacks elsewhere in the West. Nor would the Taliban sweep back into power if all Western troops left Afghanistan tomorrow; the other players are still in the game.

Everybody who dies in this conflict is dying for nothing, because it will not change what happens when the foreign troops finally go home. As they eventually will.

Has Obama really drunk the Kool-Aid? Maybe, but maybe not.

When he announced in December 2009 that he would send another 30,000 troops to Afghanistan in early 2010, bringing the total reinforcements that he had committed to the country since taking office to over 60,000, he also stated that he would start withdrawing them again in 2011. This could just be overconfidence, but it could also be a way of signalling to the Taliban, "I'm sending more troops now to placate the hawks at home, but I'm really on the way out of Afghanistan. Go relatively quiet for a while and let it look like I'm making progress militarily, and I'll be out of your hair in no time. Then make whatever deal you can with Karzai or his successors in Kabul, or just roll over them if you have the power."

That's basically what Henry Kissinger, President Nixon's Secretary of State, told the North Vietnamese negotiators at the Paris peace talks in 1973, and he got the Nobel Peace Prize for it.

3.

CLIMATE I

As recently as 2005, climate change was just another subject that I wrote about from time to time. It was a big problem for the future, probably, but so were lots of other things. As Calvin Coolidge remarked: "If you see ten troubles coming down the road, you can be sure that nine will run into the ditch before they reach you."

Then, by the late summer of 2005, the Arctic sea ice cover crashed by almost 50 percent, and the real outlines of the crisis had become visible, even to an overworked journalist with a short attention span.

When I went back to the articles I had written in 2006, I was quite startled to see how clear and fast my shift was from distant concern to tight focus. During the first three months of that year, I wrote three articles on apparently unconnected topics that ended up being very connected indeed. It's the way the mind works, or at least mine does—I don't always know how an article is going to end when I start it—and my mind was obviously working hard to put the pieces together.

Mind you, I had a lot of help from Jim Lovelock, who was willing to say the things other scientists worried about only in private.

January 18, 2006
THE ONE-HUNDRED-THOUSAND-YEAR FEVER

"We are in a fool's climate, accidentally kept cool by smoke, and before this century is over billions of us will die and the few breeding pairs of people that survive will be in the Arctic where the climate remains tolerable." If anybody but James Lovelock had said that, you'd dismiss him as an attention-seeking panic-monger. But it was Lovelock himself.

A couple of centuries from now, Lovelock's reputation as an original and influential thinker in the life sciences may rival Charles Darwin's. On the other hand, it's possible that nobody will remember either him or Darwin two centuries from now, because there may be no civilization left. It is already too late to stop drastic global warming, he says, and the catastrophes that follow may sweep everything away.

Lovelock's great scientific insight began with a question: why is the Earth's climate, and even the very composition of the atmosphere itself, so radically different from what it would be on a dead planet? The Earth's two neighbours, Venus and Mars, have atmospheres that are almost entirely carbon dioxide, whereas the carbon dioxide in our own atmosphere is only one-third of 1 percent. That makes all the difference because it keeps our world cool.

At our planet's distance from the Sun, a carbon dioxide atmosphere would give the Earth an average surface temperature of 290 degrees Celsius, far too hot for life. Venus, only one-third closer to the Sun than us, but blanketed with carbon dioxide, has a temperature of 465 degrees Celsius. So, what, exactly, removed the carbon dioxide here, gave us this lovely, thin, oxygen-and-nitrogen atmosphere, and maintained the Earth's average surface temperature at between ten and twenty degrees Celsius for the past 3.5 billion years? Life, of course.

The Earth's early atmosphere was almost all carbon dioxide. On a lifeless world, the carbon dioxide would gradually have gotten thicker (it comes from volcanoes and accumulates over time), and the planet would have gotten hotter and hotter. But here, early life forms incorporated the carbon from the carbon dioxide into their bodies and released the oxygen into the atmosphere as a waste product. New forms then evolved that could use the oxygen to run a far more efficient metabolism, and the whole biosphere took off.

The Earth teems with life because the temperature is liveable, and that is so because the atmosphere stays largely free of carbon dioxide. In fact, the average surface temperature on this planet has varied only within a narrow range of ten or fifteen degrees Celsius over the past 3.5 billion years, despite all the ice ages and warming spells that seem to bring such dramatic changes. The Sun's heat output has increased by about 20–30 percent during that time, and still the climate hasn't changed. Something is actually *keeping* it stable.

To explain the phenomenon, in the 1970s Lovelock hypothesized that as living things evolved on this planet, they actually shaped their environment through complex chemical feedback loops that maintain the average temperature, the salinity of the oceans, and various other key variables at the levels best suited to life.

Lovelock was going to call this complex mechanism the "biocybernetic universal system tendency," but a neighbour of his, Nobel Prize–winning novelist William Golding, persuaded him to call it "Gaia" instead. It was a mistake. New Age romantics embraced the concept, but their enthusiasm actually slowed down scientific acceptance of the concept. Only in the past decade has Lovelock's theory, now renamed "Earth system science," been widely accepted among mainstream scientists.

Lovelock has worried aloud about global warming for thirty years because though the living feedback mechanisms that keep the atmospheric carbon dioxide down are good at dealing with gradual changes, they are unable to cope with the speed at which the level has been rising since the industrial revolution. "The Earth is about to catch a morbid fever that may last as long as one hundred thousand years," he warns, with temperatures rising five degrees Celsius worldwide and as much as eight degrees Celsius near the poles by 2100.

We are living in a "fool's climate," Lovelock says. Our climate seems normal only because atmospheric pollution in the northern hemisphere is reflecting much sunlight back into space and keeping global temperatures low. At some point, however, something will cause a major industrial downturn—a war that doubles the price of oil, a flu pandemic, whatever—and within weeks the smoke will thin out dramatically. Then we will find out how hot it really is already.

There will be repeated episodes of this sort as the carbon dioxide builds up during this century, he predicts, and in the long run, civilization will collapse in most places. Much of the densely populated tropics will become desert and scrub, massive population movements will overwhelm borders, billions will die of hunger, and war will take care of most of the rest.

Now Lovelock is saying that it's already too late to avert that outcome: "We will do our best to survive, but sadly I cannot see the United States or the emerging economies of China and India cutting back in time, and they are the main source of emissions. The worst will happen . . ."

I don't know if Lovelock is right, but I take him very seriously. He is, as he says, a "cheerful sod," and he didn't used to talk like this. It's very worrisome.

I still don't accept that this outcome is inevitable, but I take Lovelock's point: people and countries will have to behave in more responsible and far-sighted ways than they normally do if we are to have a decent chance of averting the worst outcome. And there's not much sign of such a change, is there?

The following month, I started writing a piece about China, and ended up with approximately the same conclusion.

February 12, 2006
UNSUSTAINABLE GROWTH

It's exactly the sort of document that an American think tank would have produced in the year 1900, if they had had think tanks in 1900. This time it's the Chinese Academy of Sciences, the leading research institute in the world's most populous country, and the document is called *China Modernization Report 2006*.

That imaginary American think tank of a century ago would certainly have predicted massive urbanization and far higher incomes in the United States by 1950, as those trends were already well established at the time. It might not have forecast that half the American population would own automobiles by 1950, let alone that tens of millions of Americans could afford to travel abroad by then, but another, bolder forecaster might have done so. Either way, when it all came true, nothing terrible happened as a result.

Alas, the Chinese Academy of Science's predictions won't come true because terrible things will start to happen in China long before 2050. This is deeply unfair: all that China wants for its citizens is the same lifestyle that most Western countries had achieved by 1950. But we got away with it because we were the first countries to industrialize, and China won't because it is so big and because it has come so late to the game.

The report, published on February 9, glows with enthusiasm for the predicted rise in Chinese incomes—tenfold by 2050, to $1,300 CAD a month—for the five hundred million peasants who will move to the cities and for the six hundred million city dwellers who will move out into hi-tech suburban homes. Half of China's people will own their own cars and be able to afford overseas travel, the report predicts. But I don't think so.

The Chinese people deserve prosperity, and they have waited too long for it, but they cannot have it in the classic Western style. Take the cars alone. Within a decade, China will be the second-largest automobile manufacturer on the planet—but for half the Chinese population to own cars, the world's total stock of motor vehicles must almost double. For half of Indians and Brazilians and Russians also to own cars (and all these people have similar expectations), the number of cars on the planet must triple.

It doesn't work at the local level (nine of the world's ten most polluted cities are already in China), and it doesn't work at the global level either. It is taboo to say so outside of scientific and environmental circles, because the rapid growth of the Chinese and Indian economies is now the main motor driving world economic growth, but it cannot go on like this.

At the beginning of the Second World War, the world had two billion people, about one-quarter of whom lived in industrialized countries—but few of them owned cars, or ran air conditioners, or travelled abroad.

Forty years later, there were four billion people. Those who lived in fully industrialized societies consumed far more energy and produced far more waste, as a "modern" lifestyle now included cars, meat in most meals, electrical appliances galore and, for many people, foreign travel, but they were still only one-quarter of the world's population. Total human pressure on the environment? Up five- or sixfold in forty years.

Now we have six-and-a-half billion people in the world, and one-quarter of the human race is living in developed countries, so the pressure on the environment is roughly ten times what it was in 1940. But the predicted development of China by 2050 (and the comparable growth of India, Brazil and Russia) will raise the share of the human race living in high-consumption industrial economies to more than half of the global population—which will exceed eight billion by that time. Total human pressure on the environment? Perhaps twenty-five times higher in a single century.

It's China's turn, and it's monstrously unfair that it cannot just follow the same development path that Britain first carved out in the late 1800s, and the rest of the West followed in the 1900s. But it can't. You cannot get away with that style of development anymore when the world is already as damaged as it is now.

The most frightening map I have ever seen is one published in James Lovelock's new book, *Revenge of Gaia*: it shows what proportion of the Earth's surface would remain suitable for agriculture if the average global temperature went up by five degrees Celsius. None of China is habitable (above desert population densities) except Manchuria. None of India makes it either, except the foothills of the Himalayas, and none of the United States, except the Pacific Northwest.

That is a completely unacceptable outcome of headlong "modernization" in the old style, and it makes the *China Modernization Report 2006* look like a fantasy. Somewhere between now and the future China envisages for 2050, the negative consequences of continuing down the present path will become so large and undeniable that the current pattern of development will be abandoned. It may not be abandoned soon enough to avoid terrible consequences for China and the world, but the day will never arrive when half of China's population owns cars.

On the other hand, the day *must* arrive when China's people (and India's and Brazil's and Indonesia's) live as well as Americans, or else there will be hell to pay. So the day may well arrive when more than half of all Americans don't own cars either. The future, as usual, is not going to be like the present.

The "car" is merely a metaphor for industrial-era consumption, of course. I can actually imagine a decarbonized future in which everybody would still have their personal transportation device, known as a "car," but the energy supply would have to come from entirely different sources. Meanwhile, in the real world, China became the world's largest car manufacturer a decade early, in 2009, and it is building old-fashioned, petroleum-fuelled cars.

So we're still headed for the bad future of famines and wars, as the folks in the think tanks already realize.

March 17, 2006
BRITISH NUKES: TAKING THE LONG VIEW

Last November, when Britain was having a public debate about the government's intention to proceed with a whole new generation of nuclear weapons that would take the country into the mid-twenty-first century, I wrote a column mocking Defence Secretary John Reid for not even knowing why he wanted the weapons. How could he justify such a major expenditure and such a provocative policy, I asked, with the lame excuse that "It is impossible in most cases to predict where your enemy will come from . . . Whether we might have a nuclear enemy in fifteen years' time is a difficult question to answer, other than to say history probably suggests we will."

Perhaps I owe John Reid an apology: I think I now understand why he wanted the nuclear weapons, and why he was not willing to get specific about it.

Some time this month or next, the Intergovernmental Panel on Climate Change (IPCC) will send a draft report to the world's governments that drastically raises its prediction of global warming increases to be expected this century. In its last report, the IPCC suggested that the average global temperature might increase as little as 1.5 degrees Celsius over the next hundred years. This would have a significant but still manageable impact in terms of wilder weather, coastal flooding and changing rainfall patterns.

The IPCC's experts now believe that merely raising the concentration of carbon dioxide in the atmosphere by 30 percent over the pre-industrial level of 270 parts per million has already produced major changes in sea ice, glaciers, droughts, floods, ecosystems and ocean acidification. They have redone their calculations on the amount of warming to be expected from doubling the amount of carbon dioxide in the atmosphere—the level we will reach by 2050, if we stay on our present course—while taking into account positive feedback effects that they had not previously allowed for. The results are disturbing, to say the least.

The IPCC's new estimates for global warming during the twenty-first century range from a minimum of 2 degrees to a maximum of 5.8 degrees Celsius. The planet has not been that hot since the start of the Eocene era fifty-five million years ago, when a huge release of carbon gases of uncertain, perhaps volcanic origin, drove global temperatures up for two hundred thousand years.

Natural processes eventually sequestered most of the carbon and restored a normal climate, but during the long hot spell the equatorial regions and most of the mid-latitudes, where the bulk of the world's population now lives, were barren semi-deserts.

These revised estimates, in other words, are very bad news for most countries. If you are Spanish or Brazilian or Thai—or American, for that matter—most or all of your country is going to turn into a desert, unless we all cut carbon dioxide emissions radically starting yesterday. Indeed, at least two-thirds of the world's existing farmland would become sterile, and billions would have to move or risk dying.

These estimates will have no immediate impact in the United States, where disbelief in climate change is still strong. President Bush's principal adviser on these matters, James Connaughton, recently expressed the view that we may be able to double the atmospheric concentration of carbon dioxide, perhaps even triple or quadruple it, without changing the climate. (Physics and chemistry work differently on his planet.) But elsewhere, most governments are paying close attention to the implications of all this.

Within the scenario of general climate catastrophe, some countries come out relatively unharmed, mainly because they are in the high latitudes. Unfairly, they are mostly the older industrialized countries that bear the largest share of the responsibility for setting the disaster in motion: Canada, Britain, Germany, Russia and Japan. Some of them, with long land borders, can expect to be overwhelmed by more numerous refugees from the south, if this disaster actually comes to pass. But Britain is an island—a very crowded island with little room for refugees.

The British government makes lots of mistakes, but there is no government in the world that puts as much effort into modelling long-term scenarios and thinking them through. I would be astonished if there were not some cell in London that spends much of its time imagining the future consequences of extreme climate change and feeding its conclusions to its political masters.

The first duty of British politicians is to protect the British people. If the worst comes to pass, that could well involve a capability to stop too many refugees from swamping Lifeboat Britain. In a world where nuclear weapons would almost certainly be more widespread than they are now, a credible British nuclear deterrent would be an indispensable part of such a policy, and I'll bet next month's mortgage that exactly that argument got made last year somewhere in Whitehall.

So, apologies to John Reid for not taking him seriously enough. And apologies to the rest of you for ruining your breakfast.

The boy finally got it. Took him a while, though.

What followed, in terms of the public debate, was a couple of years in which we began to explore the political implications of climate change. Suddenly it looked like it was going to take over the whole agenda, both domestically and internationally, for the indefinite future. Some very interesting ideas came up, but then the global warming file was shelved in order to deal with the global economic meltdown.

December 14, 2006
GETTING RADICAL ABOUT CLIMATE CHANGE: THE SHAPE OF THINGS TO COME

Here's the plan. Everybody in the country will get the same allowance for how much carbon dioxide they can emit each year, and every time they buy some product that involves carbon dioxide emissions—filling their car, paying their utility bills, buying an airline ticket—carbon points are deducted from their credit or debit cards. Like Air Miles, only in reverse.

So if you ride a bike everywhere, insulate your home, and don't travel much, you can sell your unused points back to the system. However, if you use up your allowance before the end of the year, you will have to buy extra points from the system.

This is no lunatic proposal from the eco-radical fringe. It is the brain-child of Britain's environment secretary, David Miliband, who hopes to launch a pilot program soon, with the goal of moving to a comprehensive national scheme of carbon rationing within five years.

Ever since a delegation of scientists persuaded prime minister Margaret Thatcher, a scientist herself, to start taking climate change seriously back in the late 1980s, British governments of both parties have been in the forefront on the issue, but Miliband's initiative breaks new ground. It has, he says, "a simplicity and beauty that would reward carbon thrift."

A huge share of total emissions is driven by the decisions of individual consumers. Miliband thinks that the least intrusive, most efficient way of shaping those decisions is to track everybody's use of goods and services that produce a lot of greenhouse gases, and to reward the thrifty while imposing higher costs on the profligate. The world's carbon emissions have to stop growing within ten to fifteen years, he says, and Britain must cut its total carbon emissions by 60 percent in the next thirty or forty years.

"We are in a dangerous place now," Miliband told the *Guardian* on December 11, "and it is going to be very difficult to get into a less dangerous place. The science is getting worse faster than the politics is getting better. People know the technology exists to get a lot of this done . . . but there is a huge chasm of mistrust between countries about how to do this . . . The developing countries won't take on any carbon reduction targets until they believe the countries that have caused the problem do so."

The science certainly is "getting worse," in the sense that every new forecast is worse than the one before. The most recent assessment of the state of the Arctic by the Intergovernmental Panel on Climate Change, whose full fourth report is due next year, was published last week in the journal *Geophysical Research Letters*, because its forecast was so alarming.

If current trends persist, the scientists reported, the Arctic Ocean will be entirely ice-free in the summertime by 2040, not in 2080, as previous forecasts suggested. That's just thirty-three years from now. Then, at that point, the dark ocean surface will absorb much more heat than the reflective ice did, another element of feedback kicks in, and the speed of warming increases again.

Those in the know are very frightened, but there is still that "huge chasm of mistrust." The developing countries, which are only now beginning to emit large amounts of greenhouse gases, look at the mountain of past emissions produced by the developed countries, and they want the rich countries to cut back very deeply—deeply enough to leave the developing countries some room to raise their consumption, without dooming us all to runaway climate change.

That's where the long-range target of 60 percent emission cuts for Britain comes from. Britain only produces 2 percent of global greenhouse-gas emissions, so a 60 percent cut in Britain alone is still only a drop in the bucket, but the aim is to set an example: see, we can do this without impoverishing ourselves, so other developed countries can too. And if they succeed, then a deal to control the growth of emissions in the developing countries is within reach.

So individual carbon credit accounts for all, and if you want to do things that produce more carbon dioxide than your annual allowance, you pay for it. The frugal and the poor can sell their unused credits back into the system—and every year or so, as the average carbon efficiency of transport or food production or power generation improves a little bit, the size of the free personal carbon allowance is reduced a little bit. This, I suspect, is the shape of things to come.

Maybe, but not quite yet. Miliband's proposal elicited no enthusiasm from any quarter, and was never discussed again. It is going to be a very long haul—maybe too long, given how fast things are moving. The Arctic Ocean is now generally expected to be largely ice-free at the end of the summer melt season within ten to twenty years, with the most pessimistic prediction saying 2013.

November 21, 2007
CHINA'S SHOES

The United States is off the hook: last year China overtook it to become the world's biggest emitter of carbon dioxide. "The tall tree attracts the wind," and from now on China will be the main target of the criticism that used to be directed at the United States for its refusal to accept binding limits on its greenhouse-gas emissions.

What's particularly striking is the speed with which China has surged into the lead. In 2005, China's carbon dioxide emissions were 2 percent lower than those of the U.S.; in 2006, they were 8 percent higher. While China has four times the population, the average Chinese is nothing like a quarter as rich as the average American. In fact, the vast majority of Chinese don't even own cars. So why does China produce so much carbon dioxide?

One reason is cement. The pace of building in China is so intense that the country produces 44 percent of the world's cement (the U.S. produces 4 percent), and cement production is a major source of greenhouse gases. The main culprit, however, is coal, which accounts for 70 percent of China's energy consumption.

China already burns more than twice as much coal as the U.S., and almost as much as everybody else in the world combined. In the race to keep up with soaring energy demand, it is building 550 new coal-fired power stations (they are currently opening at the rate of two a week), and nobody has the time to experiment with "clean-burning" coal technologies that are still new, even in the West. The result? China's emissions will continue to race ahead of everybody else's.

How can they let this happen? Don't they understand that emissions growing at this pace will pitch the world into runaway climate change, and that they will be among the worst sufferers if that happens? Well, yes and no. The Chinese public mostly does not understand where this is leading because there has been little discussion of climate change in their media, but also because their attention is focused closer to home.

"China's position today is similar to that of the U.S. or Europe during the seventies, when people first started to be concerned about pollution and the destruction of ecosystems," explained climate change expert Li Zou of Renmin University of China in Beijing. "We have only just started being concerned about local environmental issues. When we become richer and richer . . . people will have more time and more resources to pay attention to something not directly linked to themselves."

But climate change *will* affect the lives of ordinary Chinese people, and the government and the experts know it. One government study last year predicted a 37 percent fall in crop yields within the next fifty years if current trends persist. Since we may assume that climate change will have comparable effects elsewhere, and that even a rich China will be unable to make up the shortfall by importing food, that prediction implies mass starvation. Don't they care?

Of course they care. But they are in a high-stakes poker game and they cannot afford to blink. There will have to be a global agreement on curbing greenhouse-gas emissions within the next five to ten years; if not, the world will face runaway climate change. But countries like China and India must get special terms or their hopes of a prosperous future are doomed.

Put yourself in China's shoes. Five hundred years ago, average incomes in Europe, India and China were about the same. Then the Europeans got the jump on everybody else technologically, grew unimaginably rich and powerful, and conquered practically the whole world. They also industrialized, and for two hundred years it was their industries, their cities, their vehicles that poured excess carbon dioxide and other greenhouse gases into the atmosphere.

Now the rich countries are concerned about the consequences. Now they are even willing to curb their emissions (though some rich countries less so than others) — but they can easily afford to because they are already rich and bound to remain so. If China imposes the same kind of curbs on its emissions, then it will not become a country where most people are prosperous and secure in this generation, or perhaps ever. The same goes for India and all the other once-poor countries that are now experiencing very rapid economic growth. So, the deal must be that they get to keep on growing fast, and the rich countries take the strain.

There are two main ways for the developed countries to take the strain. One is to cut their own emissions very deeply, leaving room for the developing countries to expand theirs. The other way is to pay directly for cuts in the emissions of the developing countries: pay them to adopt clean-burning coal technologies; pay them to build renewable energy sources; pay them not to cut the rainforests down. Pay them quite a lot, in fact, because otherwise we will all suffer.

The developing countries will never get that deal unless they demonstrate that they are unwilling to curb emissions without it. Their refusal to cut emissions until they get that deal may seem selfish or blind, but they understand what kind of game they're in. It's not poker; it's a game of chicken.

4.

Given my own lack of belief, it's remarkable how much I have written about religion over the years. I wrote this piece when Pope John Paul II died in 2005, and it is, in its own way, confessional.

April 3, 2005
MY GREATEST JOURNALISTIC MOMENT

In the days to come, we will be hearing a great deal about Pope John Paul II's impact on the Catholic Church, the candidates for the succession, and what kind of straw they burn with the ballots to get that black smoke. This is the first time that a pope has died in twenty-seven years, and that finally gives me a hook for my story about how the last pope died. Or rather, about how I covered the previous pope's death. Or actually, how I didn't cover it.

It was late September of 1978, and I had been driving across the Alps all night from Germany with Mati and Tom—two hot-shot young journalists just like me. We were doing a radio series on war, and were passing through Italy on our way to Rome's Ciampino airport and then on to an aircraft carrier out in the Mediterranean. But first, we planned to stop in Rome for a day or two, so I'd arranged for us to stay at my friend Fareeda's flat in Trastevere, an area near the Vatican.

We stopped at a service area an hour north of Rome to phone Fareeda, because we needed to get the key before she left for work. We left Mati sleeping in the car, and when we came back he told us this weird story about how a truck driver had tried to tell him something. Mati hadn't understood a word—the only languages he spoke were Estonian and English—but he was a great mimic, and he parroted what the man had said.

"Il papa è morto," the man had said, and Mati had looked blank, so the truck driver repeated it in German: "Der Papst ist gestorben." Then he'd put his hands together and laid his head on them, as if he were going to sleep—or dying. "That means 'The Pope is dead,'" I said, and we all laughed at the poor trucker. How could anybody be so out of touch? The old pope had died over a month ago; Cardinal Albino Luciani had already been elected in his place, and had chosen the papal name John Paul.

We drove on into Rome. (There was nothing on the radio but hymns, so we switched it off.) We got to Trastevere too late to catch Fareeda before she left for work, so we went to the centre of town and had a second breakfast, then sat in a café and drank some wine.

Meanwhile, back in London, they were frantic to get in touch with us. They knew we were due in Rome that day, and we were just about the only English-speaking radio journalists in town. There were hundreds of them in town last month, when the new pope was crowned, but they'd all gone home. However, this was well before the age of mobile phones, so we sat there in blissful ignorance and had some more wine. And some more.

It was about three in the afternoon when I noticed a man walking by with a paper folded under his arm and the headline showing: "Il papa è morto." Oh, bugger. The new one had died, too. We're in trouble now.

We sent Tom off to phone London with some cock-and-bull story about how we were trapped all night in an Alpine pass and had just arrived in

Rome, while Mati and I dashed over to St. Peter's Square to get some vox pop. By the time we got there, alas, everybody was long gone. Earlier the square had been full of weeping old ladies on their knees, but then they all went home to make lunch and didn't come back. People do love an excuse to mourn together in public, but there was a limit to what you would do for a man who had only been pope for thirty-three days.

There was nobody around except for a few desperate journalists interviewing each other, so we did the same and "pigeoned" the resulting sorry effort off to London with an obliging Alitalia stewardess. (Yes, technology was once that low.) Mercifully, it got lost in transit. We solemnly vowed that we would never tell anybody else about the day, and sealed the pact with another bottle of wine.

The only thing I learned from all this was the real source of the Beatles song "Maxwell's Silver Hammer." The chorus had always seemed a bit obscure: "Bang! Bang! Maxwell's silver hammer / came down upon her head / Clang! Clang! Maxwell's silver hammer / made sure that she was dead." But Paul McCartney had been born Catholic, and soon the media were once again full of trivia about Vatican rituals—like the deathbed one where a cardinal bangs the late pope on the forehead five times with a silver hammer, while calling out his real name, to make sure that he is dead.

Albino Luciani didn't reply, so the brief reign of Pope John Paul I was declared over and Karol Wojtyla got the chance to remake the Catholic Church in his own authoritarian and ultra-conservative image. His rock-star charisma deflected attention from the collapse in church attendance, the hemorrhaging of priests (an estimated one hundred thousand quit the priesthood during his papacy), and the end of the Catholic monopoly in Latin America (where up to a quarter of the poor have converted to evangelical Protestant sects in the past quarter-century). How different it all might have been if Luciani hadn't had his heart attack.

I never did like John Paul II. Just after he took over, I did a four-continent tour of the Catholic Church for a radio series. At that point, it was an institution in a ferment of new ideas: liberation theology, feminist critiques of the traditional hierarchy, social activism of every sort. Karol Wojtyla shut all of that down, and left the Church a poorer place than he found it. But he did do one thing right.

April 8, 2005
WHAT JOHN PAUL II REALLY DID

It was the biggest photo op in world history, and everybody who is any-body was there. Even the Protestant president of the United States and the Muslim clergyman who is president of the Islamic Republic of Iran felt obliged to show up for the Pope's funeral. But the media circus is already moving on to the next global event, and we have one last oppor-tunity to consider the life of Karol Wojtyla.

Forget all the stuff about how he smothered all the new thinking and decentralization that were beginning to transform the Catholic Church when he was chosen pope in 1978. It's true, but he was elected precisely to carry out that task. The conservatives in the Roman Curia who had been sidelined by Vatican II were determined to stop the rot (as they saw it), and they were well aware that Wojtyla was a man in their own mould when they pushed him forward as the dark-horse candidate to succeed John Paul I.

He acted as they expected that he would, and it would be foolish to condemn him for it. He held those conservative beliefs long before he became pope, and he never hid them. But there was one thing he did that astonished and appalled the conservatives; and that one thing will continue to define Catholic Church policy centuries from now.

Most of John Paul II's policies are eminently reversible, if a subsequent generation of church leaders should decide that a different line on con-traceptives or women priests is more in accord with divine teaching. That isn't likely to happen any time soon, given the way that John Paul II has packed the College of Cardinals with like-minded individuals, but with enough time, many things become possible. What later generations are most unlikely to reverse is his acknowledgement that Judaism is a valid alternative path to God.

We are not just talking "apology" here—although Christians certainly owed apologies to the Jews for two millennia of slander and persecu-tion—nor even "reconciliation." John Paul II went far beyond that, though few members of the general public realized it at the time: he recognized Judaism as a true religion.

There is an old saying, beloved of Catholic theologians, that "error has no rights." It drives the ecumenical crowd crazy, but it is perfectly logical: if you believe that your religion is true, then the others are false. John Paul II was perfectly affable and hospitable to various Protestant Christians who came to visit, but he truly believed that they were wrong, wrong, wrong—and he refused to enter into the equal relationships that they imagined possible between the various Christian sects.

He was more open to the Orthodox Christian world, both because he came from Eastern Europe himself and because the quarrel between the Orthodox churches and the Church of Rome has always been about hierarchical and stylistic matters, not basic doctrinal issues. It was in his relations with non-Christian religions also in the lineage of Abraham, however, that John Paul II broke decisively with Christian and Catholic tradition.

After fourteen hundred years of constant and intimate contact between the Muslim and Christian peoples around the Mediterranean, he was the first pope ever to enter a mosque. He doubtless continued to believe that Christianity was the one true successor to Judaism and that Islam was a post-Jewish, post-Christian heresy, but he was the first pope to argue that cordial relations between them were possible and desirable. And, in the case of the Jews, he went much further.

It's understandable that the new religion of Christianity, struggling to distance itself from its Jewish roots, should have insisted that the Christian revelation had invalidated and replaced the older faith. By implication, however, that meant that those Jews who refused to convert were in revolt against God—and from that mindset came the Christian image of Jews as "Christ killers," and two millennia of savage Christian persecution culminating in the European Holocaust of 1942–45.

Karol Wojtyla was a witness to that Holocaust, which may be why he did the extraordinary thing that he did. On his visit to Israel in 2000, he posted a prayer in a niche in Jerusalem's Wailing Wall that said: "God of our fathers, you chose Abraham and his descendants to bring your name to the nations. We are deeply saddened by the behaviour of those who in the course of history have caused these children of yours to suffer, and asking your forgiveness we wish to commit ourselves to genuine brotherhood with the people of the covenant."

By posting that prayer in the wall, he acknowledged that this uniquely Jewish method of communicating with the Almighty is valid; and by its contents, he accepted that the Jewish covenant with God is still in force.

It was a thing done in a moment, but it ended two thousand years of Christian rejection of Judaism. The Catholic Church, while still advocating the conversion of everybody else, no longer seeks the conversion of the Jews, which is as close as it can get to acknowledging the equal validity of the Jewish faith.

That was the Big Thing that John Paul II did, and it is more important and will last far longer than all the other things he did put together.

Doctrinal disputes, within or even among the three great Abrahamic religions, are of limited interest to those who do not share their particular beliefs, but the political relations among these three great religions matter a lot. The Israeli-Palestinian dispute poisons the relationship between Jews and Muslims everywhere. The Christian-Muslim relationship has been fraught from the very beginning, when half of the then-Christian world was conquered by Muslim armies in little more than a century. Unlike the localized, and to some extent encysted, quarrel between the Israelis and their neighbours, moreover, the Muslim-Christian relationship implicates more than half of the world's people.

June 23, 2006
UPDATE ON THE FAMILY QUARREL

The past year has been one of the worst in recent history for relations between Muslims and "the West" (as the part of the world formerly called "Christendom" is now known). According to the Pew Global Attitudes Project for 2006, an opinion survey conducted in thirteen mainly Christian or Muslim countries by the Pew Research Center in Washington, D.C., the majorities who saw relations between the West and Islam as "generally bad" ranged from 53 percent in Russia and Indonesia to highs of 70 percent in Germany and 84 percent in Turkey.

There were purely local causes for some of the extreme reactions, like resentment among Turks at being seen as problem candidates for European Union membership simply because they are Muslims. The violent uproar in January over Danish newspaper cartoons lampooning the Prophet Muhammad doubtless influenced the answers of many respondents, both Muslim and Western, in a poll conducted only months later. But military confrontations that killed a lot of people were the core problem: Western armies fought local insurgents in two occupied Muslim countries, Iraq and Afghanistan; suicide bomb attacks by young British Muslims killed fifty-two people in London; and the nightmare images of 9/11 were never far from the surface in the United States. Furthermore, the Arab-Israeli fight over the land between the Jordan River and the Mediterranean Sea had entered its seventieth bloody year.

Seventy years, give or take a few, depending on whether you date that long conflict from the great Palestinian revolt against Jewish immigration in 1936 or from some other clash of that period. Without that open sore, however, the deep resentment of Muslims at having been conquered by European empires—as they all were, apart from the Turks—would probably have mostly died down by now. It is the Israeli-Palestinian dispute that has kept it alive for generations of Muslims from Morocco to Indonesia.

The U.S. and British invasion of Iraq was a ghastly mistake that confirmed existing suspicions in the Muslim world: its declared motives were so transparently false that Muslims everywhere were driven to look for ulterior, undeclared motives—like a Western crusade against Islam. On the other hand, Muslims have remained in denial about how their own internal conflicts have spilled over into anti-Western terrorism. Majorities in most of the Muslim countries polled still refuse to believe that Arabs carried out the 9/11 attacks in the United States, taking refuge in fantasies about Zionist or CIA plots.

Descend from high politics to cultural stereotypes, and it starts to look like a classic family quarrel. A majority of Muslims see Westerners as violent and immoral, while the view from the reverse perspective is that Muslims are violent and fanatical. Majorities in every Western country polled see Muslims as disrespectful of women, and majorities in every Muslim country polled (except Turkey) see Westerners as disrespectful of women. But then, it *is* a family quarrel.

Just the same, you cannot really have a "clash of civilizations" between Muslims and "Westerners" (Christians and Jews, by belief or at least by cultural descent) because they are members of the same civilization—the twin descendants of the old classical civilization of the Near East and the Mediterranean world. That world was divided almost fourteen centuries ago between competing but clearly related religions—the Christians of seventh-century Syria and Egypt who were the first to face Muslim armies surging out of Arabia saw Islam as a new Christian heresy—but it remains a single civilization whose fundamental cultural values are largely shared.

The surviving half of the former Christian world subsequently spread its faith and its genes across the Americas and Australia, while Islam conquered much of southern Asia (and the two religions divided Africa between them). Together, they account today for more than half of the world's population, so the old family quarrel affects a lot of people.

Muslim-Western disputes are so emotional precisely because they are between family members: neither of the estranged twin cultures brings the same amount of reproach and resentment to its occasional disputes with peoples who belong to entirely different traditions. But the fact that they do share so much history and so many values—they are all, as Muslims put it, "peoples of the Book"—means that the possibility of reconciliation is also ever present.

The most interesting statistics in the Pew survey are those about Muslim minorities living in the West, who were interviewed as a separate group for the first time this year. Muslims elsewhere may see Westerners as disrespectful of women, but Muslims who actually live among Westerners say the opposite—by a 73 percent majority in Germany, a 77 percent majority in France, an 82 percent majority in Spain. Even in Britain, despite the police harassment that has alienated so many Muslims since last July's bombs in London, a narrow majority agrees.

The same phenomenon is evident across a broad range of issues—and the huge non-Muslim majorities in Britain, France and the United States also have largely positive views of the Muslims in their midst, despite all the old history and all the recent clashes and controversies. To know them may not be to love them, exactly, but it does seem to breed tolerance, and maybe even solidarity.

What a respectful non-believer, I can hear a few of you murmur. He must be a deeply spiritual person despite his inability actually to believe.

Well, no, actually. The sociology and the political behaviour of religions is interesting to me. Even the various competing theologies have a certain weird fascination: how can people believe that stuff? Especially, how can they believe it just because they were born into families and communities that believe it, when they know that other people, just as intelligent and well educated, believe equally weird but entirely contradictory things because they were born into different families and communities? Isn't anybody paying attention here?

If I had a magic wand to wave, I would expunge all religion tomorrow: not just the institutions, but the whole body of superstition and fear of the unknown that underpins religion. I do not have such a wand, so I will only call your attention to the following article. Suspicions confirmed.

March 17, 2007
RELIGION AND GOOD BEHAVIOUR

They published an opinion poll in Britain recently in which 82 percent of the people surveyed said that they thought religion does more harm than good. My first reaction, I must admit, was to think: that's what they would say, isn't it? It's not just that suicide bombers give religion a bad name. In "post-Christian Britain," only 33 percent of the population identify themselves as "religious persons," and if you stripped out recent immigrants—especially Polish Catholics, West Indian Protestants, Pakistani Muslims, Indian Hindus—then the number would be even lower.

So that's what the British would say, isn't it? In the United States, where over 85 percent of people describe themselves as religious believers, the answer would surely be very different, as it would be in Iran or Mexico. But then I remembered an article that was published a couple of years ago in the *Journal of Religion & Society* entitled (sorry about this) "Cross-National Correlations of Quantifiable Societal Health with Popular Religiosity and Secularism in the Prosperous Democracies: A First Look," in which Gregory Paul set out to test the assertion that religion makes people behave better.

If that is true, then the United States should be heaven on Earth, whereas Britain would be overrun with crime, sexual misbehaviour and the like. Paul examined the data from eighteen developed countries, and found just the opposite: "In general, higher rates of belief in and worship of a creator correlate with higher rates of homicide, juvenile and early adult mortality, venereal disease, teen pregnancy, and abortion," while "none of the strongly secularized, pro-evolution democracies is experiencing high levels of measurable dysfunction."

How interesting. Now, to be fair, only one of the eighteen countries examined (Japan) was not Christian or "post-Christian," so this might just show that high levels of *Christian* belief correlate with a variety of social ills. There's really no way of testing that, since, apart from the countries of East Asia, there are no non-Christian countries where the level of religious belief has yet fallen below 60 percent.

There's not even any way of knowing if other religions will eventually experience the same decline in belief as the people who used to believe in them get richer, more urban and better educated. Even in what used to be Christendom, the United States didn't follow that path, after all. But the question is not whether religion will continue to flourish. It is whether religion makes people behave better, and the data say no.

Even within the U.S., Paul reported, "the strongly theistic, anti-evolution South and Midwest" have "markedly worse homicide, mortality, sexually transmitted disease, youth pregnancy, marital and related problems than the North-East, where societal conditions, secularization and acceptance of evolution approach European norms." As the most religious country of the eighteen surveyed, the U.S. also comes in with the highest rates for teenage pregnancy and for gonorrhea and syphilis. (A sidebar: boys who participate in sexual abstinence programs are more likely to get their partners pregnant, presumably because they are in denial about what they are doing.)

What are we to make of this? I never thought that religion really made people behave any better, but apart from the occasional pogrom or religious war, it hadn't occurred to me that it would actually make them behave worse. But there may be a clue in the fact that the more religious a country is, the fewer resources it puts into social spending, perhaps on the assumption that God will provide.

There is a very strong linkage between how secular a country is and how much it spends on social welfare and income redistribution. There is an equally strong correlation between high levels of social spending and a good score in Paul's survey—which makes sense, as all the ills he measured, from homicide to high infant mortality to teen pregnancy, are far more likely to affect the poor than the rich.

It's not that religious people choose to do bad things more often— indeed, they are probably more likely to get involved in charitable activities. Maybe it's just that when they talk about transforming people's lives, they don't think in terms of big state-run systems—and if you don't, lots of people fall through the cracks. Whereas the Godless, all alone under the empty sky, decide that they must band together and help one another through large amounts of social spending because Nobody Else is going to do it for them.

Or maybe there is some other reason entirely. But the numbers don't lie: the more religious a country is, the worse people behave in their private lives. Thank God they didn't do a survey on the correlation between strong religious belief and war.

Amen to that.

5.

ISRAEL-PALESTINE I

I'm beginning this section in the middle, so to speak, because 2007 was the fortieth anniversary of the Six Day War, and that was the event that changed everything for both the Israelis and the Palestinians. If you want to understand what's really going on in the region, you always have to start in 1967.

May 31, 2007
THE WAR OF SIX DAYS AND FORTY YEARS

On June 5, 1967, Israel launched a pre-emptive war against Egypt, Syria and Jordan. In six days, it annihilated the Arab air forces, defeated the Arab army and conquered the Sinai Peninsula, East Jerusalem, the West Bank, the Gaza Strip and the Golan Heights. It seemed like a decisive victory at the time, but forty years later the outcome is still in doubt.

By June 10, 1967, the amount of territory under Israeli control had tripled. Most of it was the empty desert of the Sinai Peninsula, which was returned to Egypt eleven years later in exchange for a peace treaty. The Israeli government also decided in principle in 1967 to give the Golan Heights back to Syria in return for a peace treaty, although that deal has still not happened. But no decision was ever taken to "give back" East Jerusalem, the West Bank and the Gaza Strip.

From the start, the Israeli-Palestinian dispute has been about demography and land. If Israel was to be a Jewish state, then most of the Palestinian Arab population had to be removed, and that deed was accomplished during the independence war of 1948–49. Some of the Arabs fled and others were driven out, but by the end of the war, the Arab population of the land under Israel's control, which had been close to a million, was only two hundred thousand.

As Benny Morris, the doyen of the "new generation" of Israeli historians, put it in the *Guardian* in 2004: "Pillage [by Jewish fighters] was almost *de rigueur*, rape was not infrequent, the execution of prisoners of war was fairly routine during the months before April 1948, and small- and medium-scale massacres of Arabs occurred during April, May, July and October to November. Altogether, there were some two dozen cases." So, by 1949, Israel was an overwhelmingly Jewish state.

David Ben-Gurion, the country's first prime minister, noted in his diary: "We must do everything to ensure they [the Palestinian refugees] never do return." We would now call this "ethnic cleansing"—no matter why refugees flee, if you don't let them return home when the shooting stops, that's what you are doing—but it was vital to the project of founding a Jewish state in former Palestine. And for twenty years, it worked.

Before 1967, Israel was militarily insecure but demographically triumphant: 85 percent of the people within its frontiers were Jewish. Then, with the victory of 1967, it showed that it had become militarily unbeatable, a fact confirmed by the last full-scale Arab-Israeli war in 1973. But the conquests of 1967 also revived its old demographic insecurities, for most of the Palestinian refugees of 1948 were now back in the same political space as the Jews, that is, in the West Bank and Gaza Strip.

Many Israelis saw the danger, and urged that the West Bank and the Gaza Strip be handed back to the Arabs (though almost no one was willing to give back East Jerusalem). A few brave souls even argued that the occupied territories should become the Palestinian state promised in the United Nations resolution of 1948, which partitioned Palestine and created Israel, but most succumbed to the lure of the land.

Jewish settlement in the West Bank began almost immediately, and now, forty years on, there are 450,000 Jews in former East Jerusalem and the West Bank (plus another 17,000 in the Golan Heights). None of this settlement growth could have happened without the 1967 victory, but it's also true that the separation of the populations that happened in 1948 has been undone.

All the land between the Jordan River and the Mediterranean Sea is effectively a single political territory, as Israel ultimately controls all of it. There are now ten million people living in that space, but only a bare majority of them are Jews: 5.5 million, versus 4.5 million Palestinians, and because the Palestinians have a much higher birth rate they will become the majority by 2015.

This is what Israelis call the "demographic problem," but it is really a political and territorial problem. If they want to hang on to the land, then they are stuck with the Palestinians who live on it. If Israel is truly democratic and grants all these people the vote it will cease to be a Jewish state. If it chooses to remain Jewish by excluding them, then it is no longer democratic. And yet it cannot bring itself to let the occupied territories go.

The 1967 victory has brought Israel two generations of military occupation duties, two Palestinian uprisings and a chronic terrorist threat. It has also brought it an existential political threat, because 1967 essentially reunited the Palestine that had been divided in 1948. What if, one day, the Palestinians simply accept that fact?

Ehud Olmert, now Israel's prime minister, put it bluntly in an interview with *Yedioth Ahronoth* in 2003. "We are approaching the point where more and more Palestinians will say: 'We have been won over. We agree with [extreme right-wing Israeli politician Avigdor] Lieberman. There is no room for two states between Jordan and the sea. All that we want is the right to vote.' The day they do that is the day we lose everything."

Now rewind a couple of years, to an event that only makes sense if you understand the dilemma that 1967 created for the Israelis. As a commando leader, as a hero general in the 1973 war, and as a deeply controversial defence minister, Ariel Sharon, the prime minister in 2004, had established a reputation as an efficient and enthusiastic killer of Arabs and the godfather of the settlement movement. So why was he now planning to close down the Jewish settlements in the Gaza Strip and hand the land back to the Palestinians?

September 16, 2004
A CURSE ON SHARON

The way his enemies and even his allies are talking, you'd think that Israeli Prime Minister Ariel Sharon had suggested giving the country back to the Arabs. In fact, he accused his critics last Wednesday of trying to spark a civil war in Israel, so extreme are their condemnations of his plan to evacuate Jewish settlers from the Gaza Strip by the end of next year.

Early last week, seventy thousand people, including many members of his own Likud Party, rallied in Jerusalem to denounce him as a "traitor" and a "dictator." His chief rival within the Likud Party and the government, former prime minister Binyamin Netanyahu, has demanded a referendum on Sharon's Gaza pullout plan. And a settler-rabbi, Yaël Dayan, has announced that he is prepared to put a death curse on Sharon.

Yaël Dayan has a track record in this matter. He conducted a similar mystical ceremony to put a death curse on then-prime minister Yitzhak Rabin shortly before he was murdered by an ultra-nationalist Israeli Jew in 1995. The thought of Ariel Sharon being murdered because he is soft on the Arabs boggles the mind, but right now he probably is more at risk of being assassinated by a fanatical Jewish settler than by a suicide bomber from Hamas. Can this be the Sharon we all know and love?

Relax, he hasn't really gone soft on us. He's just not as totally blind to inconvenient realities as the more extremist Jewish settlers in the occupied territories. In the West Bank, which is more than one-third as large as Israel itself and close to the most densely settled areas of that country, the 230,000 Jewish settlers are more than one-tenth of the total population and effectively control about half the land. With few exceptions, their settlements are relatively easy to protect from the hostile Palestinian majority around them.

The Gaza Strip is different. It is a tiny, mostly barren strip of land, right on the Egyptian border and far from Israel's main population centres, packed tight with 1.3 million Palestinians whose parents or grandparents fled or were driven from their homes farther north in Israel proper in 1948. Amid them live only eight thousand Jewish settlers—but those settlers control one-third of the land, and require an approximately equal number of Israeli soldiers to guard them from the Palestinians who surround them.

The Gaza settlements make no economic or military sense, and while many of the Jewish settlers there are driven by a religious vision, the secular Israeli governments that authorized the enclaves probably always saw them as bargaining chips in some potential future deal with the Palestinians. Sharon is certainly using them as bargaining chips, though he has no intention of making a deal with the Palestinians.

Sharon's strategy aims to separate Israelis from Palestinians as much as possible, while still retaining almost all the Jewish settlements in the West Bank and carving the Palestinian areas up into enclaves separated by Israeli-patrolled roads and military checkpoints. The Gaza pullout will save Israel money and troops while also letting Sharon throw the world a bone: look, Israel is withdrawing voluntarily from some settlements. But about 96 percent of the Jewish settler population, up in the West Bank, will remain where it is.

Asked last week about what would happen after the Gaza withdrawal, Sharon replied: "Israel will continue its war on terrorism, and will stay in the territories that will remain." Still, the furious arguments in Israel over the Gaza withdrawal serve to divert foreign attention from all that, and make Sharon appear to be a beleaguered moderate assailed by wild-eyed fanatics. If Yaël Dayan hadn't volunteered to put a death curse on him, Sharon would gladly have paid him to do it.

It is vintage Sharon: brilliant tactics, but not even a hint of strategic vision. Sharon was the main political patron of the settlers from the start, and though he does not share their religious fanaticism he retains a deep emotional attachment to the territories they have settled. Now he has turned the more extremist settlers against him, but he still wants to keep almost all of the land. The problem is that this means no deal with the Palestinians, and a future of endless war.

The late Yitzhak Rabin was at least as tough a general and as dedicated to Israel as Ariel Sharon, but he was a great deal wiser. He thought long-term, and understood that the day must eventually come when Israel no longer enjoys all its current strategic advantages. It was therefore necessary for Israel's survival to reach a lasting settlement with the Palestinians before it lost the upper hand.

Sharon and his allies deny that a deal is possible because "there is nobody to negotiate with," and by now they have managed to discredit or kill most of their potential Palestinian negotiating partners. The truth is they don't really want a deal anyway. They are unwilling to contemplate the sacrifices that it would require, and have no coherent vision beyond endless military occupation of the territories and an endless war on the consequent terrorism.

Journalists did not get to "know" Ariel Sharon, but I had dealings with him. He was a bully and a blowhard, qualities that served him well.

I did get to know Yitzhak Rabin a bit, and I found him serious, wise and altogether admirable. Israel lost its best chance to make a lasting peace when he was murdered.

As for Yasser Arafat, he ended up as self-caricature, and intellectually he was just not up to the task he had set himself. Nevertheless, he did leave two major accomplishments behind.

October 29, 2004
ARAFAT'S LEGACY

Yasser Arafat isn't dead yet. The "blood disorder" that forced him to desert his besieged headquarters in Ramallah and fly to Paris for medical treatment may not kill him, but he is probably never going home again, and his long reign as the undisputed leader of the Palestinian people is certainly over. So it is time to write his political obituary, if not his personal one.

Frantic speculation has already begun about who will succeed him, but it's unlikely that any single successor will command the support and respect that Arafat enjoyed in the deeply divided Palestinian community at home and in exile. The notion that a new Palestinian leader might be able to reopen peace talks with Israel is built on the myth that they only failed because of Arafat's stubborn personality. His career seems to be ending in failure—and yet he did achieve something.

He should have died at least ten years ago, of course. It would have been better for his reputation, for he never had the skills to run a proto-state like the Palestinian Authority: even as "President" of the PA, he remained at heart a guerrilla chieftain who ruled through cronies and relatives, co-opted his opponents with bribes of one sort or another, and never failed to appoint at least two rivals to any position of power.

His death then would also have been better for peace in the region, for a more astute Palestinian leader might just have pulled off a final peace agreement at the Camp David talks with Israeli prime minister Ehud Barak in 2000. It was already late in the game. The 1995 assassination of Israeli prime minister Yitzhak Rabin, Arafat's partner for peace in the Oslo Accords, and the subsequent delaying tactics of prime minister Binyamin Netanyahu in 1996–99, used up most of the available political time and patience, but a more flexible and imaginative man than Arafat might just have managed it.

Arafat was too cautious, and so the Camp David deal failed. A month later, Ariel Sharon, guarded by hundreds of Israeli soldiers and snipers, marched onto the square in front of the al-Aqsa Mosque in Jerusalem with the manifest intention of provoking a violent Palestinian response. The Palestinians threw rocks, the snipers opened fire, and that triggered the intifada, just as Sharon (and maybe Barak, too, by that time) intended. Four years later, all the peace plans lie in ruins and nothing awaits the Palestinians and the Israelis but endless violence.

So what did Arafat do right? Just two things, but they were big. First, he broke the hold of Arab governments who tried to control the Palestinian resistance movements for their own purposes. Then, even more importantly, he made the whole world acknowledge the existence of the Palestinian nation. He did that, for the most part, by successful acts of terrorism.

When Arafat created the Fatah guerrilla movement in 1959, the Palestinian refugees who had fled or been driven from their homes in 1948, in what is now Israel, were known simply as "refugees": stateless Arabs who could theoretically be "resettled" anywhere. Arab governments resisted this definition, but in the West it was universal. Arafat changed all that.

The key event in his life was the Six Day War of 1967, in which Israel conquered the West Bank and the Gaza Strip, where most of the 1948 "refugees" had ended up. In response to that disaster, Arafat took his guerrilla movement, Fatah, into the Palestinian Liberation Organization in 1968, became the PLO's leader the following year, and launched the campaign of international terrorism that made him famous.

It was universally condemned in the West, and all the authorities vowed that terrorism would never succeed, but by the time Arafat called off the campaign in 1989 he had achieved his goal. The world no longer talked about "refugees"; it talked about "Palestinians," and giving them that name implicitly recognized their right to a particular territory. The result: American and Israeli recognition of Arafat as a valid negotiating partner, the Oslo Accords of 1993, and the peace negotiations that took up most of the 1990s.

The peace negotiations failed, and Arafat bears a share of the blame (though only a share). As he departs from power and perhaps from the land of the living, the future of the Palestinians and the Israelis has rarely looked grimmer. But the history of the future is just as long as the history of the past; we just don't know it yet. There is still hope, and the historians of the future may be kinder to Yasser Arafat than the judgment of his contemporaries.

Yasser Arafat died in November 2004, and Mahmoud Abbas replaced him as head of the PLO and president of the Palestinian National Authority. Like any change of personnel or circumstances in the claustrophobic Israeli-Palestinian relationship, this led to an outburst of optimism about the "peace process." It didn't last long.

July 17, 2005
ISRAEL AND PALESTINE: THE END OF THE "CALM"

Palestinian leader Mahmoud Abbas called for a "period of calm" when he took over the late Yasser Arafat's job in January, and for a while some people allowed themselves to believe that peace was within reach. But that delusion depended on the belief that Arafat had been the main obstacle to a permanent peace agreement, and it is now melting in the summer sun.

"This calm is dissolving," said General Dan Halutz, the Israeli military's chief of staff, last Friday. Mushir al-Masri, a spokesman of the radical Hamas movement that rejects a permanent peace deal with Israel, sort of agreed: "The calm is blowing away in the wind, and the Zionist enemy is responsible for that." But the truth is that neither Halutz's political superiors nor al-Masri's expected the calm to last.

Israel would prefer the Palestinians to remain quiet, of course, but Prime Minister Ariel Sharon's strategy does not include serious negotiations with them. He is instead going for an imposed peace that leaves all the main Jewish settlement blocks in the West Bank under Israeli control, and last August, he got official U.S. support for that policy.

Sharon is building a "security fence" along the border between Israel and the West Bank—but cutting deep into the Palestinian territories in a number of places to include the major Jewish settlement areas— that translates that policy into a de facto new border for Israel. He is expanding Jewish settlements around predominantly Arab East Jerusalem to cut it off from the West Bank and to eliminate the possibility that it could ever serve as the capital of a Palestinian state. And Washington has promised to put no pressure on him for concessions to the Palestinians until he completes the "disengagement," the unilateral withdrawal of some 8,500 Jewish settlers from the Gaza Strip that is due to begin next month.

In reality, as Sharon's chief of staff, Dov Weisglass, explained last October, the disengagement process is intended to supply "the amount of formaldehyde that is necessary so there will not be a political process with the Palestinians . . . When you freeze that process, you prevent the establishment of a Palestinian state, and you prevent a discussion on the refugees, the borders and Jerusalem. Effectively, this whole package called the Palestinian state, with all that it entails, has been removed indefinitely from our agenda . . . all with a presidential blessing and the ratification of both houses of Congress."

Sharon spoke bluntly about his strategy to the Knesset in April: "I am doing everything I can to preserve as much [of the West Bank settlements] as I can." He is succeeding: by the time the Gaza withdrawal is complete, so should be the wall that cuts through the West Bank and defines the new de facto border between Israel and the occupied territories. But since Palestinians understand all this, they have concluded that Mahmoud Abbas's gamble that a "period of calm" would lead to genuine peace negotiations with Israel has failed.

Palestinians are turning more and more to Islamist movements that reject the whole notion of a permanent division of the land between Israel and a Palestinian state. Hamas's popular support has risen so fast that Abbas postponed the parliamentary elections scheduled for this summer, since a vote now might give Hamas and its allies a majority of seats. The Bush administration has given Sharon a green light, and he is going to move as fast as he can.

Later in 2005, Sharon's leadership of the Likud Party was challenged by Binyamin Netanyahu, who had been prime minister between 1996 and 1999. Their real goals were identical—to preserve the West Bank settlements and prevent the emergence of a Palestinian state—but Netanyahu tried to exploit the gap between what Sharon could say in public and what he actually intended to do in order to paint him as a traitor to the settlers' cause and a sell-out to the left.

Sharon saw Netanyahu's challenge off, but was felled by a stroke shortly before the elections of March 2006. Further intrigues between Netanyahu and the radical settler faction in Likud had driven Sharon to walk out of the party, taking the less extremist members with him, and to found a new centre-right party, Kadima. With Sharon permanently incapacitated, it was Ehud Olmert who led Kadima to victory in the elections—and by then, Hamas had also won the Palestinian parliamentary elections. On both sides, the whole-hoggers were in charge.

March 23, 2006
AFTER THE ISRAELI ELECTION

"It's a trade-off," said Dror Etkes, director of the Israeli organization Settlement Watch, just after Prime Minister Ariel Sharon carried out the dramatic withdrawal from the Jewish settlements in the Gaza Strip last August. "The Gaza Strip for the settlement blocks; the Gaza Strip for Palestinian land; the Gaza Strip for unilaterally imposing borders. They don't know how long they've got. That's why they're building like maniacs."

But they are going to have lots of time: Ariel Sharon may be in a permanent coma but his project is doing just fine. Nor is there any doubt about what acting Prime Minister Ehud Olmert will do once he is prime minister in his own right, with a solid majority behind him. In far blunter terms than Sharon had used in recent years, Olmert sketched out the new government's policy last month.

"Reality today obliges us to separate ourselves from the Palestinians and to remodel the borders of the state of Israel," said Olmert, "and this is what I will do after the elections. This will force us to evacuate [some] territories currently held by the state of Israel [in the West Bank, but] we will hold on to the major settlement blocks. We will keep Jerusalem united. It is impossible to abandon control of the eastern borders of Israel."

In other words, there will be no more peace negotiations: the Palestinians will just have to live within the 680 kilometres of tall fences that mark out Israel's new borders, in a pseudo-state surrounded and almost cut in half by Israeli settlements. The whole Jordan valley will stay in Israel's hands, cutting Palestinians off from the rest of the Arab world except for one Israel-controlled border crossing into Jordan at the Allenby Bridge and one that crosses into Egypt from the Gaza Strip.

The two hundred thousand Arabs living in the old city of Jerusalem are already cut off from the rest of the Palestinian territories by a ring of new Jewish suburbs and a maze of gates that they cannot pass through without magnetic cards. New settlements linking the existing Jewish suburbs east of Jerusalem with the settlement block of Ma'ale Adumim will push Israel's frontier most of the way across the West Bank in the centre, effectively cutting off the northern West Bank from the southern part.

All the big settlement blocks in the West Bank—Ariel, Gush Etzion and Ma'ale Adumim—will formally become part of Israel, sheltering behind the wall that divides them from the misery and desperation on the other side. Some isolated settlements will be abandoned, and the estimated 60,000 Jews who live in them will be moved to join the 185,000 people who already live in the bigger blocks. The Israeli army will police the areas that remain Palestinian, making incursions as necessary. And there you have it: the permanent solution to the Israeli-Palestinian problem.

Israelis justify this unilateral "solution" with the argument that there is nobody on the Palestinian side to negotiate with, and with the victory of the radical Hamas Party in Palestinian elections two months ago, that argument sounds almost plausible. But we arrived at this sorry situation because Israel was unwilling to negotiate fairly with any of the previous, more reasonable incarnations of the Palestinian leadership. The settlements always got in the way.

For twenty years, while one peace initiative after another died due to Israeli stalling and the patience of moderate Palestinians eroded, the settlements doubled and redoubled in population, taking up more and more Palestinian land. So now, since the Palestinians are too radical to talk, the settlements must become part of Israel. Most Israeli voters are willing to accept this logic for the time being, but it does not serve Israel's long-term security.

At the moment, Israel holds all the cards in the Middle East. Its army and economy are incomparably stronger than those of its Arab neighbours. It has hundreds of nuclear weapons, and they have none. And it has 110 percent support from the United States, the world's only superpower. But a prudent Israeli leader would conclude that now is therefore the right time to make a permanent peace with the Arabs, including the Palestinians, because nobody can be certain that Israel will still hold all of these cards in twenty-five or fifty years' time.

Israel cannot have a permanent peace and the settlements, too. It is making a bad trade.

Actually, Israel cannot have the settlements with or without a peace deal, because the international law changed after 1945. It is illegal to change a border by force, and the international community (that is, all the other countries in the world) will not recognize such a change.

April 13, 2006
OLMERT: DREAMING IN TECHNICOLOUR

"We have a very tight timetable [for drawing Israel's final borders], because we seek the support of the U.S. administration and President Bush. It has to be done by November 2008," said Yoram Turbowicz in an interview with the *Yediot Ahronoth* newspaper on April 11.

Turbowicz, who will be chief of staff to prime minister Ehud Olmert when the latter takes over as prime minister of Israel's new government, was only saying publicly what most members of the Kadima Party think in private, but it's interesting how foolish it looks when you see it in cold print.

Olmert imagines that he can carry out Sharon's grand plan, since he has the letter that President Bush wrote to Sharon last year that drastically changed U.S. policy, declaring that Israel could not be expected to return to its pre-1967 borders, "in light of new realities on the ground, including already existing major Israeli population centers." Just get it all done in the next thirty-two months, as Yoram Turbowicz said, before Mr. Bush leaves office at the end of 2008.

One of Turbowicz's assumptions is dead right: Israel cannot expect to have Washington's support for expanding its borders in such a dramatic way from any successor administration, whether Republican or Democratic. No previous administration in Washington would have backed such a project either. The Bush administration is an aberration, both in its contempt for international law and in its belief that American national interests and the desires of the current Israeli government are identical. So the deadline is real.

But Turbowicz is dead wrong in assuming that U.S. support will be enough to make the change in Israel's borders legal, permanent and widely accepted. The world does not work like that, and even if America's power were as great as Olmert seems to think it is, Washington could not make other countries accept such a gross breach of international law.

The post-1945 international law, written into the United Nations Charter, states that territorial changes imposed by force will not be recognized by UN members. Full stop. It's about taking the profit out of war and thereby reducing the temptation to go to war, and for more than sixty years, it is the one UN rule that has almost never been broken. Indonesia conquered East Timor and held it for a quarter-century, for example, but nobody ever recognized East Timor's annexation as legal and finally Indonesia had to leave.

Israel conquered East Jerusalem (together with the West Bank, the Gaza Strip and the Golan Heights) in the Six Day War of 1967, and immediately proclaimed that a unified Jerusalem (including Arab East Jerusalem) was its new capital forever more. The Israeli Ministry of Foreign Affairs and all the other government departments moved from Tel Aviv to Jerusalem, and, since 1967, Israeli domestic law has treated East Jerusalem as just another part of Israel. But no foreign government recognized the annexation of East Jerusalem as legal, and no foreign embassies moved from Tel Aviv—not even the U.S. embassy.

Look at the website of the U.S. embassy in Tel Aviv, and you'll read that "the information contained in this website applies specifically to American citizens residing in or travelling through the Tel Aviv Consular District (which is comprised of "greenline" Israel) [that is, the country within its pre-1967 borders]; residents of Jerusalem, the West Bank and Gaza should visit http://jerusalem.usconsulate.gov/." The U.S. State Department knows the law, and it applies it.

It is possible (though unlikely) that the Bush administration might yet browbeat the State Department into "recognizing" not only Israel's annexation of East Jerusalem but the far greater expansion of Israel's borders that Olmert now has in mind. But it is simply inconceivable that President Bush could persuade other countries to accept such a gross violation of international law.

Olmert cannot deliver; the deadline is meaningless. His government can build walls, dig ditches, move settlers around, proclaim that Israel's eternal borders are now some distance to the east of where they were last week, maybe even get the Bush administration to agree to the change, but none of it will have any legal force. The whole exercise will take up enormous amounts of time, effort and newsprint over the next few years but it is, in the end, only a charade.

6.

MISCELLANY.I

September 7, 2006
SMEED'S LAW

I was in a taxi in Beijing this morning, in heavy traffic moving very slowly, when a truck tried to change lanes and push in front of us. The taxi driver was having none of that, so he nosed forward to block the truck. The truck driver held his course, the taxi driver pushed forward again, and fifteen seconds later came the inevitable crunch. Small accident, nobody hurt.

You see this sort of thing almost every day here, and you sometimes wonder why Chinese drivers are such idiots. But they aren't. They're just first-generation drivers.

China still has less than one car for every fifty people, but even ten years ago, more than one hundred thousand people were dying on its roads annually. The death toll is probably much greater now, because car ownership has grown at least fivefold since then. But I'll bet that it is already falling in terms of deaths per vehicle-kilometre driven. There is a national learning curve in driving, and China is climbing it. So is the rest of the developing world.

Around the world, about 1.2 million people are killed in road accidents each year. An astounding 85 percent of those deaths happen in developing countries, although they own less than one-fifth of the world's cars and trucks. There's no getting round it: they are very, very bad drivers in China, India, Africa and the Middle East. (And they are almost as bad in Southeast Asia, Eastern Europe and Latin America.)

Take Liberia, for example. If the Liberian death rate per million kilometres driven were transposed to the United States, six million Americans per year would be killed on the roads. Actual American road deaths are about forty thousand per year, so it is 150 times more dangerous to drive in Liberia than in the U.S. You can't blame all that on poor brakes and bad roads. What *can* you blame it on?

Back in 1949, R. J. Smeed, Professor of Traffic Studies at University College London, proposed a statistical "law"—more a rule of thumb really—which was, to say the least, counterintuitive. He said that a growing number of cars on the road leads to a *decrease* in the number of accidents per vehicle. A growing car population means a big, persistent annual fall in the death rate per million kilometres driven.

Common sense tells us the opposite. It says that, other things being equal, the number of single-vehicle accidents (driving into trees, running over pedestrians) ought to increase more or less in direct proportion to the number of cars on the road. Two-car crashes and multi-car pileups ought to increase as the *square* of the number of vehicles. But it doesn't work like that.

The amount of road traffic in the United States has grown fourteenfold since 1925. If the number of American deaths per million kilometres driven had stayed steady at the 1925 rate, there would now be three hundred thousand deaths per year on American roads, not forty thousand. Americans have become much better drivers—and eventually everybody else will, too.

Smeed offered no explanation for this phenomenon, but I think that there is a collective learning process as more and more people become experienced drivers, and particularly as the generations turn over and children grow up in families that already own cars.

In thirty years, the mass stupidity that was Mexico City's road scene in the 1970s—make six lanes where there are only three, block the intersections, and blow your horn incessantly—has morphed into the relatively disciplined, relatively silent Mexico City traffic of today, which flows more smoothly now even with three or four times as many cars on the road.

Between 1925 and 1984, the U.S. road death rate per million kilometres driven fell steadily by 3.3 percent per year. In Britain, between 1949 and 1974, it fell by 4.7 percent per year. You can't just attribute this to safer cars because even modern cars in the hands of first-generation, Third World drivers still achieve kill rates as high as those of 1920s Americans in their Model T Fords. Better engineered roads may make a bit of difference, but, on the other hand, there are far more cars on the road.

Eventually, you hit diminishing returns: in the last ten years, U.S. road deaths per million kilometres driven have fallen at less than 2 percent a year. When almost everybody is a third-generation driver, what's left to learn? But Smeed's Law still holds, because the number of kilometres driven per year in the U.S. isn't growing fast anymore either.

So this year's 1.2 million traffic deaths will not soar to five or ten million when all the people in the developing countries get cars, too. It will rise for a while, due to the huge surge of new drivers, and then it will fall back as they gain experience, perhaps even below the current figure.

Which leaves only two problems. The long-term one is that the world will go into climate meltdown because of those two or three billion cars on the road. (The current global car population is about five hundred million.) The short-term one is that Beijing, where an extra thousand cars are put on the road every day, will achieve total gridlock just in time for the 2008 Olympics.

Wrong again: they avoided gridlock in Beijing by banning half the vehicles from the road (licence plates ending in odd numbers one day, even numbers the next) for a month before the Olympics and a month afterwards. Prophecy is an art, not a science.

And so, on to the ever-popular topic of gun control, on which I have repeatedly been wrong in the past. But I think I finally got it right.

April 16, 2007
GUN COUNTRY

You can imagine lots of countries where a candidate for the presidency might lie about owning a gun so as not to alienate the voters, but only in the United States would he lie and say he does own a gun when he doesn't. That was Republican presidential candidate Mitt Romney's sin earlier this year—and he compounded it by claiming that he was a lifelong hunter. Diligent reporters checked and found that Romney had never taken out a hunting licence anywhere. (Where were they when President Bush claimed that Saddam Hussein had "weapons of mass destruction"?)

The notion that the voters might punish a candidate for not owning a gun would seem simply bizarre in most jurisdictions, but it is a serious political reality in the U.S. That's why hardly anybody in the U.S. is using the latest mass slaughter by some enraged loser (thirty-three dead at Virginia Tech) to argue for more gun control. There's not even pressure to renew the federal law banning the sale of assault rifles, which was recently allowed to lapse.

Gun control is a dead issue in the United States, and it isn't coming back. There is a sound political reason for this, and there is also a rational explanation for it (which isn't the same thing).

The political reason was simplicity itself: the Democratic Party realized that it wasn't going to win back a majority in either house of Congress if it didn't stop talking about gun control. The party's leaders looked at the political map after the 2004 election, a sea of Republican red with a narrow strip of Democratic blue on either coast, and realized that their problem was more than just George W. Bush's fatal charm. They weren't winning in "heartland" states because they were seen as trying to take Americans' guns away.

There are other issues even in Montana, of course, but enough people care passionately about their guns in Montana that it's hard to get elected there if you are seen as anti-gun. So now the Democratic Party's national platform commits it to uphold the Second Amendment—the right to keep and bear arms—and in the 2006 election, it won both the Senate seat that was being contested in Montana and the governorship of the state, for decades a Republican stronghold.

The campaign manifesto of the new Democratic senator from Montana, Jon Tester, claimed that he would "stand up to anyone—Republican or Democratic—who tries to take away Montanans' gun rights." The new Democratic governor of Montana, Brian Schweizer, says that he has "more guns than I need but not as many as I want . . . I guess I kind of believe in gun control: you control your gun, and I'll control mine." It's a whole new image for Democrats, and it won them control of both houses of Congress in 2006. (Yes, the war helped, too, but by itself it wouldn't have been enough.)

The Democrats were not going to lose the coastal states (where the effete intellectuals and most of the old urban working class live) even if they did drop gun control. They were not going to win in the heartland (where the born-agains and the Marlboro Men live) if they didn't drop gun control. So they dropped it, and now no large party supports it. That's the politics of it, and it's hard to argue the point.

There is another, quite rational reason why gun control doesn't get much traction in American politics anymore. It's simply too late. This is a society that owns approximately equal numbers of wristwatches and guns: around a quarter-billion of each. There's no going back—and if practically everybody else has guns, maybe you should have one, too.

As various commentators will be pointing out soon, if just one of those thirty-three murdered students had been carrying a concealed handgun, maybe the killer would have been stopped sooner. It is perfectly legal to carry concealed weapons with a permit in Virginia, but not on college campuses. This loophole must be closed.

More fundamentally, the gun control argument may be missing the cultural point. Most Swiss and Israeli households with a male between the ages of eighteen and forty-five also contain a fully automatic weapon, because the national military mobilization model in those countries requires reservists to keep their weapons at home. Yet the Swiss and Israelis don't murder one another at a higher rate than people in countries like Britain or Turkey, where there is relatively strict gun control.

"Guns don't kill people; people kill people" is the best-known slogan of the National Rifle Association, the most effective pro-gun lobbying organization in the United States. But it's really a cultural thing: the British have bad teeth, the French smell of garlic, Americans tend to have more bullet holes in them than other people. The slogan should actually go: "Guns don't kill Americans; Americans kill Americans."

My two favourite types of fiction are alternative histories and science fiction. One genre imagines different ways that the past might have played out; the other imagines ways that the future may unfold. I'm a romantic about the future, and I suspect that the human adventure may have just begun, although I know that there are several ways in which it could end quite abruptly. At any rate, I am living at the right time.

March 9, 2009
WE ARE PROBABLY NOT ALONE

The real wonder of our age is that you can go on the Web, type in Planet Quest: New Worlds Atlas, or The Extrasolar Planets Encyclopedia, or NASA Star and Exoplanet Database, and directly access the data on 340 new planets that have been discovered in the past five years.

That number is set to grow very fast now, for last Saturday NASA (the U.S. National Aeronautics and Space Administration) successfully launched the Kepler telescope, which will find many more planets, including potentially Earth-like ones. It will stare unblinkingly at an area of space containing about one hundred thousand relatively near stars, watching for the tiny dimming of a star that happens when one of the star's planets passes between the star and us.

I enjoyed writing that last sentence. I couldn't have written it ten years ago because at that time we still didn't know whether it was normal for a star to have planets. Maybe planets were very rare, and life a thousand times rarer, and we were the only intelligent life in the galaxy. That always seemed pretty unlikely but you couldn't prove otherwise.

Well, now we know that planets are as common as dirt. Another new technique, which can see past the blinding glare of the parent star to pick out the faint light reflected from a planet's surface, has found planets revolving around more than a hundred nearby stars. It's like spotting a candle burning next to a lighthouse from a thousand kilometres away, but it works.

The Kepler telescope mechanizes the search. If any of those one hundred thousand stars have planets that orbit in a plane that causes them to pass between the star and us, Kepler will spot them by the dimming they cause as they pass in front of the star. Probably thousands of the stars have planets orbiting in that plane, so now the tally of "exoplanets" (planets orbiting other suns) is going to rise very quickly.

Even in that tiny section of sky, Kepler will probably miss tens of thousands of other planets whose orbits don't bring them between their star and the Earth. Moreover, the great majority of the planets it does find will be gas giants like Jupiter and Saturn, because gas giants orbiting close to their stars are the easiest planets to spot. But those are planets that cannot support our kind of life; the real triumph will be finding planets like Earth.

The closest astronomers have come so far is a planet called Gliese 581 c. It's the middle planet of three orbiting Gliese 581, a star about twenty light-years from here. It may have other planets, but we can't see them, and it's only one-and-a-half times the diameter of Earth. It is a rocky planet like our own, not a gas giant, and it is in the "Goldilocks Zone" around its star, where the temperature is neither too hot nor too cold to permit liquid water on the surface.

Gliese 581 c is not another Earth. The gravity is much higher; it is very close to its sun (which is smaller, dimmer and cooler than our own); and it whips around its sun every 13 days compared to our 365 days. But it could potentially support our kind of life—which makes it, for the moment, the second most interesting object in the universe after our own planet.

We still cannot see if it has an atmosphere, and if so, whether it contains the telltale gases that indicate the presence of life, but a new generation of orbiting observatories planned for the next decade—NASA's Terrestrial Planet Finder and the European Space Agency's Darwin project—could give us the answers. Darwin, for example, is going to survey one thousand of the closest stars, looking for small, rocky planets and seeking signs of life on them.

Two big consequences are going to come out of all this. One is a long and tempting list of Earth-like planets in our own stellar neighbourhood, with, quite likely, evidence of life on many of them.

Unless we can discover some loophole in the laws of physics, we may never reach them—the distances involved are immense—but they will always be there, beckoning us to come and visit, even to come and settle them. The knowledge that there is a destination worth going to can be a powerful spur to innovation.

The other consequence is a huge question about intelligent life in the universe. If planets capable of supporting life are so commonplace — last month Dr. Alan Boss of the Carnegie Institution for Science told the annual meeting of the American Association for the Advancement of Science in Chicago that there could be a hundred billion such planets in this galaxy alone — then where is everybody?

Is intelligence a rare accident in the evolutionary process, or such a self-destructive attribute that intelligent species don't usually survive more than a couple of centuries after they industrialize? Are they all observing radio silence because there is something dreadful out there? Or have we just not figured out yet how mature galactic civilizations communicate?

I enjoyed writing that paragraph, too.

I feel compelled to write a piece about the "war on drugs" every year or so because it's the stupidest war of all and by far the easiest one to end. Doing so would also save more lives than any other war we might end, but writing about it usually feels like shouting down a well.

Occasionally, however, a little bit of hope breaks through.

September 4, 2009
THE LONGEST WAR

It's too early to say that there is a general revolt against the "war on drugs" the United States has been waging for the past thirty-nine years, but something significant is happening. European countries have been quietly defecting from the war for years, decriminalizing personal consumption of many of the banned drugs in order to minimize harm to their own people, but it's different when countries like Argentina and Mexico do it.

Latin American countries are much more in the firing line. The U.S. can hurt them a lot if it is angered by their actions, and it has a long history of doing just that. But from Argentina to Mexico, they are fed up to the back teeth with the violent and dogmatic U.S. policy on drugs, and they are starting to do something about it.

In mid-August, the Mexican government declared that it will no longer be a punishable offence to possess up to half a gram of cocaine (about four lines), five grams of marijuana (around four joints), fifty milligrams of heroin or forty milligrams of methamphetamine.

At the end of August, Argentina's Supreme Court did something even bolder: it ruled that, under the Argentine constitution, "Each adult is free to make lifestyle decisions without the intervention of the state," and dismissed a case against youths who had been arrested for possessing a few joints.

In an ideal world, this ruling would have a powerful resonance in the United States, whose constitution also restricts the right of the federal government to meddle in citizens' private affairs. It took a constitutional amendment to enable the U.S. Congress to prohibit alcohol in 1919 (and another amendment to end alcohol prohibition in 1933), so who gave Congress the right to criminalize other recreational drugs nationwide by the Controlled Substances Act of 1970? Nobody—and the U.S. Supreme Court has yet to rule on the issue.

Half a million Americans a year went to jail last year for drug-related "crimes" that hurt nobody but themselves, and a vast criminal empire has grown up to service the American demand for drugs. Over the decades, hundreds of thousands of people have been killed in the turf wars between the gangs, the police–dealer shootouts, and the daily thousands of muggings and burglaries committed by addicts trying to raise money to pay the hugely inflated prices that prohibition makes inevitable.

Most users of illegal drugs are not addicts, let alone dangerous criminals. Legalization and regulation, on the pattern of alcohol and tobacco, would avoid thousands of violent deaths each month and millions of needlessly ruined lives each year, although psychoactive drug use would still take its toll on the vulnerable and unlucky, just as alcohol and tobacco do.

But what about the innocent children who will be exposed to these drugs if they become freely available throughout society? Nothing that doesn't happen to them now. There are no cities and few rural areas in the developed world where you cannot buy any illegal drug known to man within half an hour, for an amount of money that can be raised by any enterprising fourteen-year-old.

Indeed, the supply of really nasty drugs would probably diminish if prohibition ended, because they are mainly a response to the level of risk the dealers must face. (Economist Milton Friedman called it the "Iron Law of Prohibition": the harder the police crack down on a substance, the more concentrated that substance becomes—so cocaine gives way to crack cocaine, as beer gave way to moonshine under alcohol prohibition.)

But there is little chance that American voters will choose to end this longest of all American wars any time soon, even though its casualties far exceed those of any other American war since 1945. The "War on Drugs" will not end in the United States until a very different generation comes to power.

Elsewhere, however, it is coming to an end much sooner, and one can imagine a time when the job of the history books will be to explain how this berserk aberration ever came about. A large part of the explanation will then focus on the man who started the war, Richard Nixon—so let us get ahead of the mob and focus on him now.

We can do that because of the famous Nixon tapes that recorded almost every word of his presidency. It turns out that he started the war on drugs because he believed that they were a Jewish plot. We know this because researcher Doug McVay from Common Sense on Drug Policy, a Washington-based non-governmental organization, went through the last batch of tapes when they became available in 2002 and found Nixon speaking to his aides as follows:

"You know, it's a funny thing, every one of the bastards that are out for legalizing marijuana is Jewish. What the Christ is the matter with the Jews, Bob? What is the matter with them? I suppose it is because most of them are psychiatrists."

Nixon had much more to say about this, but one should not conclude that he was a single-minded anti-Semite. He was an equal-opportunity paranoid who believed that homosexuals, Communists and Catholics were also plotting to undermine America by pushing drugs.

"Do you know what happened to the Romans? The last six Roman emperors were fags . . . You know what happened to the popes? They were laying the nuns; that's been going on for years, centuries. But the Catholic Church went to hell three or four centuries ago. It was homosexual . . .

"Dope? Do you think the Russians allow dope? Hell no . . . You see, homosexuality, dope, uh, immorality in general: these are the enemies of strong societies. That's why the Communists and the left-wingers are pushing it. They're trying to destroy us."

The reason for this thirty-nine-year war, in other words, is that President Richard Nixon believed that he was facing a "Jew-homo-doper-Commie-shrink-lefty-pope" conspiracy, as *Washington Post* writer Gene Weingarten put it in a gloriously deadpan article in 2002. But that is just plain wrong. As subsequent developments have shown, it is actually a Jew-homo-doper-Commie-shrink-lefty-pope-*Latino* conspiracy.

7.

TERRORISM I

You will note that I have some difficulty in curbing my contempt for most of the discussions of the "terrorist threat" that have been inflicted on us in the past few years. This is because I remember a time when the military, at least, understood that terrorism is a political strategy, not just "mindless violence," and that the biggest mistake you can possibly make is to over-react. Doing so is falling into the trap they have laid for you.

Once upon a time, all of the professional armed forces of the Western world understood that, because they spent the fifties, sixties and seventies fighting various revolutionary movements in the Third World that used terrorism extensively as a tool in their struggle. By the seventies, indeed, all the military staff colleges, where they trained the next generation of senior officers, devoted a large part of the curriculum to guerrilla wars and terrorism. But that generation is gone from the armies now, and so are most of the insights that came at a very high price.

September 2, 2004
VICTORY IN THE WAR ON TERROR

"With the right policies, this is a war we can win, this is a war we must win, and this is a war we will win," said Democratic presidential candidate John Kerry in Tennessee on August 31. "The war on terrorism is absolutely winnable," repeated his vice-presidential running mate, Senator John Edwards. That is utter drivel, and they must privately know it, but truth generally loses to calculated lies in politics.

This outburst of bravado was prompted by President George W. Bush's brief brush with the truth about terrorism the previous weekend, when he told an interviewer that he did not really think you can win the war on terror, but that conditions could be changed in ways that would make terrorists less acceptable in certain parts of the world. For a moment there, you glimpsed a functioning intellect at work. Such honesty rarely goes unpunished in politics.

This heroic attempt to grapple with reality was a welcome departure from Mr. Bush's usual style—"I have a clear vision of how to win the war on terror and bring peace to the world," he had claimed as recently as August 30—and his opponents pounced on it at once. "What if President Reagan had said that it may be difficult to win the war against Communism?" asked John Edwards, in one of the least credible displays of indignation in American history.

Mr. Bush promptly fled back to the safe terrain of hypocrisy and patriotic lies. "We meet today in a time of war for our country, a war we did not start, yet one that we will win," he told a veterans' conference in Nashville on September 1. But it is not "a time of war" for the United States, and it cannot "win."

Some 140,000 young American soldiers are trapped in a neo-colonial war in Iraq—where there were no terrorists until the U.S. invasion—and their casualties are typical of colonial wars: fewer than 1 percent killed per year. As for the three hundred million Americans at home, exactly as many of them have been killed by terrorists since 9/11 as have been killed by the Creature from the Black Lagoon in the same period. None.

The rhetoric of a "war on terror" has been useful to the Bush administration, and terrorism now bulks inordinately large in any media where the agenda is set by American perspectives. On the front page of the

International Herald Tribune that carried the story on Mr. Bush's return to political orthodoxy on terrorism, four of the other five stories were also about terrorism: "Twin bus bombs kill 16 in Israel," "Blast leaves 8 dead in Moscow subway," "12 Nepal hostages slain in Iraq," and "French hold hectic talks on captives."

In other words, thirty-six of the quarter-million people who died on this planet on August 31 were killed by terrorists: close to one in eight thousand. No wonder the *International Herald Tribune* headlined its front page "A Deadly Day of Terror," although it would have been on firmer statistical ground if it had replaced the headline with "A Deadly Day for Swimming" or even "A Deadly Day for Falling Off Ladders."

Actually, more than thirty-six people were killed by "terrorists" on August 31 — perhaps as many as fifty or sixty. The rest were killed in wars that the United States is not all that interested in: in Nepal, Peru, Burundi and in other out-of-the-way countries, where the local guerrillas are not Muslims and have no imaginable links with the terrorists who attacked the U.S.

Governments fighting Muslim rebels — such as the Israelis fighting the Palestinians in the Israeli-occupied territories or the Russians fighting the Chechens in Russia — have had more success in tying their local counter-insurgency struggles to the U.S. "war on terror," and as a result Washington doesn't criticize their human-rights violations much. But the only terrorists the U.S. government really worries about — and this would be equally true under a Kerry administration — are terrorists who attack Americans. There aren't that many of them, and they aren't that dangerous.

George W. Bush spoke the truth, briefly, at the end of August, when he said that the "war on terror" cannot be won. It cannot be won *or* lost because it is only a metaphor, not an actual war. It is like the "war on crime," another metaphor — but nobody ever expects that the "war on crime" will one day end in a surrender ceremony where all the criminals come out with their hands up, and afterwards there is no more crime. It is a *statistical* operation, and success is measured by how successful you are in getting the crime *rate* down. Same goes for terrorism.

You could do worse than to listen to Stella Rimington, the former director of MI5, Britain's intelligence agency for domestic operations: "I'm afraid that terrorism didn't begin on 9/11 and it will be around for a long time. I was very surprised by the announcement of a war on terrorism because terrorism has been around for thirty-five years . . . [and it] will be around while there are people with grievances. There are things we can do to improve the situation, but there will always be terrorism. One can be misled by talking about a war, as though in some way you can defeat it." As Mr. Bush said before his handlers got the muzzle back on.

One small fact that will help to clarify the following story: London was awarded the 2012 Olympics on July 6, 2005, the day before the suicide bombers struck several targets in the city.

July 7, 2005
LONDON: NOT EXACTLY THE BLITZ

Tony Blair flew down from the G8 summit in Scotland to be with Londoners in their time of trial, and you can hardly blame him. It's not that we needed him to take charge—it was only four smallish bombs, and the emergency services were doing their job just fine—but the tabloid newspapers would have crucified him if he hadn't shown up and looked sympathetic in public.

No doubt he was feeling sympathetic, too, but the words he used rang false. The accent was British, but the words were the sort of thing that comes out of the mouth of George W. Bush—all about defending British values and the British way of life. He didn't mention God, so he's still British under it all, but I'm pretty sure I even heard him use Mr. Bush's favourite words, "freedom" and "resolve." I'm also pretty certain that this cut very little ice with most Londoners.

This is a town that has been dealing with bombs for a long time. German bombs that fell during the Blitz in September–December 1940 killed 13,339 Londoners and seriously injured 17,939 more. In 1944, London was the first city in the world to be hit by cruise missiles (the V-1s or "buzz bombs") and, later that same year, it was the first to be struck by long-range ballistic missiles (the V-2s, which carried a ton of high explosives).

During the Second World War about thirty thousand Londoners were killed by German bombs and three-quarters of a million lost their homes. Then, between 1971 and 2001, London was the target of 116 bombs set by various factions of the Irish Republican Army, although they only killed fifty people and injured around one thousand. And not once during all those bombings did people in London think that they were being attacked because of their values and their way of life.

It was quite clear to them that they were being attacked because of British *policies* abroad, or the policies of Britain's friends and allies. The people who organized the bombings wanted Britain out of the Second World War, or British troops out of Northern Ireland, or the British army out of the Middle East (or maybe, in this instance, the whole G8 to leave the rest of the world alone). Nasty things, bombs, but those who send them your way are usually rational people with rational goals, and they almost never care about your values or your way of life. It's political, not personal.

Londoners understand this, and such knowledge has a remarkably calming effect: once you have grasped this basic fact, you are no longer dealing with some faceless, formless, terrifying unknown, but a bunch of people who are willing to kill at random in order to get your government to change its policies. Moreover, they can't hurt all that many people. In a large city, the odds are very much in your favour: it will almost always be somebody else who gets unlucky.

This knowledge breeds a fairly blasé attitude towards bombings, which was much in evidence this morning when I had to go in to Harley Street at noon to pick up my daughter from school. (They didn't let school out early; it was just the last day.) The buses and the London Underground weren't running and a lot of streets were blocked off by the police, but everybody was finding ways round them, on foot and in cars. You pull over to let the emergency vehicles pass, and then you carry on.

What happened to the victims of the bombs was horrible, and the British media did their best to stir up panic and fury, but it didn't work. In fact, several times during the day, I overheard people say something along the lines of "Bloody terrorists. Always get it wrong. If only they'd done this two days ago then we wouldn't be lumbered with the bleeding Olympics."

One would-be terrorist eventually got the Nobel Peace Prize.

July 4, 2006
MANDELA THE TERRORIST

The oddest bit of news this week has been the tale of the hunt for Nelson Mandela's pistol, buried on a farm near Johannesburg forty-three years ago. It was a Soviet-made Makarov automatic pistol, given to Mandela when he was undergoing military training in Ethiopia. (He also went to Algeria, to learn from the revolutionaries who had just fought a savage eight-year war of independence to drive out their French colonial rulers.) A week after he buried the gun, he was arrested by the apartheid regime's police as a terrorist and jailed for life.

It's very hard now to imagine Nelson Mandela as a terrorist. He is the most universally admired living human being, almost a secular saint, and the idea that he had a gun, and was prepared to shoot people with it, just doesn't fit our picture of him. But that just shows how naïve and conflicted our attitudes towards terrorism are.

Nelson Mandela never did kill anybody personally. He spent the next twenty-seven years in jail, and only emerged as an old man to negotiate South Africa's transition to democracy with the very regime that had jailed him. But he was a founder and commander of Umkhonto we Sizwe (Spear of the Nation), the military wing of the African National Congress (ANC), and MK, as it was known, was a terrorist outfit. Well, a revolutionary movement that was willing to use terrorist tactics, to be precise, but that kind of fine distinction is not permissible in polite company today.

As terrorist outfits go, MK was at the more responsible end of the spectrum. For a long time, it only attacked symbols and servants of the apartheid state, shunning random attacks on white civilians even though they were the main beneficiaries of that regime. By the time it did start bombing bars and the like in the 1980s, Mandela had been in prison for twenty years and bore no direct responsibility for MK's actions—but neither he nor the ANC ever disowned the organization. Indeed, after the transition to majority rule in 1994, MK's cadres were integrated into the new South African Defence Force alongside the former regime's troops.

There's nothing unusual about all of this. Jomo Kenyatta in Kenya, Archbishop Makarios in Cyprus, Robert Mugabe in Zimbabwe, and a dozen other national leaders emerged from prison to negotiate independence after "terrorist" organizations loyal to them had worn down the imperial forces that occupied their countries. In the era of decolonization, terrorism was a widely accepted technique for driving the occupiers out. South Africa was lucky to see so little of it, but terrorism was part of the struggle there, too.

Terrorism is a tool, not an ideology. Its great attraction is that it offers small or weak groups a means of imposing great changes on their societies. Some of those changes you might support, even if you don't like the chosen means; others you would detest. But the technique itself is just one more way of effecting political change by violence—a nasty but relatively cheap way to force a society to change course, and not intrinsically a more wicked technique than dropping bombs on civilians from warplanes to make their government change its policies.

Neither terrorism nor military force has a very high success rate these days: most people will not let themselves be bullied into changing their fundamental views by a few bombs. Even in South Africa's case, MK's bombs had far less influence on the outcome than the economic and moral pressures that were brought to bear on the apartheid regime. But that is not to say that all right-thinking people everywhere reject terrorist methods. They don't.

What determines most people's views about the legitimacy of terrorist violence is how they feel about the specific political context in which force is being used. Most Irish Catholics felt at least a sneaking sympathy for the IRA's attacks in Northern Ireland. Most non-white South Africans approved of MK's attacks, even if they ran some slight risk of being hurt themselves. Americans understandably see all terrorist attacks on the United States and its forces overseas as irredeemably wicked, but most Arabs and many other Muslims are ambivalent about them, or even approve of them.

We may deplore these brutal truths, but we would be foolish to deny them. Yet in much of the world at the moment, it is regarded as heretical or even obscene to say these things out loud, mainly because the United States, having suffered a major attack by Arab terrorists in 2001, has declared a "global war on terror." Rational discussion of why so many Arabs are willing to die in order to hurt the United States is suppressed by treating it as support for terrorism, and so the whole phenomenon comes to be seen by most people as irrational and inexplicable.

And meanwhile, on a former farm near Johannesburg that was long ago subdivided for suburban housing, they have torn down all the new houses and are systematically digging up the ground with a backhoe in search of the pistol that Saint Nelson Mandela, would-be terrorist leader, buried there in 1963. If they find it, it will be treated with as much reverence as the Holy Hand Grenade of Antioch. The passage of time changes many things.

They never did find the pistol. But here's another valuable find . . .

October 30, 2006
THINKING LIKE A TERRORIST

What are they thinking, those terrorists who hate America's values, as the United States prepares to vote in the 2006 mid-term Congressional elections? Do they think that a terrorist bombing somewhere in the United States in the next few days would drive Americans back into President Bush's arms, or discredit his strategies further? And which result would they prefer: do they want the Republicans to lose control of Congress, or not?

To discuss these questions sensibly, you must first accept that terrorists are not just hate-filled crazies. They are people with political goals and rational (though vicious) strategies for achieving them. So put your prejudices aside for a moment, and try to think like a terrorist.

Happily, a document has come into my hands that will help us to figure out their strategy. True, it reads like a script written for an amateur dramatic society, but it comes from one of the Western intelligence agencies that certified the existence of weapons of mass destruction in Iraq, so there can be little doubt about its authenticity. I have taken the liberty of translating it into English.

A heavily guarded compound in Waziristan. Three bearded men in robes enter the courtyard.

Osama bin Laden (for it is he): So do we blow something up in America before the election this time, or not? We skipped 2002 and 2004. Surely it wouldn't hurt to do something this time.

First Henchman: Well, I don't know, boss. Not blowing more stuff up in America has worked for us so far. Bush got the credit for keeping the terrorists away, and that gave him the freedom to invade Iraq, and so the Americans never put enough troops into Afghanistan, and now they're losing both wars. I say leave him alone. It's coming along just fine.

Second Henchman: Besides, we don't really have . . .

Osama bin Laden (interrupting): I bought that argument in 2002, and I bought it again in 2004, but now it's different. Bush will be in power until 2008 no matter how Americans vote, so the U.S. soldiers will still be pinned down in Iraq until then anyway. He's not going to pull them out. And he's not going to send a lot more troops to Afghanistan, either, no matter who controls Congress, so our Taliban friends will be all right. We have nothing to lose. Let's blow something up. It will humiliate the Americans and make us look good.

Second Henchman: That's all very well, but . . .

First Henchman (interrupting): You know, I think the boss is right. It can't hurt now. Activate the sleeper cells in America, and have them blow up a few car bombs.

Second Henchman: Will you stop talking and listen for a minute! We don't have any sleeper cells in America. We never did. We had to bring the 9/11 guys in from abroad, and they're all dead. This whole discussion is pointless, and furthermore . . . [At this point the transcript ends]

On second thought, I do wonder if this document is entirely genuine. There's something about the style that doesn't sound quite right. But the logic is exactly right: this is how terrorists think.

The 9/11 attacks on the United States were meant to provoke an American military response. The point was to lure Washington into invading Afghanistan (where Bin Laden's bases were), so that they would become trapped in another long guerrilla war like the one he and his colleagues had waged (with U.S. support) against the Soviet invaders of Afghanistan in the 1980s. The images from such a war, of high-tech American forces smashing Afghan villages and families, would reverberate across the Muslim world and radicalize so many people that the Islamist revolutions Bin Laden dreamed of would at last become possible.

George W. Bush dodged that bullet by overthrowing the Taliban regime without causing vast destruction in Afghanistan (it was done almost entirely by American Special Forces and their local allies), so there was no guerrilla war there at first. Bin Laden's gamble had failed. But then Bush invaded Iraq, providing Arab extremists with the guerrilla war they wanted and images of horror in profusion. He even abandoned most of the effort to rebuild Afghanistan in order to concentrate on Iraq, so the Taliban got the chance to recover there, too.

That's where we are now, and Osama Bin Laden has little incentive to try to discredit President Bush with the American electorate by carrying out further terrorist attacks. The project is on track, and the Americans will be largely gone from the Middle East in a few years anyway.

And besides, there are no sleeper cells in America. There never were.

8.

SOUTH ASIA

One of the abiding themes of the last decade has been the American court-ship of India as a potential alliance partner in the "containment" of China. Washington wasn't really sure that it would end up in a military confrontation with China, and was also pursuing a policy of "engagement" with Beijing—the twin policies being known colloquially as "congage-ment"—but it wanted India on its side as an insurance policy.

India had a tradition of non-alignment, but it was tempted by the U.S. offer: privileged access to the next generation of American military technol-ogy, and an end to the U.S. ban on the export of nuclear-power technology to India that had been imposed when New Delhi tested its nuclear weap-ons in 1998. It took most of the decade to manoeuvre that deal through the U.S. Congress and the Indian parliament, and even now it is not a full-fledged alliance. But it was quite enough to make China paranoid.

June 11, 2007
INDIA: THE PRICE OF CHOICE

Choices usually involve a price, but people persist in believing that they can avoid paying it. That's what the Indian government thought when it joined the American alliance system in Asia in 2005, but now the price is clear: China re-announced its claim to the Indian state of Arunachal Pradesh, some eighty-three-thousand square kilometres of mountainous territory in the eastern Himalayas containing over a million people.

China has actually claimed Arunachal Pradesh for a century and, during the Sino-Indian border war of 1962, Chinese troops briefly occupied most of the state before withdrawing and inviting India to resume negotiations. However, most Indians thought the dispute had been more or less ended during Chinese premier Wen Jiabao's visit to New Delhi in April 2005, when the two sides agreed on "political parameters" for settling both the Arunachal Pradesh border dispute and another in the western Himalayas.

Indians assumed that the new "political parameters" meant that China would eventually recognize India's control of Arunachal Pradesh. In return, India would accept China's control of the Aksai Chin, a high-altitude desert of some thirty-eight-thousand square kilometres next to Kashmir. And that might actually have happened, in the end—if India had not signed what amounts to a military alliance with the United States.

Informed Indians knew perfectly well that Wen Jiabao's visit was a last-minute attempt to persuade India not to sign a ten-year military co-operation agreement with the United States. Two months later, Pranab Mukherjee, then India's foreign minister, went to Washington and signed the thing. Still, most people in New Delhi managed to convince them-selves that Wen's concessions during his visit were not linked to India's decision about the American alliance.

In June 2006, I spent two weeks in New Delhi interviewing Indian analysts and policy-makers about India's strategic relations with the U.S. and China. With few exceptions, their confidence that India could "manage" China's reaction to its American alliance remained high. "India knows what it is doing," insisted Prem Shankar Jha, former editor of the *Hindustan Times*, citing confidential sources close to Prime Minister Singh. "It is not going to make China an enemy."

On the face of it, India got a very good deal in the lengthy negotiations that led up to the military cooperation agreement. It gained access not just to current U.S. military technology but to the next generation of American weapons (with full technology transfer), and the Indian military are predicted to spend $30 billion on U.S. hardware and software over the next five years. They also got all sorts of joint training deals, including U.S. Navy instruction for Indian carrier pilots. And Washington officially forgave India for testing nuclear weapons in 1998.

This was the only part of the deal that got much attention in Washington, where the Bush administration waged a long struggle (only recently concluded) to get Congress to end U.S. sanctions against exporting nuclear materials and technologies to India. The Bush administration was aware that stressing the military aspects of the new relationship with India would only rile the Chinese, who would obviously conclude that it was directed against them, especially since America's closest allies in the Asia-Pacific region, Japan and Australia, have also now started forging closer military relations with India.

It took a while, but China was bound to react. Last November, just before President Hu Jintao's first visit to India, the Chinese ambassador firmly stated that "the entire state [of Arunachal Pradesh] is a part of China." This took New Delhi by surprise, defence analyst Uday Bhaskar told the *Financial Times* last week: "The Indians had taken the [2005] political parameters [for negotiating the border issue] as Chinese acceptance of the status quo." They should have known better.

It's mostly petty irritants so far, but they accumulate over time. Last month, for example, Indian Navy ships took part in joint exercises with the U.S. and Japanese navies in the western Pacific, several thousand kilometres from home and quite close to China's east coast. Admiral Sureesh Mehta, chief of naval staff, said the exercise had "no evil intent," and two Indian warships also spent a day exercising with the Chinese navy to take the curse off it—but Beijing knows which exercise was the important one.

Also last month, India cancelled a confidence-building visit to China by 107 senior civil servants. Why? Because Beijing refused to issue a visa to the one civil servant in the group who was from Arunachal Pradesh: he was already Chinese, they said, and did not need one.

A year ago, Indian foreign-policy specialists were confident that they could handle China's reaction to their American deal. In fact, many of them seemed to believe that they had taken the Americans to the cleaners: that India would reap all the technology and trade benefits of the U.S. deal without paying any price in terms of its relationship with its giant neighbour to the north.

But there was confidence in Washington, too: a quiet confidence that once India signed the ten-year military cooperation deal with Washington, its relations with China would automatically deteriorate and it would slide willy-nilly into a full military alliance with the United States. Who has taken whom to the cleaners remains to be seen.

Benazir Bhutto must have known she was risking her life when she returned from exile to run in the Pakistani election in December 2007. It was a deal brokered by the United States to shunt General Pervez Musharraf aside and put a civilian, U.S.-friendly prime minister in power, and it was bound to anger the Islamists. She was ready to be a martyr, if necessary. But she was not really ready to be prime minister.

December 27, 2007
BHUTTO ASSASSINATION

Benazir Bhutto, a woman who very much liked her privileges and luxuries, did five years of hard time in prison, much of it in solitary confinement, after her father, Prime Minister Zulfikar Ali Bhutto, was overthrown and hanged by the worst of Pakistan's military dictators, General Muhammad Zia-ul-Haq.

I got to know Benazir Bhutto a bit in the mid-1970s, when she had finished her degree at Harvard and was doing graduate work at Oxford. She actually spent much of her time in London, in a grand flat just off Hyde Park, and if you knew a lot of people in town who took an interest in Middle Eastern and subcontinental affairs—I had been studying at the School of Oriental and African Studies—and you weren't too old or too boring, you were likely to end up at her flat once in a while, at what some would call a salon but I would call a party.

A fairly decorous party as those things went in seventies London, to be sure, with everybody showing off their sophisticated knowledge of the region's politics and nobody getting out of hand, but definitely a party.

The hostess was well informed and quite clever, and she obviously had money coming out of her ears. We knew her dad had been prime minister of Pakistan before Zia overthrew him, of course, but she was neither a serious scholar nor a budding politician.

She seemed more American than Pakistani in her style and attitudes, but beneath the Radcliffe and Harvard veneer she also seemed like thousands of other young upper-class women from Pakistan and India floating around London at the time. They called one another by girlish nicknames like "Bubbles," didn't take anything very seriously (including their studies), and seemed destined for a life of idle privilege.

Then Benazir Bhutto went back to Pakistan in 1977, just about the time that Zia sentenced her father to death in a rigged trial. He was hanged in 1979, and Benazir was thrown into jail for five years. When she came out after Zia died, she was already the head of the party her father had founded, the Pakistan People's Party, and by 1988, she was prime minister. She was only thirty-five.

She was prime minister twice, from 1988 to 1990 and from 1993 to 1996, and was removed from power both times on corruption charges. The charges have never been proven in court, but the evidence of kickbacks and commissions, especially to her husband, Asif Zardari, whom she foolishly made investment minister, is pretty overwhelming. The real problem, however, was that she never seemed to have any goal in politics, apart from vindicating her father by leading his party back to power. At the start, she was hugely popular, but she wasted her opportunity to make real changes in Pakistan because she had no notion (beyond the usual rhetoric) of what a better Pakistan would look like. Pakistan is already pretty good for her sort of people, so it should not surprise us that there was almost nothing to show for her years in office.

If she had become prime minister again, which was a quite likely outcome of the current crisis, there is no reason to believe that she would have done any better this time. Her assassination just makes it harder to solve the crisis at all.

Benazir Bhutto's party, the Pakistan People's Party, has no alternative leader with national visibility. The other major opposition party leader, Nawaz Sharif, is equally compromised by his past failures, and is currently planning to boycott the elections scheduled for January 8. Ex-general Pervez Musharraf, who had himself "re-elected" president in October and then imposed emergency rule in order to dismiss the Supreme Court judges who would have ruled his "election" illegal, is totally discredited and unlikely to last much longer. The most probable outcome is a new period of military rule under a different ruler, simply for lack of a good alternative.

It is pathetic that a country the size of Pakistan should have so few inspiring or even promising candidates for high political office. The vast majority of the politicians and of the people who run almost everything else in Pakistan apart from the armed forces, are drawn from the 3 or 4 percent of the population who constitute the country's traditional elite. It is a very shallow pool of talent, made up of people who have a big stake in the status quo and a huge sense of entitlement.

Look east to India, west to Iran, or north to China, and by comparison Pakistan's political demography is absolutely feudal. So long as that remains the case, it is absurd to imagine that democracy will solve Pakistan's problems. I admired Benazir Bhutto's courage and I am very sorry that she was killed, but she could never have been Pakistan's saviour.

In the end, they made Benazir Bhutto's son the head of the Pakistan People's Party and put her husband, Asif Zardari, in the presidency. Whether this is just an interlude before "a new period of military rule" remains to be seen.

February 15, 2009
SRI LANKA AFTER THE WAR

The greatest mistakes are made on the morrow of the greatest victories. Sri Lanka is now approaching a decisive victory in its twenty-six-year war against Tamil separatism, and it is about to make a very big mistake.

"While separatist terrorism must be eradicated," wrote Lasantha Wickrematunge, editor of the *Sunday Leader*, "it is important to address the root causes of terrorism, and urge government to view Sri Lanka's ethnic strife in the context of history and not through the telescope of terrorism. We have agitated against state terrorism in the so-called war against terror, and made no secret of our horror that Sri Lanka is the only country in the world routinely to bomb its own citizens."

Wickrematunge left that on his computer, to be published if he was murdered, which he duly was last month. He knew it was going to happen, and he believed that he knew who would be responsible: the government. This is why he addressed President Mahinda Rajapaksa directly in his post-mortem article. (It was the first time that most of Wickrematunge's readers learned that he and the president had been close friends for a quarter-century. In fact, they regularly met late at night at the president's house, alone or with a few other old friends.)

"In the wake of my death," Wickrematunge wrote, "I know you [President Rajapaksa] will make all the usual sanctimonious noises . . . but like all the inquiries you have ordered in the past, nothing will come of this one. For truth be told, we both know who will be behind my death, but dare not call his name. [Almost certainly Defence Secretary Gotabaya Rajapaksa, the president's brother.] Not just my life but yours too depends on it."

Like the United States under President Bush, Sri Lanka has ceased to respect the law in its fight against "terrorism." Since the Tamil minority began fighting for a separate state in 1983, over seventy thousand people have been killed in Sri Lanka, the majority of them civilians — and since President Rajapaksa took power in 2004, fourteen journalists have been murdered by unknown assailants.

Rajapaksa is now on the brink of destroying the rebel army, the Liberation Tigers of Tamil Eelam (Tamil Tigers). Even one year ago, they still controlled some fifteen thousand square kilometres in the north and northeast of the island, where they maintained all the institutions of a sovereign state, but the relentless offensive of the Sri Lankan army has now reduced them to only a couple of hundred square kilometres of territory.

Within a week or two that will be gone too, and what remains of the Tamil Tigers will no longer control a pseudo-state. Good riddance, for they were brutal extremists who killed their own Tamil people in order to enforce unquestioning obedience, just as readily as their suicide bombers killed the majority Sinhalese population. But that doesn't mean Sri Lanka can just go back to the kind of country it was before the fighting began in 1983. The Tamils had a reason to revolt.

Tamil-speaking Hindus have been part of Sri Lanka's complex ethnic and religious mosaic for centuries, but they are only 12 percent of the population. They got along well enough with the Sinhalese-speaking,

Buddhist majority when the island was first united under British imperial rule in the early nineteenth century, but after that the relationship
went rapidly downhill.

The British, in typical divide-and-rule style, favoured the Tamil minority in education and in civil-service jobs. Sinhalese resentment grew
rapidly, and the first Sinhalese-Tamil riots were in 1939. As in the subsequent bouts of killing, most of the victims were Tamils.

Once independence arrived in 1948, the Sinhalese used their majority to pass laws giving members of their own community preference for
university entrance and government jobs, and Sinhala was declared the
sole national language. As Sinhalese and Tamil ethnic nationalism grew
more extreme, some of the riots in the 1960s and 1970s verged on anti-
Tamil pogroms.

By the late 1970s, the process of setting up a shadow Tamil state in
the north and northeast had begun. Open war broke out in 1983, with the
Tamil Tigers rapidly eliminating the rival Tamil separatist groups and
establishing totalitarian control over the population under their rule.

Twenty-six years later, the Tamil Tigers' army has finally been crushed,
and the Sri Lankan state (in practice, the Sinhalese state) is triumphant.
But the 12 percent of the population who are Tamils will still not accept
unequal status, and they are not going away.

This is the time when a peace that gives the Tamils equal rights and
autonomous local governments in the areas where they are a majority
could secure the country's future, but it is most unlikely to happen.

Sinhalese nationalism is as intolerant as ever, and now it is triumphalist
to boot. Moreover, the rapid growth of a "national security state" under
President Rajapaksa has undermined democracy and largely silenced criticism of government policies. The forecast, therefore, is for a reversion to
guerrilla war in the north, and continuing campaigns of murder by both
the government and Tamil extremists in the rest of the country.

*In the afterglow of victory, Rajapaksa quickly called and won presidential
and parliamentary elections. Sarath Fonseka, the general who commanded
the Sri Lankan army in the final campaign, and who subsequently used
his fame to enter politics and run against Rajapaksa for the presidency, is
in jail facing court martial for "military offences." So far, there has been
no return to guerrilla war and terrorism.*

November 25, 2009
THE TRIALS OF BANGLADESH

If a Shakespeare should ever arise in Bangladesh, he would have plenty of tragedies around which to weave his history plays. The country is only thirty-eight years old, but the vendettas between the leading families, the murders and plots and coups, have been just as tangled and bloody as the ones in fourteenth- and fifteenth-century England that gave the great playwright so much of his material.

That kind of history may be coming to an end in Bangladesh, but it's not dead yet. Last February, at least four thousand soldiers serving in the Bangladesh Rifles, a border defence regiment, mutinied and began killing their officers. Fifty-seven officers and seventeen other people were murdered by the mutineers, who dumped the bodies in sewers and an army-run incinerator. The violence spread to military camps all over Bangladesh.

The mutineers said that they were revolting against poor pay, but many people suspected that there was a political motive behind it all. If there was, it failed. The rest of the army remained loyal, tanks surrounded the regiment's various camps, and the government promised to look into the rebels' complaints if they surrendered.

That was a lie, of course: they were all arrested. The first nine soldiers went on trial for mutiny before a military court on November 24 and more than 3,500 others will follow in various military cantonments around the country, while several hundred more will be tried before civilian courts for murder, rape and looting.

This is not the kind of blood-spattered Shakespearean ending that Bangladeshis have become much too familiar with. The trials may even answer the question of whether there was a political motive behind the military uprising. But suppose there was. What could it have been?

Another high-profile court case in Bangladesh in the past month might provide a clue. On November 19 the Supreme Court confirmed the death sentences for twelve former military officers who took part in the 1975 assassination of Bangladesh's founding father, Sheikh Mujibur Rahman. The five ex-officers who are actually in custody, and whose final appeal was rejected, now face imminent execution for their crime of thirty-four years ago.

Few countries have had a bloodier birth than Bangladesh. For a quarter-century after the partition of India in 1947, it was just the eastern wing of Pakistan, a country split in two parts that had a great deal of Indian territory between them. But the two parts never got along, and when what is now Bangladesh tried to leave Pakistan in 1971, it got very ugly.

The Pakistan army killed up to three million people in rebel "East Pakistan" before an Indian military intervention forced it to withdraw. East Pakistan then became the independent country of Bangladesh, and the country's nationalist political leader, Sheikh Mujibur Rahman (who had spent the war in jail in West Pakistan), came home to lead it.

Mujib, as he was known, was an autocratic man, and by 1975 he had closed down all the opposition papers and declared himself president for life. But he did not deserve what happened to him and his family.

In the early hours of August 15, 1975, a group of young officers stormed Mujib's house and killed everybody in it, including his wife, his three sons (one was only nine years old) and his servants. Twenty people in all. Only his two daughters, who were abroad at the time, survived. One of them, Sheikh Hasina, is now the prime minister. (I told you it was Shakespearean.)

The young officers who murdered Mujib were overthrown by a different group within months, and another coup removed that bunch before the end of the year. Eventually power ended up in the hands of General Ziaur Rahman, who was also murdered by fellow officers in 1981. His widow, Khaleda Zia, has been prime minister three times, and still leads the main opposition party.

General Zia was not involved in the murder of Mujib, but he did end up allied to the people who had killed him: officers who detested Mujib's secularism and who, in some cases, had helped the Pakistani army slaughter their own people during the independence war. They killed Zia, too, in the end, but that does not stop Zia's widow and Mujib's daughter from hating each other.

That personal vendetta has virtually paralyzed the politics of a country with half the population of the United States. Ever since democracy was restored in Bangladesh in 1990, Sheikh Hasina and Khaleda Zia have alternated in power, each woman devoting all of her time in opposition to sabotaging the other's initiatives. But now the page may have turned.

The Supreme Court's confirmation of the death sentences on the ageing conspirators of 1975 may finally enable the country to move past its obsession with those horrific murders. If there was a political motive behind the Bangladesh Rifles mutiny, it was to stop that verdict from being passed, but the insubordination did not spread.

Sheikh Hasina's Awami League won the last election by a landslide, and the army stayed loyal to the elected government right through the crisis. The Bangladeshi Shakespeare may be running out of material.

9.

IRAQ I

The Iraq War was a year and a half old when I wrote this piece, and the pattern for the next few years was already clear: a relentless guerrilla war against the American occupation, with one or more Iraqi civil wars on top. I had mostly stopped raging against the stupidity and illegality of the invasion by then, but I still couldn't get over the sheer military incompetence of the operation.

November 14, 2004
WHACK-A-MOLE IN FALLUJA

"We're going to raise the Iraqi flag over Falluja and give it back to the Fallujans," Major-General Richard Natonski told the First Marine Division at the start of the battle for the western Iraqi city. After six days of one-sided fighting (38 American soldiers and about 1,200 Iraqi resistance fighters killed), what's left of the city has indeed been captured, but most Fallujans fled weeks ago, as did most of the resistance fighters who were making it their base.

An estimated thirty to fifty thousand of the city's three hundred thousand people did stay, however, not realizing how devastating U.S. firepower would be in the final assault. Many of them are now dead or injured, though we will never know how many because the U.S. forces refuse to count the civilians killed in their operations and forbid Iraqi official organizations to do so either.

In the end nothing has been accomplished. As Falluja was being reduced to ruins, rebels were seizing the centre of Mosul, Iraq's third-largest city, and a third of the U.S. blocking force around Falluja had to be sent north to deal with it. It's like the fairground game of Whack-a-Mole: bash down one mole and up pops another elsewhere. And the U.S. has just not got enough troops in Iraq to whack all the centres of the resistance at once.

This was the main issue from the start for the U.S. Army, which was deeply opposed to the invasion plan that Defence Secretary Donald Rumsfeld forced on the professional soldiers. As Army Chief of Staff General Eric Shinseki (forced into retirement by Rumsfeld) told a Senate committee in February of last year, a force "on the order of several hundred thousand soldiers" would be needed to control Iraq after the war.

Rumsfeld retorted publicly that Shinseki's figure was "far from the mark," and his neo-conservative ally, Deputy Defence Secretary Paul Wolfowitz, said: "It's hard to conceive that it would take more forces to provide stability in post-Saddam Iraq than it would take to conduct the war itself . . ." But that's exactly what the professional soldiers did foresee.

Anybody could have invaded Iraq. With a little help on sealift and air support, Belgium could have done it. The Iraqi army was comprehensively smashed in the 1991 Gulf War, and due to UN sanctions it had neither repaired its losses nor acquired any new weapons in the following twelve years. Only the toadies in the upper ranks of Western intelligence services managed to persuade themselves that Iraq had functioning weapons of mass destruction; working-level analysts overwhelmingly doubted it. The problem wasn't the war; it was the occupation.

"All of us in the Army felt . . . that the defeat of the Iraqi military would be a relatively straightforward operation of fairly limited duration, but that the securing of the peace and security of a country of twenty-five million people spread out over an enormous geographic area would be a tremendous challenge that would take a lot of people, a lot of labour, to be done right," said Thomas White, Secretary of the Army in 2001–03, in the Public Broadcasting System's recent *Frontline* documentary "Rumsfeld's War."

If there had been three hundred thousand U.S. troops in Iraq when the war ended, the orgy of looting, the collapse of public order and public services, and all the consequent crime and privation that alienated the Iraqi public might have been averted. The U.S. armed forces could have come up with that many soldiers for a year—and if order had been maintained in Iraq and elections held a year ago it would have been over by now. But on Rumsfeld's insistence there were only 138,000 U.S. troops in Iraq.

Why did he insist on that? Because proving that he could successfully invade foreign countries on short notice with relatively small forces, and without demanding major sacrifices from the U.S. public, was key to making President Bush's new strategic doctrine of "pre-emptive war" credible. It was also essential to the neo-conservatives' dream of a lasting *Pax Americana*, which could easily involve an Iraq-sized war every couple of years. So the generals were told to shut up and follow orders.

It's too late to fix Iraq by pumping in larger numbers of U.S. troops now. As Don Rumsfeld used to say sarcastically at his press conferences back when he was sure he was right and both the media and the professional soldiers were all wrong: "All together now: 'quagmire.'"

In January 2005, the United States finally allowed a general election in Iraq. It had resisted the move for almost two years, instead imposing "interim governments" filled with its own placemen. But it was forced to hold the election by Grand Ayatollah Ali al-Sistani, who threatened a Shia general strike if it did not.

Sistani's purpose was to secure the permanent hold on power of the Shia Arab majority (60 percent of Iraq's population), and he succeeded. But the election also increased the alienation of the Sunni Arab minority (20 percent of the population), almost all of whom boycotted the event. They had lost their historic dominance in Iraqi society because of the U.S. invasion, they were already the backbone of the armed resistance to the occupation—and, in less than a year, they would end up in a civil war with the Shias. Even before that happened, American support for the war was collapsing at home.

June 29, 2005
THE LIGHT AT THE END OF THE TUNNEL

If mere rhetoric could bridge the gulf of credibility, President George W. Bush might have turned the tide with his nationally televised speech on Tuesday evening. As usual, he strove to blur the distinction between the "war on terror" (which almost all Americans still see as necessary) and the war in Iraq (which they are finally turning against), and promised viewers that all would end well if they only showed "resolve." His pitch didn't work: the audience has heard it too many times before.

A majority of Americans now understand that the terrorist attacks in Iraq are a result of the U.S. invasion, not a justification for it. Many have also seen the leaked CIA report that concluded that Iraq is producing a new breed of Arab jihadis, trained in urban warfare, who are more numerous and deadlier than the generation that learned its trade in Afghanistan. And so they don't believe the war in Iraq is making them safer, and they see no light at the end of the tunnel.

Since Vice-President Dick Cheney boasted in early June that the insurgency in Iraq was "in its last throes," more than eighty American soldiers and about seven hundred Iraqi civilians have been killed. On Monday, the new Iraqi prime minister, Ibrahim al-Jaafari, declared that "two years will be enough and more than enough to establish security"— but the previous evening, U.S. Defence Secretary Donald Rumsfeld mused aloud on U.S. television that the insurgency in Iraq might last for "five, six, eight, ten, twelve years."

Even more than it hates casualties, the American public hates defeat, and it can sense panic and confusion among the president's allies and advisers. The latest polls show a huge swing against the Iraq War in American public opinion, with around 60 percent now opposing the war and refusing to believe that the Bush administration has a clear plan for winning it. But that doesn't mean that U.S. troops will be leaving Iraq any time soon: there is still the question of saving face.

People forget that American public opinion turned against the Vietnam War in 1968, but that the withdrawal of U.S. combat troops was not completed until 1973. The intervening five years—resulting in two-thirds of all American casualties in the war—were devoted to the search for a way to get U.S. troops out of Vietnam without admitting defeat. At the very least, there had to be a "decent interval" after the U.S. left before the victors collected their prize.

In the end, the humiliation was far greater than if the United States had simply walked away in 1968—the desperate helicopter evacuation on the roof of the American Embassy in Saigon in 1975 is among the best-known images of American history—and the U.S. army became so demoralized that it was virtually useless as a fighting force for a decade afterwards. But we are dealing with human psychology here, and so the pattern is likely to be repeated in Iraq.

The current administration in Washington has identified itself with the Iraq adventure so closely that it would have great difficulty just walking away—especially since Mr. Bush is loyal beyond reason to the neo-conservative ideologues whose obsessions landed him in this mess. There will be mid-term elections to Congress in only sixteen months, but it stretches credulity to believe that U.S. forces could be extracted from Iraq by that time without having a negative effect on Republican chances in the vote.

The real deadline for a U.S. withdrawal from Iraq is the three and a half years that the Bush presidency has left. Keeping control of the White House will be the most important consideration for American Republicans in 2008, so there must be some resolution of the Iraq problem by then. What might it be?

There is the happy-ever-after ending, constantly promised by the Bush administration and its Iraq collaborators, where all the Iraq communities reconcile, the insurgency dies down, and a genuinely democratic government begins to deliver security and prosperity to the exhausted Iraqis. Such an outcome is not impossible in principle, but it is unlikely to occur while U.S. troops are still occupying the country and goading both Islamists and Arab nationalists into resistance.

There is also the roof-of-the-embassy scenario, but that is equally unlikely. The Sunni Arab insurgents in Iraq, drawn from a solid block of 20 percent of the population occupying the heart of the country, have the power to thwart any peace settlement that excludes them. But they cannot drive U.S. troops out, and they cannot re-establish their political domination over the Shia Arabs and the Kurds even if the Americans leave.

So it's going to be messy, and it's even possible that U.S. troops won't be out of Iraq three and a half years from now. In which case, the next U.S. president will be a Democrat.

The long anticipated civil war between the Sunnis and the Shias got underway about eight months later, after the bombing of the al-Askariya shrine on February 22, 2006. It was a horrific civil war—in 2006 and early 2007 an average of a hundred people a day were being kidnapped and killed, usually after horrendous torture, in the Baghdad area alone—but it never really threatened Shia control of the government. Furthermore, it actually brought the American casualty rate down, because U.S. troops were no longer the primary target of the Sunni fighters. And it may not even have raised the overall Iraqi death rate that much, because the number of Iraqi dead was already very great.

October 12, 2006
THE HUMAN COST OF THE IRAQ WAR

The final indignity, if you are an Iraqi who was shot for accidentally turning into the path of a U.S. military convoy (they thought you might be a terrorist), or blown apart by a car bomb or an air strike, or tortured and murdered just for being a Sunni or a Shia, is that President George W. Bush and Prime Minister Tony Blair will deny that your death happened. The script they are working from says (in Mr. Bush's words last December) that only "30,000, more or less" have been killed in Iraq during and since the invasion in March 2003.

So they have a huge incentive to discredit the report in the British medical journal *The Lancet* this week that an extra 655,000 Iraqis have died since the invasion in excess of the natural death rate: 2.5 percent of the population. "I don't consider it a credible report," said Mr. Bush, without giving any reason why not. "It is a fairly small sample they have taken and they have extrapolated it across the country," said a spokesman of the British Foreign Office, as if such a methodology were invalid. But it's not.

The study, led by Dr. Les Roberts and a team of epidemiologists from the Bloomberg School of Public Health at Johns Hopkins University in Baltimore, was based on a survey of 1,849 households, containing 12,801 people, at forty-seven different locations chosen at random in Iraq. Teams of four Iraqi doctors—two men and two women—went from house to house and asked the residents if anybody had died in their family since January 2002 (fifteen months before the invasion).

If anybody had died, they then inquired when and how. They asked for death certificates, and in 92 percent of cases, the families produced them. Then, the Johns Hopkins team of epidemiologists tabulated the statistics and drew their conclusions.

The most striking thing in the study, in terms of credibility, is that the pre-war death rate in Iraq for the period January 2002–March 2003, as calculated from their evidence, was 5.5 per thousand per year. That is virtually identical to the U.S. government estimate of the death rate in Iraq for the same period. Then, from the same evidence, they calculated that the death rate since the invasion has been 13.3 per thousand per year. The difference between the pre-war and post-war death rates over a period of forty months is 655,000 deaths.

More precisely, the deaths reported by the 12,801 people surveyed, when extrapolated to the entire country, indicates a range of between 426,369 and 793,663 excess deaths—and because the sample is large enough it is 95 percent certain that the true figure is within that range. What the Johns Hopkins team have done in Iraq is a more rigorous version of the technique that is used to calculate deaths in southern Sudan and the eastern Congo. To reject it, you must either reject the whole discipline of statistics, or you must question the professional integrity of those doing the survey.

The study, which was largely financed by the Massachusetts Institute of Technology's Center for International Studies, has been reviewed by four independent experts. One of them, Paul Bolton of Boston University, called the methodology "excellent" and said it was standard procedure in a wide range of studies he has worked on: "You can't be sure of the exact number, but you can be quite sure that you are in the right ballpark."

This is not a political smear job. Johns Hopkins University, Boston University and MIT are not fly-by-night institutions, and people who work there have academic reputations to protect. *The Lancet*, founded

182 years ago, is one of the oldest and most respected medical journals in the world. These numbers are real. So what do they mean?

Two-thirds of a million Iraqis have died since the invasion who would be alive if it had not happened. Human Rights Watch has estimated that between 250,000 and 290,000 Iraqis were killed during Saddam Hussein's twenty-year rule, so perhaps 40,000 people might have died between the invasion and now if he had stayed in power. (Though probably not anything like that many, really, because the great majority of Saddam's killings happened during crises like the Kurdish rebellion of the late 1980s and the Shia revolt after the 1990–91 Gulf War.)

Of the 655,000 excess deaths since March 2003, only about 50,000 can be attributed to stress, malnutrition, the collapse of medical services as doctors flee abroad, and other side effects of the occupation. All the rest are violent deaths, and 31 percent are directly due to the actions of foreign "coalition forces," that is, the Americans and British.

The most disturbing thing is the breakdown of the causes of death. Over half the deaths—56 percent—are due to gunshot wounds, but 13 percent are due to air strikes. No terrorists do air strikes. No Iraqi government forces do air strikes, either, because they don't have combat aircraft. Air strikes are done by coalition forces, and air strikes in Iraq have killed over seventy-five thousand people since the invasion.

Oscar Wilde once observed that "to lose one parent may be regarded as a misfortune; to lose both looks like carelessness." To lose seventy-five thousand Iraqis to air strikes looks like carelessness, too.

10

THE POST-SOVIET SPACE

Well, what else was I going to call it? If I'd said "Commonwealth of Independent States," everybody would look blank. The CIS *includes most of the countries that were once part of the Soviet Union. Russia accounts for more than half the population and territory of this space, but the nine full members and two associate members vary widely in language, religion and ethnicity.*

The CIS *has no authority over its members, and is mainly a device for maintaining the free trade and free travel among most of the former Soviet republics. (The Baltic states were never part of it, and Georgia quit after the Rose Revolution.) But the countries that occupy this "post-Soviet space" have shared a lot of history, much of it very painful—and their fates remain linked in some ways, mainly because most of them have Russian-speaking minorities and Russia will always be the neighbourhood superpower.*

Russia is an ethnic stew itself—at least 20 percent of its population is non-Russian—and it has done a spectacularly bad job of reconciling the

Muslim nationalities of the north Caucasus to their membership in the Russian state. Especially in Chechnya. So Moscow borrowed a page from Israel's book.

September 5, 2004
"DECONTEXTUALIZING" CHECHNYA

What would we do without Richard Perle, everybody's favourite neo-conservative? It was he who, some years ago, came up with the notion that we must "decontextualize terrorism": that is, we must stop trying to understand the reasons why some groups turn to terrorism, and simply condemn and kill the terrorists. No grievance, no injury, no cause is great enough to justify the use of terrorism.

This would be an excellent principle if only we could apply it to all uses of violence for political ends—including the violence that is carried out by legal governments using far more lethal weapons than terrorists have access to, and causing far more deaths. I'd be quite happy, for instance, to decontextualize nuclear weapons, agreeing that there are no circumstances that could possibly justify their use. If you want to start decontextualizing things like cluster bombs and napalm, that would be all right with me, too. But that was not what Perle meant at all.

Perle was speaking specifically about Palestinian terrorist attacks against Israel. The point of decontextualizing such attacks was to make it unacceptable for people to point out that there is a connection between Palestinian terrorism and the fact that the Palestinians have lived under Israeli military occupation for the past thirty-seven years and lost almost half their land to Jewish settlements.

Since the Palestinians have no regular armed forces, if we all agree that any resort by them to irregular violence is completely unpardonable and without justification, then there is absolutely nothing they can legitimately do to oppose overwhelming Israeli military force. Decontextualizing terrorism would neatly solve Israel's problem with the Palestinians—and it would also neatly solve Russia's problem with the Chechen resistance.

That is why Russian President Vladimir Putin was so quick to describe the rash of terrorist attacks in recent weeks, and above all, the school massacre in Beslan last Friday, as "a direct intervention against Russia by international terrorism." *Not* by Chechen terrorism, because that would focus attention on Russian behaviour in Chechnya, where Russia's main human-rights organization, Memorial, estimates that three thousand innocent people have been "disappeared" by the Russian occupation forces since 1999.

No, this was an act of international terrorism (by crazy, fanatical Muslims who just hate everybody else), and nothing to do with Russian policies in Chechnya. Indeed, the Russian security services let it be known that ten of the twenty militants killed in the school siege in Beslan were "citizens of the Arab world" and that the attack was the work of al-Qaeda.

And how did they know this, since it's unlikely that the dead attackers were carrying genuine identity documents? It turns out that Federal Security Service "experts" surmised it from the "facial structure" of the dead terrorists. (You know, that unique facial structure that always lets you pick out the Arabs in a crowd.)

Ever since 9/11, countries like Russia and Israel, which face serious challenges from Muslim peoples living under their rule, have been trying to rebrand their local struggles as part of the "global war on terrorism." For those countries that succeed, the rewards can be great: a flood of money and weapons from Washington, plus an end to Western criticism over the methods they use to suppress their Muslim rebels. Without 9/11, Israel would never have gotten away with building its "security fence" so deep inside Palestinian territory, and Russia would face constant Western criticism over the atrocities committed by its troops in Chechnya.

Chechnya was a thorn in Russia's side—and the Russians were an almost unlimited curse for the Chechens—long before anybody had heard of Osama bin Laden. The Chechens, less than a million strong even now, were the last of the Muslim peoples of the Caucasus to be conquered by the Russian Empire in the nineteenth century, holding out for an entire generation, and they never accepted that they had a duty of loyalty to the Russian state.

When the old Soviet Union broke up in 1991, Chechnya immediately declared independence, and successfully fought off a Russian attempt to reconquer it in 1994–96, though the fighting left tens of thousands dead and Grozny, the capital, in ruins. That should have been the end of it, but Vladimir Putin launched a second war against Chechnya in 1999, just after Boris Yeltsin chose him as his successor.

The deal was that Putin could be president if he promised to protect Yeltsin from corruption charges after his retirement. But the practically unknown Putin still had to persuade the Russians to vote for him in a more or less honest election, so he restarted the war in Chechnya in order to build his image as a strong man with Russian voters.

Five years later, Chechnya is a war-torn landscape patrolled by about a hundred thousand Russian soldiers, many thousands are dead, and the Chechen resistance is carrying out terrorist attacks in Russian cities. There may be a few foreign volunteers from other Muslim countries involved in the struggle, but this is not part of some international terrorist conspiracy. It is not even a Russian-Chechen war, really. It is Putin's war, and you can't decontextualize that.

The fighting in Chechnya has died down, and a Russian-backed local warlord now ensures that almost everybody in Chechnya stays quiet and does what they are told. There are still guerrillas in the hills, but not many.

The terrorist attacks on Russian territory have not stopped, however, and Moscow still gets very cross if you question its line that they are the product of some international Islamist conspiracy against Holy Russia. When it was first published, the above piece brought a shower of protests from Russian embassies in various countries; five years later, when Chechen suicide bombers caused carnage on the Moscow subway system in early 2010, I made essentially the same points in another article, and had to deal with identical protests from the same Russian embassies.

But the collapse of the Soviet Union in 1991 was not followed by war in most places. In fact, it was a remarkably non-violent process. Apart from the Caucasus, where Armenians fought Azerbaijanis, Georgians fought their own minorities, and Chechens fought Russians, the whole transformation was accomplished with only a few hundred lives lost. If only the aftermath had been as well managed.

March 9, 2006
BELARUS: A CASE OF ARRESTED DEVELOPMENT

The ten million citizens of Belarus don't go to the polls until March 19, but the outcome is already certain: Alexander Lukashenko will win a third term as president. Most other governments in Europe will express their dismay and claim that the election was unfair. They will be right in the sense that the opposition has been mercilessly harassed and that the counting of the votes probably won't meet international standards. But they will be wrong if they really think that Lukashenko would have lost a fair election.

"It is necessary . . . to take a stand against this post-Soviet autocrat and his efforts to totally suppress what remains of independent initiatives in Belarus," said former Czech president Vaclav Havel last year, but Lukashenko does not see autocracy as a bad thing. As he told Belarusian radio early this month: "An authoritarian ruling style is characteristic of me, and I have always admitted it. Why? . . .You need to control the country, and the main thing is not to ruin people's lives."

Belarus has more policemen per capita than any other country in the world, and a few of Lukashenko's harshest critics have simply "disappeared." Opposition politicians are regularly beaten up or jailed, and people can go to jail for up to two years simply for openly criticizing the president. It is an ugly, petty, oppressive regime that is reminiscent in many ways of the old Communist tyrannies—but Lukashenko has won two elections and a referendum in the past dozen years, all with more than 70 percent of the vote.

Although many people in Belarus feel intimidated by his rule, if they were really a majority then the tool for their liberation would be readily available. In the last five years, disciplined crowds of non-violent protestors have overthrown similar "post-Soviet autocrats" in several other post-Soviet states, and if the problems are just unfree elections and intimidation, why don't Belarusians get rid of their faintly Chaplinesque dictator that way?

The answer is to be found in the results of an international opinion poll published last week by the Social Research Institute in Budapest. The survey was conducted last year in eleven Central and Eastern European countries that were ruled by Communist tyrannies for at least a generation until the revolutions of 1989–91. The only country where a majority of the people polled preferred the "democratic" systems (some real, some sham) that they have lived in since then was the Czech Republic, where 52 percent actively supported democracy and only a small minority longed to have Communism back.

In most of the former Soviet-bloc countries, the nostalgia for Communist rule remained strong, peaking at 38 percent in Bulgaria and 36 percent in Russia (where only 13 percent favoured democracy). But this is hardly surprising when you consider that most people's experience, in most of these countries, was that the end of Communist rule brought a steep fall in living standards and a sharp rise in insecurity and inequality. For Russia, it also brought the loss of a centuries-old empire, the "exile" of tens of millions of Russians as minorities in newly independent countries, and a huge decline in the country's power and influence in the world.

These things are not what normally accompanies the advent of democracy elsewhere. They happened in Central and Eastern Europe partly because the social and economic costs of converting from a centrally planned economy to a free market were bound to be very high, and partly because the former Communist elite seized the opportunity to "privatize" the state's former assets (that is, almost everything) into their own pockets. It was an experience that has given democracy a very bad name in the former Soviet bloc, and only time and the rise of a new generation will erase these attitudes.

And here we have Belarus, where a former collective-farm manager legitimately elected to power in 1994 halted the privatization process before it had properly got underway. Lukashenko has preserved both the good and the bad elements of the Communist system almost unchanged (except that the actual Communist Party no longer rules), and as a result there has not been the same crash in living standards in Belarus and none of the soaring inequality and unemployment experienced by almost all of its neighbours.

There is also no free media and the secret police are everywhere. Belarus has the drab conformity typical of late-period Communist states, with occasional state violence against "dissidents," but Lukashenko would probably have won a majority of the votes honestly in every election and referendum he has held.

Why has it happened this way in Belarus and not elsewhere? Partly pure chance, but Belarus was also an ideal candidate because it has a very weak national identity (most people there actually speak Russian). Also, there is little of the nationalism that helped most other former Soviet countries to persevere with the changes, and many Belarusians would be happy to be reunited with Russia. But even if this were to happen they would still have to undergo many of the painful changes that they have so far avoided by choosing to live in this time-warp.

Sooner or later, they will have to go through those changes anyway, but not yet. Not in this election.

If you like the Caucasus, you'll love Central Asia. With the obvious excep-tions of Afghanistan and Pakistan, all the 'stans are former Soviet repub-lics, and they sometimes seem engaged in a race to the bottom. They are former Russian colonies, and, as in post-colonial Africa, the successor regimes tend to be both autocratic and incompetent. The roads are crum-bling in Central Asia, too.

And just like post-colonial Africa, Central Asia has become an arena for strategic competition between the great powers.

May 8, 2006
CHENEY AND KAZAKHSTAN: USEFUL HYPOCRISY?

Had U.S. Vice-President Dick Cheney declared during his visit to Kazakhstan last weekend that "in many areas of civil society—from religion and the news media to advocacy groups and political parties— the government has unfairly and improperly restricted the rights of the people," human-rights groups would have cheered. But he said that in Russia, a few days earlier.

What Cheney told Kazakhstan's dictator, Nursultan Nazarbayev, was that "all Americans are tremendously impressed with the progress that you've made in Kazakhstan in the last fifteen years. Kazakhstan has become a good friend and strategic partner of the United States."

Admiration for Kazakhstan's progress is not actually a leading conver-sational topic in the United States. The man whom the *Financial Times* recently and memorably described as "the Bush administration's Lord Voldemort" was merely engaging in a little useful hypocrisy, or so he imagined. The question is whether it really is useful.

Cheney's blunt condemnation of the Russian government's behaviour certainly roused a vehement reaction in Russia. President Vladimir Putin's drift towards a "soft dictatorship" has the support of most Russians, who are still smarting from the anarchy, corruption and poverty of the first post-Communist decade under Boris Yeltsin. Now the anarchy has been suppressed, the corruption is better hidden and the economy is growing, so the Russian media's bitter response to Cheney's strictures really did match popular attitudes.

Under the headline "Enemy at the Gate," the Moscow business daily *Kommersant*, normally a critic of the Kremlin, said that "the Cold War has restarted, only now the front line has shifted." An overreaction, of course, but Cheney's criticisms would have been less offensive if he were not so obviously applying a double standard. Kazakhstan will become one of the world's top ten oil producers in the next decade. It is a close ally of the United States, and even sent a small contingent of Kazakh troops to Iraq. But Kazakhstan is not a democracy, and Nursultan Nazarbayev is not a democrat.

When Dick Cheney became Secretary of Defence in the administration of the elder George Bush in 1989, Nursultan Nazarbayev was the First Secretary of the Kazakh Communist Party. By 1990, he was president of the Kazakh Soviet Socialist Republic and a member of the Soviet politburo in Moscow. And, by the end of 1991, he was the president of an independent Kazakhstan and a keen advocate of the free market, as if his Communist past had been merely an adolescent foible.

Fifteen years and three "elections" later, Nazarbayev is still president of Kazakhstan, re-elected last December with a 91 percent majority in a vote that foreign observers condemned as fraudulent. His daughter, Dariga Nazarbayeva, who controls the Khabar media conglomerate and leads the "opposition" Asar Party, is expected to take power when his current seven-year term expires in 2012. ("I can't swear it will never happen," she says coyly.)

Nazarbayev's regime does not boil people in oil like the regime of his neighbour in Uzbekistan, President Islam Karimov (who was First Secretary of the Uzbekistan Communist Party in 1989). It is not as megalomaniacal as the regime of President-for-Life Saparmurat Niyazov in Turkmenistan, who has renamed the month of January after himself, April after his mother, and May after his father. (Niyazov became First

Secretary of the Turkmenistan Communist Party in 1985.) Indeed, among the 'stans, Nazarbayev's Kazakhstan is only the third- or fourth-worst dictatorship, but it is a far less democratic and tolerant society than Putin's Russia. So why did Dick Cheney castigate Russia's imperfect democracy while saying not a word about Kazakhstan's shameless travesty of the democratic system? Oil, obviously, but how could he be so ignorant of Nazarbayev's priorities?

Senior oil company executives know that you sometimes have to kiss the nether regions of local potentates in order to make the deals happen, but they generally only do so when it seems fairly certain that the deal will really go through as a result. This one won't.

What Cheney wants out of Nazarbayev is commitment to pipelines that will move Kazakh oil and gas to Europe by routes that do not cross Russia—which means pipelines under the Caspian Sea. In turn, what Nazarbayev wants is a solid American offer that he can take to the Russians, so that he can demand a higher price for his gas exports to them through the existing pipelines. He will also take it to the Chinese and suggest that they build pipelines to bring his oil and gas to China. In short, he has been playing the game at least as long as Cheney, and he holds a better hand.

Nursultan Nazarbayev is holding out for the best price, and the winning bid is unlikely to come from the United States. Cheney's kowtowing to Nazarbayev is as futile as his chiding of Putin. And although his hypocritical moralizing about the shortcomings of Russian democracy probably has little direct effect on the calculations of a strategist as cool as Vladimir Putin, it does poison the relationship at many other levels. And that still matters because Russia is coming back as a force in the world.

Russia is not coming back as a coequal superpower to the United States, of course. That role is reserved (if they want it) for the Chinese. But it is coming back as a dominant regional power with a sphere of influence that other great powers respect, just as the other great powers respect the dominant role of the United States in Central America and the Caribbean.

I am too fond of the Russians, so I may be an unreliable guide in these matters, but I do think that Russia will evolve into a modern democracy one of these days. Generational turnover solves a lot of problems and, in the end, I think it will erase the bad memories of the 1990s and make democracy respectable again in Russia. Although many Russians (and many Europeans) would dispute it, Russia is a European country, and democracy has become the European norm.

June 26, 2006
RUSSIA: CUCKOO IN THE NEST

On Sunday, July 1, the Russian rouble will become a fully convertible currency, traded under the same rules as dollars, euros, pounds and yen. The date was obviously chosen to impress President Vladimir Putin's guests at the G8 meeting in St. Petersburg in mid-July with Russia's economic progress. And there really has been quite a lot of progress on that front since he took over. But the Group of Seven, "the world's most exclusive club," was originally meant to be an annual gathering of the leaders of the biggest industrialized *democracies.*

It would be stretching the term to say that the new member of the Group of Eight, as it became in 1996, is a democracy anymore. While sections of the Russian press still conduct raucous political debates, the all-important medium of television has been brought under direct or indirect state control, and more and more power has been concentrated in Putin's hands. He speaks of a "managed democracy," but his chief economic adviser, Andrei Illarionov, resigned last December saying that Russia was no longer free or democratic.

It's equally questionable whether Russia is really an industrialized power anymore. The Russian economy resembles Nigeria's or Iran's more than those of its fellow G8 members: oil and gas account for 70 percent of the country's export earnings and 30 percent of its entire economy. Even after six years of Putin's rule, Russian oil production has not risen back up to the level of the early nineties, and only the high price of oil worldwide gives Russia some prosperity at home and some clout abroad.

Since the whole purpose of inviting Russia to join the G8 was to encourage the growth of democracy and a modern free-market economy in the ex-Communist giant, Russia's fellow G8 members are filled with consternation at the way things have turned out. However, they are at a loss for how to deal with the cuckoo in their nest. Quiet persuasion doesn't seem to work, but neither does noisy outrage.

Putin simply doesn't feel the need to listen—and neither do Russians in general. The remarkable thing about Putin's rule is that after six years in office he continues to have the approval, according to reasonably reliable opinion polls, of 77 percent of his fellow citizens. Indeed, although Putin will obey the constitutional ban on a third consecutive presidential term and leave power after the 2008 election, there is huge popular support for changing the constitution to allow him to stay on for another four years (59 percent yes, 29 percent no). What's the matter with the Russians? Doesn't everybody want democracy?

No, not everybody wants democracy. According to Leonid Sedov, a senior analyst at the VTSIOM-A polling agency, about 80 percent of Russians say they dislike democracy, although they are less clear on what they do like. Only 3 percent want the return of the tsars, some 16 percent want a tough authoritarian ruler like Stalin, and the rest are scattered all over the political map. But they like Putin because he has given them back stability, prosperity and self-respect.

It's a reaction to the chaotic process of de-Communization under Boris Yeltsin in the 1990s, which was misleadingly called "democratization," and it doesn't necessarily mean that Russians would dislike real democracy. (They were keen enough on it in 1989–91, before "democratization" impoverished most of them.)

Russians are still among the best-educated populations on the planet, and once the middle class feels prosperous and secure enough, the demand for democracy is likely to re-emerge. But that may be years away, and what are the democratic majority in the G8 to do with this authoritarian cuckoo in their nest in the meantime?

Put up with it, and pretend not to notice that it doesn't really fit in. Nag it about its more severe human-rights abuses, and demand that it give at least lip service to its democratic principles, but don't drive the regime out into the cold. When the tide finally turns in Russian society, the survival of formal democratic structures and the rule of law, however much abused in practice, will make the task of building a genuine democracy in Russia a lot easier.

In effect, that is what the other seven members of the G8 have decided, and they are probably right. Of course, the fact that Russia has all that oil and gas to sell may have influenced their decision, too.

I have only met Georgia's President Mikheil Saakashvili once, and have no special insight into his character. (I was not in the region when the war broke out in 2008, and had no access to special sources of information.) So why was it obvious to me that it was the Georgians who had started the war, while the English-language news media, with a few honourable exceptions (the British Broadcasting Corporation, the English service of Al-Jazeera and one or two others), fell for the Georgian claim that they were being attacked by the Russians?

All the early reports placed Georgian troops well inside South Ossetia, some of them right in Tskhinvali, the capital. What the hell were they doing there if the Russians had started the war? And yet the Western media fell for the old stereotypes of big bad Russia and gallant little Georgia that Saakashvili started pushing as soon as his little smash-and-grab operation went wrong.

The Georgians' greatest blunder was that they did not give absolute military priority to getting a blocking force into place at the exit from the Roki/Roksky Tunnel under the main Caucasus range, a 3.6-kilometre tunnel that connects North Ossetia, part of the Russian Federation, with the rebel Georgian province of South Ossetia. There were barely a thousand lightly armed Russian peacekeeping troops in South Ossetia when the Georgians attacked them, but leaving that tunnel open meant that they would be facing major Russian armoured forces within twenty-four hours. That is exactly what happened, and three days later the Georgian army broke and fled. Stupid, stupid, stupid.

August 10, 2008
SOUTH OSSETIA: A MONUMENTAL MISCALCULATION

The war in South Ossetia is essentially over, and the Georgians have lost. This was Georgia's second attempt in eighteen years to conquer the breakaway territory by force, and now that option is gone for good. So are the country's hopes of joining the North Atlantic Treaty Organization (NATO). Yet sections of the Western media are carrying on as if the Russians started it, and are now threatening to invade Georgia itself.

President George W. Bush has condemned Russia's "disproportionate and dangerous" response, although there is no evidence that Russian ground troops have violated the borders of Georgia proper. Nor are they likely to.

Much is made of Russian air attacks on targets inside Georgia, and especially of the inevitable misses that cause civilian casualties, but the vast majority of the two thousand civilians allegedly killed so far in this conflict were South Ossetians killed by Georgian shells, rockets and bombs. Some shooting and bombing will continue until all the Georgian troops are cleared out of South Ossetia—including the 40 percent of its territory that they controlled before the war—but then it will stop.

Meanwhile, Georgian President Mikheil Saakashvili is playing on old Cold War stereotypes of the Russian threat in a desperate bid for Western backing: "What Russia is doing in Georgia is open, unhidden aggression and a challenge to the whole world. If the whole world does not stop Russia today, then Russian tanks will be able to reach any other European capital." Nonsense. It was Georgia that started this war.

The chronology tells it all. Skirmishes between Georgian troops and South Ossetian militia grew more frequent over the past several months, but on Thursday, August 7, Saakashvili offered the separatist South Ossetian government "an immediate ceasefire and the immediate beginning of talks," promising that "full autonomy" was on the table. Only hours later, however, he ordered a general offensive.

South Ossetian's president, Eduard Kokoity, called Saakashvili's ceasefire offer a "despicable and treacherous" ruse, which seems fair enough. Through all of Thursday night and Friday morning Georgian artillery shells and rockets rained down on the little city of Tskhinvali, South Ossetia's capital, while Georgian infantry and tanks encircled it. Russian journalists reported that 70 percent of the city was destroyed, and by Friday afternoon it was in Georgian hands.

The offensive was obviously planned well in advance, but Saakashvili didn't think it through. He knew that the world's attention would be distracted by the Olympics, and he hoped that Russia's reaction would be slow because Prime Minister Putin was off in Beijing. Given three or four days to establish full military control of South Ossetia, he could put a pro-Georgian administration in place and declare the problem solved. But his calculations were wrong.

There was no delay in the Russian response. A large Russian force was on its way from North Ossetia by midday on Friday, and Russian jets began striking targets inside Georgia proper. By the time Putin reached the North Ossetian capital of Vladikavkaz on Saturday morning, the Georgian forces were already being driven out of Tskhinvali again.

By Saturday evening, Georgia was calling for a ceasefire and declaring that all its troops were being withdrawn from South Ossetia to prevent a "humanitarian catastrophe." Saakashvili's gamble had failed — and, as Putin put it, the territorial integrity of Georgia had "suffered a fatal blow."

Not just South Ossetia has been lost for good. Georgia's hope of ever recovering its other breakaway province, Abkhazia, has also evaporated. On Saturday, the Abkhazian government announced a military offensive to drive Georgian troops out of the Kodori gorge, the last bit of Abkhazian territory that they control. How much does all of this matter?

It matters a lot to the three hundred thousand Georgians who fled from Abkhazia and South Ossetia when the two ethnic enclaves, which were autonomous parts of the Georgian Soviet Socialist Republic in Soviet times, declared their independence after the old Soviet Union collapsed in 1991. Georgia's attempts to reconquer them in 1992–93 were bloody failures, and after this second failure, it is clear that the Georgian refugees will never go home.

There is reason to rejoice for most Abkhazians and Ossetians. Although they are Orthodox Christians like the far more numerous Georgians, they are ethnically distinct peoples with different languages, and they always resented Stalin's decision to place them under Georgian rule. Whether they ultimately get full independence or simply join the Russian Federation, they will be happy with either outcome.

The Bush administration's bizarre ambition to extend NATO into the Caucasus mountains is dead. Russians are pleased with the speed and effectiveness of their government's response. And nobody else really cares.

There is no great moral issue here. What Georgia tried to do to South Ossetia is precisely what Russia did to Chechnya, but Georgia wasn't strong enough and South Ossetia had a bigger friend. There is no great strategic issue either: apart from a few pipeline routes, the whole Transcaucasus is of little importance to the rest of the world. A year from now the Georgians will probably have dumped Saakashvili, and the rest of us may not even remember his foolish adventure.

I wrote that article only sixty hours after the fighting started late on August 7, 2008, and I got a few things wrong. The civilian death toll in South Ossetia was in the low hundreds, not two thousand as first reported. Russian troops did subsequently push thirty or forty kilometres into Georgian territory for a while, to destroy military supply dumps and the like, but they left again. And Saakashvili, astonishingly, is still in power despite his huge blunder.

A year after the war ended, a special commission set up by the European Union concluded that Georgia started the war, but the Georgian government still insists that it was an unprovoked Russian invasion. It is taking quite a while for the post-Soviet space to settle down, but at least the tense Ukrainian-Russian relationship seems on the way to a sensible resolution.

November 13, 2008
REALISM IN UKRAINE

The brawl in the Ukrainian parliament last Tuesday was an undignified ending to the country's two-month political crisis, but something important has changed. In the immediate aftermath of the Orange Revolution of 2004, the more extreme Ukrainian nationalists fantasized that the country could break all its links with Russia and become an entirely Western state, but now realism is starting to prevail.

To the extent that abstract generalizations play a role in Ukrainian politics, they are mainly generalizations about Russia. Is it a friendly neighbour, close to Ukrainians in language, culture and history, or is it a perpetual threat to Ukraine's independence? The answer people give depends mainly on whether they speak Ukrainian or Russian at home (and about half of Ukraine's citizens do speak Russian at home).

The more extreme nationalists would deny that, insisting that the great majority of the country's citizens speak Ukrainian, but that is a wish rather than a fact, as a walk down the streets of any big Ukrainian city, except Lviv in the far west of the country, will quickly reveal. Centuries of Russian political domination mean that Russian is the dominant language of urban culture almost everywhere in Ukraine, and in the heavily industrialized east of the country even the ethnic Ukrainians mostly speak Russian.

Many, perhaps most, Ukrainian nationalists believe that Ukraine can safeguard its independence only through integration with major Western institutions. Since the old ex-Communist elite was finally forced from power by the Orange Revolution in 2004, President Viktor Yushchenko, the leader of that non-violent revolution, has been pushing hard for membership in the European Union and NATO. But not all the leaders of that revolution agree with this strategy.

Yulia Tymoshenko, with her trademark braided hair, became almost as famous as Yushchenko during the events of 2004 and, afterwards, she became prime minister. She subsequently fell out with Yushchenko, but was back as prime minister by December of last year. She is unquestionably a Ukrainian nationalist, but she was uncharacteristically silent when the conflict between Georgia and Russia blew up last August.

President Viktor Yushchenko, now her bitterest rival, was outspoken in his backing of Georgia against the Russian "invasion," and urged the European Union and NATO to speed up their response to Ukraine's applications for membership. But Ukraine is deeply divided on those questions, with around half the population opposing NATO membership. In the end, neither Western organization responded to the applications with an unequivocal yes.

Tymoshenko didn't say much about that, either, and then in September her party in parliament voted along with the pro-Russian Party of the Regions in a move to curb the president's powers. President Yushchenko saw this as a betrayal, since Tymoshenko's party and his own "Our Ukraine" group were in a coalition in parliament.

Quite a few people in Ukraine suspect that Tymoshenko has made a secret deal with the Russians. She intends to run for the presidency against Yushchenko next year, and the theory is that she promised to keep quiet about Georgia and not push for Ukrainian membership in the European Union and NATO in return for Moscow's tacit support in the presidential election.

Tymoshenko was quite right not to offer Georgia her automatic support, since it was the Georgians who started the war. She is right not to push NATO membership for Ukraine either, since that would infuriate Moscow and split Ukraine right down the middle. But that doesn't mean she didn't make that secret deal with the Russians. In fact, she probably did.

Moscow is very unhappy with the openly anti-Russian stance of President Yushchenko, and the September vote to curb his powers was just what it wanted to see. It couldn't have passed without Tymoshenko's support, and many see it as proof that she has made her deal. She is positioning herself as a Ukrainian nationalist who is not anti-Russian, and that may be enough to win her the presidency next year. But it unleashed two months of political chaos in Ukraine.

So Tymoshenko and Moscow win—but so, perhaps, does Ukraine, for the extreme pro-Western and anti-Russian positions taken up by Yushchenko were not wise. Moscow does not appear to harbour any ambition to regain the control over Ukraine it had in Soviet and Tsarist times, but it would see a Ukrainian government that joined NATO as an enemy of Russia. Ukraine's independence is probably safer outside NATO than it would be inside it.

In fact, Tymoshenko didn't win the 2010 presidential election. She lost narrowly to another pro-Russian candidate, Viktor Yanukovych. Foreign observers judged the election to be fair: Ukrainian voters were just facing up to reality. Ukraine's relationship with Russia is in many ways like Canada's with the United States—the shared history and geography, the economical and cultural ties and the huge disparity in power—so it was always a bad idea for Ukraine to talk about joining NATO. (Imagine what would have happened during the Cold War if Canada had started talking about joining the Warsaw Pact.)

Ukraine doesn't have to be a Russian satellite but if its government completely ignores Russian concerns it will have problems, even with a substantial proportion of its own citizens.

11.

IRAN

Relations between Iran and the West started getting really bad in 2005, because that's when the man with the mouth, Mahmoud Ahmadinejad, won the presidency. He really did win it, too, even though nobody saw it coming. And all the domestic and international tensions of the next five years followed almost automatically.

June 25, 2005
THE IRANIAN SURPRISE

It doesn't make sense. In the previous two presidential elections, in 1997 and 2001, Iranians voted more than two-to-one for the reformist candidate, Mohammad Khatami. It did them little good: the Islamist clerics who have veto power over the elected parts of the Iranian government blocked Khatami's attempts to liberalize the system. But it seemed clear that younger Iranians in particular were fed up with clerical domination of politics. Since the 2001 election, unemployment has gotten worse and the poor have gotten poorer. So why have Iranian voters now elected the hardest of hard-liners, Mahmoud Ahmadinejad, to the presidency with a two-thirds majority?

There's no point in pretending that Ahmadinejad didn't really win. There may have been some stuffed ballot boxes in the first round of the presidential election on June 17, when half a dozen candidates were running, but last Friday's runoff was decisive: more than seventeen million votes for Ahmadinejad and ten million for his opponent, Akbar Hashemi Rafsanjani. They didn't stuff that many ballot boxes.

Ahmadinejad is a staunch supporter of the Islamic state, an instructor in the Basij, the voluntary youth militia that monitors people's dress and behaviour, and a close associate of the Supreme Ruler, Ayatollah Ali Khamenei. He is definitely not a "reformer," though he does promise to attack corruption. Why did he win?

Iran's partial democracy first came under serious attack in last year's parliamentary election, when the ruling clerical elite concluded that the reformers were growing too popular. The Guardian Council disqualified three thousand parliamentary candidates from running on the grounds that they were not Islamic enough, including eighty sitting members of parliament (out of 290). President Khatami's feeble protests were ignored, parliament fell under Islamist control, and Iranians who opposed the regime began to lose faith in electoral politics.

The Guardian Council tried to pull the same trick with this year's presidential election, disqualifying all the reformist candidates, but the opposition responded by threatening to boycott the election, which would have reduced it to a farce. Ayatollah Khamenei intervened, and two reformist candidates were allowed to run together with one "moderate" (Rafsanjani, formerly president between 1989 and 1997 and a cleric himself) and four hard-liners.

Mahmoud Ahmadinejad was one of the hard-liners, but only three weeks ago, the opinion polls gave him a scant 5 percent of the vote. Then, suddenly, a miracle: he was ahead of all the other hard-liners and catching up with Rafsanjani and the reformist candidates.

On June 17, the moderate Rafsanjani came first, with 21 percent of the votes, but Ahmadinejad came a close second with 19.5 percent.

There may have been some skulduggery at the polls, but the main reason for his relative success is that the Islamic authorities, fearing that no pro-regime candidate would make it into the runoff, ordered their loyal supporters in the armed forces, the Revolutionary Guard and the Basij militia, to swing all their votes to Ahmadinejad.

Appalled at the prospect of a radical Islamist as president, the defeated reformers urged their supporters to hold their noses and back Rafsanjani in the second round. And yet it ended in a landslide victory for Ahmadinejad. What happened?

It was actually a very small landslide. Back when Iranians believed that electing a reformist president could bring change, voter turnout was huge, but it has been plummeting as they lost hope: from 83 percent in 1997 to 67 percent in 2001; then down to 62 percent in the first round of voting this month, and only 47 percent in the second round. Ahmadinejad's "landslide" was less than 30 percent of qualified voters.

His votes came from religious radicals and the "pious poor," who back him because he is devout but *not* one of the clerics who have used their power to enrich themselves. He played up to more sophisticated voters by promising to concentrate on economics, not dress codes—"The country's true problem is unemployment and housing, not what to wear," he explained—but he is nevertheless the Supreme Leader's choice as president, and most people know it. That's why they didn't vote.

The hard-line Islamists now control every branch of Iran's government, appointed or elected, and for a while they will have their way. But what really happened last week was that a majority of Iranians abandoned the electoral path to reform as hopeless. At some point in the future, therefore, they may try the path of non-violent revolution—and they might win.

That was my Prediction of the Year, and I'm quite proud of it. But I did not foresee that the next few years would bring a steady escalation in the military threats that the United States made against Iran.

In the thirty years that the mullahs have been in power they have not attacked any neighbouring state. When Saddam Hussein's Iraq invaded Iran in the 1980s, they fought a bitter eight-year war to repel the invasion, but accepted a negotiated peace that simply restored the status quo. There was the suspicion that Iran was working on nuclear weapons, but even if that were true it was not exactly an imminent danger. So why was the Bush administration apparently so eager to attack Iran? Maybe they were watching the wrong movies.

March 16, 2007
300: A PROPAGANDA FAILURE

Being cultural adviser to Iran's President Mahmoud Ahmadinejad must be one of the more thankless jobs on the planet, but Javad Shamghadri manages to keep busy. His latest foray is into the cultural space occupied by the teenage bloodlust demographic.

What bothers Shamghadri—and quite a lot of other people in Iran—is the new Hollywood hit 300, an animated comic book of a film that shows impossibly buff and noble Greeks rebuffing an attempt by evil Persians to strangle Western civilization in its cradle 2,487 years ago. They think it's "psychological warfare" against present-day Iranians, thinly disguised as a story about their wicked Persian ancestors.

Shamghadri is so clueless about the workings of Hollywood that you really want to take him gently by the hand and walk him through it. "Following the Islamic Revolution in Iran [in 1979]," he says, "Hollywood and cultural authorities in the U.S. initiated studies to figure out how to attack Iranian culture. Certainly, the recent movie is a product of such studies."

After pausing for a moment to savour the notion of "cultural authorities in the U.S.," let's move on to the Tehran newspaper *Ayandeh-No*, which is quite close to the regime. Under a headline screaming "Hollywood declares war on Iranians," it complains that "the film depicts Iranians as demons, without culture, feeling or humanity, who think of nothing except attacking other nations and killing people. It is a new effort to slander the Iranian people and civilization before world public opinion at a time of increasing American threats against Iran."

Now, I must admit that I haven't seen 300 (and neither has anybody in Iran). I suppose I should have gone to see the movie before I wrote about it, but a) I'm in Cuba at the moment, where it isn't playing; and b) I did see the trailer for the movie, which gave me quite enough sense of the thing's style.

I don't know many teenage males who could resist the lure of 300, but as a somewhat-more-than-teenage male, I found myself more in sympathy with the nameless Internet reviewer who wrote: "I feel comfortable enough in my masculinity to say that if I had to stand in the presence of these [ultra-macho Greek heroes] for more than ten seconds, I'd spontaneously grow a pair of ovaries."

So, can we all just laugh at those stupid, paranoid Iranians for getting their knickers into a twist about a dumb, harmless splatter film cleverly disguised as art? 'Fraid not. It really is war propaganda of the crudest, nastiest kind, even though there are no "American cultural authorities" and the people who made the movie have probably never had a consciously political thought in their money-grubbing lives.

We all swim in the same sea of images, and we all get the same short list of "things to worry about right now" from the media. It's not a plot, it's just how things work, and in this case the filmmakers had a great story to work with: the battle of Thermopylae in 480 BC really did save Greece from conquest by the nearest Asian empire, Persia (although all the Greeks at Thermopylae died). Plus, they had the extraordinary images from Frank Miller's comic-book retelling of the story, and they knew that Iran is next on the U.S. hit list.

For several decades now, the bad guys in American action films with an international setting have mostly been Middle Easterners (or at least, the rough ones are; the smooth ones are still generally British). Iranians actually do live in the Middle East, so lay it on with a trowel.

As for the stiff, super-patriotic, over-the-top macho dialogue, most of it comes straight from Miller's comic book. He presumably just picked it up from the general culture in the United States, which has been deeply infected by that sort of thing for the past number of years.

So, no plot, nobody to blame, and yet the film is everything the Iranians say it is. The Persians are depicted as "ugly, dumb, murderous savages" (in the words of *Ayandeh-No*) who want to conquer the free people of the world, while the Spartans are clearly Americans, spouting the same slogans about "liberty" and "freedom" that are sprinkled on all political discourse in the United States like sugar on corn flakes.

What's more, the Spartans are underdogs. In almost all U.S.-made action films with an international setting, the American heroes are underdogs fighting against enormous odds, even though they actually come from the most powerful country in the history of the world. Just the same, you know that they are in the right because in the movies the underdogs are always in the right, and they always win in the end.

So the gallant Spartan-Americans triumph over the evil Persians, and let that be a lesson to evildoers everywhere. But our Iranian friends should not worry that this film is juicing up American youth for an invasion of their country, because the kids just won't get it. Down in the teenage bloodlust demographic, practically nobody knows that the Persians of ancient times and the Iranians of today are the same people.

It was Iran's alleged drive for nuclear weapons that gave American hostility to the country some resonance in the rest of the world. But the American accusations were never substantiated, and they may not be correct.

September 25, 2007
IRAN'S NUCLEAR ASPIRATIONS

Iranian President Mahmoud Ahmadinejad's two speeches in New York this week, at Columbia University and then at the United Nations General Assembly, have stirred up the usual storm of outrage in the Western media. He is a strangely naïve man, and his almost-but-not-quite denial of the Holocaust—he called for "more research," as if rumours had recently cropped up suggesting that something bad happened in Nazi-occupied Europe—was as bizarre as his denial that there are any homosexuals in Iran.

But he is not a "cruel dictator," as Columbia University's president, Lee Bollinger, called him. Indeed, in the areas that matter most to foreigners—foreign policy, defence and nuclear questions—Ahmadinejad has no power at all. Those subjects are the sole responsibility of Iran's unelected parallel government, Supreme Leader Ayatollah Ali Khamenei and the Guardian Council.

So ignore the capering clown on the stage. The real questions are: Does Iran have a nuclear-weapons program? Could it "threaten the world" even if it did? And why does American rhetoric about the Iranian nuclear threat sound so much like American rhetoric about the Iraqi nuclear threat five years ago?

We know that there once was an Iranian nuclear-weapons program, but that was under the Shah, whom Washington was grooming as the policeman of the Gulf. After the revolution of 1979, the new leader of the Islamic Republic of Iran, Ayatollah Ruhollah Khomeini, cancelled that program on the grounds that weapons of mass destruction were un-Islamic, although he retained the peaceful nuclear-power program.

Then came the Iran-Iraq War of 1980–88, in which the United States ultimately backed Saddam Hussein, although he had clearly started the war. Saddam was known to be working on nuclear weapons, so despite their Islamic reservations, the Iranian ayatollahs sanctioned the restarting of the Shah's nuclear weapons program in 1984 to counter that threat.

That is when Iran began work on the uranium enrichment plant at Natanz that figures in so many American accusations. When the Iran-Iraq War ended in 1988, however, work at Natanz slowed to a crawl. And once UN inspectors dismantled all of Iraq's nuclear facilities, after Saddam Hussein's invasion of Kuwait in 1990 and his subsequent defeat in the first Gulf war, Natanz seems to have stopped functioning entirely.

Why did Iran then restart work at Natanz seven or eight years ago? Probably in response to Pakistan's nuclear weapons tests in 1998 and the subsequent overthrow of the elected government there. Iran is Shia, whereas Pakistan is largely Sunni and home to some very militant Sunni extremists. The extremists were not yet in power, but Iranians worried that one day they might be, so they took out an insurance policy.

Iran started building Natanz in secret because, back in 1984, there were daily Iraqi air-raids across the country. Natanz stayed secret after the war because there was no legal requirement to reveal its existence to the International Atomic Energy Agency (IAEA) until six months before it began to process nuclear fuel, and Iran feared an Israeli attack on the facility.

Iran was embarrassed when the existence of Natanz was revealed in 2002, and immediately suspended work there for three years, but the plant is not illegal and it does not prove that Iran is currently seeking nuclear weapons. Other countries have similar enrichment facilities to upgrade uranium as fuel for nuclear reactors, and that is what Iran says it is doing, too.

No doubt the Iranian government also knows that, in a crisis, it could run the fuel through the centrifuges many more times and turn it into weapons-grade uranium, but so do other governments. This is called a "threshold" nuclear-weapons capability, and it is a very popular option.

The IAEA found no evidence that Iran is working on nuclear weapons, so, in 2005, the United States has the issue transferred to the UN Security Council, where political rather than legal considerations decide outcomes. The Security Council imposed mild sanctions on Iran, and Washington is pressing for much harsher ones. It also threatens to use force against Iran, but for all its rhetoric, there is still no evidence that Iran is doing anything illegal.

The enrichment facilities may be solely for peaceful nuclear power now, but they would give Iran the ability to build its own nuclear deterrent much more quickly in a panic. President Ahmadinejad is a profound embarrassment to his country, but the grown-ups are still in charge in Iran.

The Nuclear Non-Proliferation Treaty (which Iran has signed) guarantees the "inalienable right" of every signatory to develop the ability to enrich uranium for nuclear power generation under full IAEA safeguards, but the Bush administration wasn't interested in legalisms. In November 2007, White House spokesperson Dana Perino offered a simple proof of Iran's wickedness. Tehran, she said, is "enriching and reprocessing uranium, and the reason that one does that is to lead towards a nuclear weapon." Case closed.

Apart from the nine nuclear-weapons powers (the U.S., Britain, France, Russia, China, India, Pakistan, Israel and North Korea), four other countries already have plants on their territory for "enriching and reprocessing uranium" under IAEA safeguards: Japan, Germany, the Netherlands and Brazil. Argentina, Australia and South Africa are also building or actively considering uranium enrichment facilities, again under IAEA safeguards. So there was some rapid back-pedalling at the White House when a journalist inquired if all these countries are also seeking nuclear weapons.

U.S. National Security Council spokesperson Gordon Johndroe was wheeled out to "clarify" Dana Perino's statement. "Each country is different, but obviously Dana was asked and was talking about Iran," he explained. In other words, the real proof that Iran is seeking nuclear weapons lies in the fact that we know in our hearts that it is evil.

By late 2007, there was good reason to fear that the Bush administration was getting ready to attack Iran before it left office—so the U.S. intelligence agencies set out to discredit the rhetoric of their own government.

December 7, 2007
IRAN AND THE INTELLIGENCE PROCESS

For four years the Bush administration told us that Iran must be subject to sanctions, and maybe to military attack, because it was secretly working on nuclear weapons. Suddenly, last week, the U.S. intelligence agencies tell President Bush that for the past four years Iran has *not* been working on nuclear weapons. So he announces that unless Iran abandons its civil nuclear-power program it must be subject to sanctions and maybe to military attack anyway, because "what's to say they couldn't start another covert nuclear weapons program?"

The sixteen U.S. intelligence agencies (sixteen!) that produce the National Intelligence Estimate (NIE) didn't expect to shake Bush's determination to go after Iran. That's why they insisted that the new NIE be declassified and published so quickly. It was a pre-emptive strike against the White House, to make it more difficult politically for Bush to press ahead despite the evidence.

Like the U.S. armed forces, the intelligence services are in a state of near-mutiny as they watch President Bush drag the country towards another unnecessary and unwinnable war. But how come the same intelligence agencies were telling us two years ago with "high confidence" that Iran was developing nuclear weapons?

I have been saying all along (with moderate confidence) that Iran probably has no immediate intention of developing nuclear weapons. Others have been saying this too, of course, and if they come forward I'll gladly join them in a bid to take over the provision of strategic intelligence to the U.S. government.

We'd do it for half the current budget, give back a billion dollars every time we got it wrong, and still end up rolling in wealth. Whereas the intelligence agencies have a huge and cumbersome array of electronic and human "assets" that feed them a torrent of mostly irrelevant or misleading information in little bits and bites, we outsiders would just apply common sense and a little local knowledge to the process.

Common sense is no help at all when you are trying to figure out radio frequencies, missile ranges, and all the other technical details that the military want to know about the armed forces of a potential opponent. For that, you need electronic intelligence-gathering and/or spies.

Strategic intelligence is a quite different matter, however, and here all the clutter of electronic and human data must be subordinated to a political analysis of the other country's interests and intentions. This rarely happens in practice.

Take the comment in the latest NIE report that the suspension of Iran's nuclear weapons program in 2003, in response to international pressure, showed that Tehran's decisions "are guided by a cost-benefit approach rather than a rush to a weapon irrespective of the political, economic and military costs." Gosh, what a revelation! And here we all thought that the Iranian regime were a bunch of mad mullahs who desired nothing more than nuclear martyrdom.

Well, not all of us thought that, but I suspect that the political analysis of the Tehran regime's goals and strategies inside the U.S. government did not rise far above that level. Obviously, if you just assume that the people running Iran are rational human beings and put yourself in their shoes, you can pretty easily figure out what their strategic concerns and priorities will be.

They wouldn't dream of attacking Israel with nuclear weapons even if they had them because that would unleash a nuclear Armageddon on their own country. Israel has hundreds of nuclear weapons, and the only imaginable use for a few Iranian ones would be to deter Israel from a first strike because of the risk of Iranian retaliation. And why would Iran suddenly want such a deterrent now, when it has been a target for Israeli nuclear weapons for at least thirty years?

We know that Ayatollah Khomeini cancelled the Shah's nuclear-weapons program after the revolution in 1979 because it was "un-Islamic." We know that Tehran started the program up again in the mid-eighties during the Iran-Iraq War, when it became clear that Saddam Hussein was working on nuclear weapons, and that it stopped again after international inspectors declared Iraq nuclear-free in 1994. We think that it was restarted once more in 1999 or 2000, and now we are told that it stopped again in 2003. What was that about?

Pakistan tested nuclear weapons in 1998 and then had a military coup, which must have worried the Iranians a lot. Then, after 9/11, the United States began claiming that Iraq was working on nuclear weapons again, which must have frightened them even more. So Tehran started working on nuclear weapons yet again—and then stopped in 2003, after Saddam

Hussein was overthrown by the U.S. and Pakistan turned out to be relatively stable after all.

That was also the year when it became known that Iran was working towards a full nuclear fuel cycle for its civil nuclear power program. That's quite legal, but as it also gives the possessor the potential ability to enrich uranium to weapons grade, Iran came under international pressure to stop—so it suspended the enrichment program for three years and stopped the weapons program.

It all makes sense, and you don't need a single spy to figure it out. In fact, given the motives of most spies, you're probably better off without them entirely.

A properly trained and disciplined military will go along with an unnecessary war because they do not presume to second-guess the judgment of their political superiors, but they will often resist an unwinnable war. It's they who would have to die in it, after all. So when it came to Iran, the U.S. intelligence services had a powerful although silent ally in the Pentagon.

Despite the huge disparity in military power between the United States and Iran the latter would win any military confrontation in the Gulf. Overcommitted in Iraq and Afghanistan, the U.S. could not come up with the huge number of extra troops that would be needed to invade and occupy a mountainous country of seventy-five million people. It could bomb Iran to its heart's content, hitting nuclear, military and port facilities, but then it would run out of options.

Iran's options, on the other hand, are very broad. It could just stop exporting oil. Pulling only Iran's 3.5 million barrels per day off the market, in its present state, would send oil prices into the stratosphere. Or it could get tough and close down all oil-tanker traffic that comes within range of its missiles—which would mean little or no oil being exported from Iraq, Saudi Arabia and the smaller Gulf states. That would mean global oil rationing and industrial shutdowns.

"Our coast-to-sea missile systems can now reach the length and breadth of the Gulf and the Sea of Oman," boasted Major-General Yahya Rahim Safavi, commander-in-chief of the Revolutionary Guards, in mid-2007, "and no warships can pass in the Gulf without being in range of our coast-to-sea missiles." The latest generation of Iranian sea-skimming missiles have mobile, easily concealed launchers, and the missiles would

come in fast and low from anywhere along almost two thousand kilometres of Iran's Gulf coast.

Iran could close the whole of the Gulf and its approaches to oil-tanker traffic: sink the first half-dozen tankers, and insurance rates for voyages to the Gulf would become prohibitive, even if you could find owners willing to risk their tankers. It's very unlikely that U.S. air strikes could find and destroy all the missile launchers, so Iran wins.

After a few months the other great powers would find some way for the United States to back away from the confrontation and let the oil start flowing again, but the U.S. would suffer a greater humiliation than it did in Vietnam, while Iran would emerge as the undisputed arbiter of the region. This is the war that the Pentagon did not want to fight, and it was quite right. By mid-2008, the likelihood of a U.S. attack on Iran was sinking fast.

July 11, 2008
SIX-TO-ONE AGAINST

The Iranians have clearly concluded that all the American and Israeli threats to attack them are mere bluff. This explains the bravado of Iran's little propaganda show on July 9, when it test-launched a number of ballistic missiles, including one that has the ability to carry a nuclear weapon and the range to strike Israel. This elicited the usual veiled threats of an attack on Iran from both Washington and Jerusalem, but the Iranians don't believe them anymore.

The main purpose of the tests was to strengthen the position of hardliners in domestic Iranian politics. They want to keep the confrontation with the United States and its allies alive, because they fear that other elements in the regime might bargain away Iran's right to enrich nuclear fuel for civilian use.

If neither the United States or Israel intends to attack Iran, this is a cost-free strategy: you win the domestic political struggle and nothing bad happens to you internationally. If you miscalculate, however, you get a war out of it. What are the odds that the Iranians are miscalculating?

Many institutions try to analyze this question, and some of them will charge you quite a lot for an answer. However, all of them are essentially guessing what goes on in the minds of the U.S. president and/or the

Israeli prime minister, both of whom are men in a hurry. Bush leaves office in January, and Ehud Olmert may be gone by September as the result of a corruption scandal.

Prime Minister Olmert's coalition government might collapse if he chose to attack Iran alone, and the Israeli military are clearly divided on the feasibility of such an attack. Besides, Israel could not do such a thing without Washington's approval—Israeli aircraft would have to fly through Iraqi airspace, which is under U.S. control—so it all comes back to what Bush decides.

He probably doesn't know himself yet, and his main concern must be that senior soldiers and spies in Washington would go public to oppose such an adventure. In circumstances like these, I generally consult the International Institute for Discussing Current Affairs Over Dinner, whose advice can be had for the price of a good meal.

Membership is limited to myself, my wife and my many talented children. Like me, they are experts in everything, and one of our most effective analytical tools is an exercise called Setting the Odds. A quorum of the Institute's membership is currently on holiday in southern Morocco, and we deployed this technique at dinner last night.

I offered my colleagues two-to-one odds that neither the United States nor Israel would attack Iran this year, and they laughed in my face. Their response was the same at odds of four-to-one. At six-to-one, one showed a mild interest, but still declined the offer. From which I deduce that for all the huffing and puffing in Washington and Jerusalem, an actual attack on Iran this year is extremely unlikely.

You may object that this technique lacks scientific rigour. I would reply that so does everybody else's, and at least you get a nice meal out of this one. Moreover, we have a good track record, mainly because we assume that, while individual leaders may lose the plot, large institutions like governments and armed forces are generally more rational in their choices.

There are occasions when whole countries are so traumatized by some shock that truly bizarre decisions become possible—the United States after 9/11 was like that for a while—but this is not one of those times. The U.S. military has been war-gaming possible attacks on Iran since the 1990s, and it has never managed to find a scenario that resulted in a credible U.S. victory.

Some people in the White House have convinced themselves that the Iranian people will rise up and overthrow their government as soon as the first American bombs fall, but the professional soldiers in the Pentagon don't believe in fairy tales. Six-to-one says that there will be no U.S. or Israeli attack on Iran this year.

Then, finally, in 2009, the spotlight switched back to Iran's domestic politics. Ahmadinejad rigged the presidential elections with the full support of the Supreme Leader, Ayatollah Khamenei, and the outraged crowds came out on the streets. At first I expected a replay of the 1978-79 experience, but I was wrong.

July 21, 2009
REVOLUTION WITHOUT MARTYRDOM?

Young Iranians were back out on the streets in Tehran on Monday night, after almost a month's hiatus. They were there again on Tuesday, despite the fact that there were many arrests. Their numbers will probably grow in the next week, for we are now nearing forty days since the regime's Basij thugs brutally crushed the first round of demonstrations.

In Iran's Shia Muslim culture, forty days of mourning for the dead are usually followed by public demonstrations of grief. During the revolution against the Shah in 1978–79, that was when the crowds came out on the streets again, to be mown down once more by the Shah's army. The cycle continued until the army, sick of killing unarmed fellow-countrymen, began to refuse the Shah's orders.

At least twenty young demonstrators, and possibly many more, were killed by the current regime's paramilitary forces in late June. Will that old cycle of protest, killing, mourning and more protest repeat itself and lead to the overthrow of the Supreme Leader, Ayatollah Ali Khamenei, and the president whose disputed re-election he so firmly defends, Mahmoud Ahmadinejad? Probably not, but they could still lose.

There will be no rerun of 1978 because today's young Iranians are strikingly different from their parents' generation thirty years ago. Those crowds had little to lose except their lives, and they were driven by a fatalistic courage that accepted death almost without demur. If you are fifteen or twenty-five or even thirty-five in Tehran today, you have lots to lose, and you do not want to die.

Like some general expecting the next war to be just like the last, I didn't understand this difference at first. But then the terrifying video clip of twenty-six-year-old Neda Agah-Soltan, shot down by a Basij sniper and dying in the street on June 21, got several million views inside Iran in twenty-four hours. After that, you could practically hear millions of young Iranians saying: "That could be me." They didn't want it to be, and the streets emptied.

So, don't expect escalating street protests to make Ali Khamenei and Mahmoud Ahmadinejad retreat. However, it's possible that cautious, limited, recurrent protests could be part of a more complex strategy that ultimately accomplishes the same goal, for the ruling elite itself is deeply split. That has not happened before.

The three "reformers" who now lead the opposition to Khamenei and Ahmadinejad are the three people who made most of the day-to-day decisions in the country from the time of the revolution until only four years ago. Mir-Hossein Mousavi, who ran against Ahmadinejad in this year's presidential election (and may really have won it), was the prime minister of Iran from 1981 to 1989; Ali Akbar Rafsanjani was president from 1989 to 1997; and Mohammad Khatami was president from 1997 to 2005.

Mousavi has always faced unrelenting hostility from the ultra-conservative Ali Khamenei. As president in 1981, Khamenei refused to accept Mousavi as prime minister (even though he had been legitimately chosen by parliament) until the Old Man himself, Ayatollah Ruhollah Khomeini, intervened and insisted that Mousavi be allowed to take office.

The strong suspicion that this time the election itself was rigged by Khamenei's supporters to exclude Mousavi from office has only made him more defiant. His website dismisses the regime's claim that the protests were inspired by Iran's foreign enemies with contempt: "Isn't it an insult to 40 million voters . . . linking detainees to foreign countries? Let people freely express their protests and ideas."

Rafsanjani, in a sermon at Tehran University last Friday, aligned himself firmly with Mousavi, demanding an end to the media clampdown and the release of people arrested during the protests. He also referred indirectly to the fact that he actually chairs the committee that elects the Supreme Leader, and can dismiss him.

Khatami went further on Monday, calling for a referendum on the alleged outcome of the election. "People must be asked whether they are happy with the situation that has taken shape," he said. "I state openly that reliance upon the people's vote and the staging of a legal referendum is the only way for the system to emerge from the current crisis." It was after that that the protestors reappeared on the streets.

They will not sweep the regime away, and if its henchmen start killing them again they will prudently withdraw from the streets for a while—but only to devise safer ways of making their resentment felt. Meanwhile, a parallel campaign will be waged within the ranks of the Islamic·clergy, mixing fine theological points with crass appeals to self-interest. This will not be an epic tale of heroism and martyrdom, but a complicated and mostly obscure contest for the future of the Islamic Republic.

The hard-liners' hope, understandably enough, was that, after a while, the outrage at Ahmadinejad's implausible re-election to the presidency would subside into a sullen acceptance of the inevitable. That has not happened. Iran is in for a lengthy struggle, with an unpredictable outcome.

12.

AFRICA

Most African countries are actually poorer now than they were when they got their independence in the 1960s or 1970s. Back then, countries like China and Malaysia were the basket cases; now they bustle and glisten, while flying over most African countries at night is like flying over the sea. There are no lights. And Africans are not just poor. They are besieged by tyranny, corruption and violence. Few people would choose to be born in Africa; nobody would choose to be born there and be female.

But things can change. Until the recent recession, Africa's average economic growth rate over the previous eight years was 5 percent. Keep that up, and the gross domestic product will quadruple in less than thirty years. All they have to do is get the politics right.

January 2, 2008
KENYA: HOPE AND BETRAYAL

More than two years ago, when Kenya's current opposition leader, Raila Odinga, quit President Mwai Kibaki's government, I wrote the following: "The trick will be to get Kibaki out without triggering a wave of violence that would do the country grave and permanent damage . . . Bad times are coming to Kenya."

The bad times have arrived, but the violence that has swept Kenya since the stolen election on December 27 is not just African "tribalism." Members of the Kikuyu tribe have been the main target of popular wrath and non-Kikuyu protesters have been the principal victims of the security forces, but this confrontation is about trust betrayed, hopes dashed and patience strained to the breaking point.

Nobody wants a civil war in Kenya, but it's easy to see why Raila Odinga rejects calls from abroad to accept the figures for the national vote that were announced last Sunday. If Odinga enters a "government of national unity" under Kibaki, as the African Union and the United States want, then he's back in the untenable situation that he was in until 2005, and Kibaki will run Kenya for another five years.

If Odinga leaves it to Kenya's courts to settle, the result will be the same: there have been no decisions yet on disputed results that went to the courts after the 2002 election. So when the opposition leader was asked by the BBC if he would urge his supporters to calm down, he replied: "I refuse to be asked to give the Kenyan people an anaesthetic so that they can be raped."

Despite the ugly scenes of recent days, Kenya is not an ethnic tinderbox where people automatically back their own tribe and hate everyone else. For example, it is clear that more than half the people who voted Mwai Kibaki into the presidency in the 2002 election were not of his own Kikuyu tribe, because the Kikuyu, although they are the biggest tribe, only account for 22 percent of the population.

Kibaki's appeal was the promise of honest government after twenty-four years of oppressive rule, rigged elections and massive corruption under the former president, Daniel arap Moi. If he had been just another thug in a suit, most Kenyans would have put up with Kibaki's subsequent behaviour in the same old cynical way, but his victory was seen as the dawn of a new

Kenya where the bad old ways no longer reigned. It is his abuse of their high hopes that makes the current situation so emotional.

By 2005, Kibaki's dependence on an inner circle of fellow Kikuyu politicians was almost total and the corruption was almost as bad as it had been under Moi. The British ambassador, Sir Edward Clay, accused Kibaki's ministers of arrogance and greed, which led them to "eat like gluttons" and "vomit on the shoes" of foreign donors and the Kenyan people. The biggest foreign donors, the United States, Britain and Germany, suspended their aid to the country in protest against the corruption.

Most of the leading reformers quit Kibaki's government in 2005, and in the weeks before last month's election, their main political vehicle, the Orange Democratic Movement, had a clear lead in the polls. That lead was confirmed in the parliamentary vote on December 27, 2007, which saw half of Kibaki's cabinet ministers lose their seats and gave the opposition a clear majority in parliament. But the presidential vote was another matter.

Raila Odinga won an easy majority in six of Kenya's eight provinces, but in Central, the Kikuyu heartland, the results were withheld until long after the vote had been announced for more remote regions. Observers were banned from the counting stations in Central and from the central tallying room in Nairobi—and on December 30, Samuel Kivuitu, the chairman of the electoral commission, declared that Kibaki had won the national vote by just 232,000 votes in a nation of thirty-four million.

It stank to high heaven. Ridiculously high turnouts were claimed for polling stations in Central—larger than the total of eligible voters, in some cases—and 97.3 percent of the votes there allegedly went to Kibaki. It was an operation designed to return Kibaki to office while preserving a facade of democratic credibility, but no foreign government except the United States congratulated Kibaki on his "victory," not even African ones, and local people were not fooled.

Within two days, Samuel Kivuitu retracted his declaration of a Kibaki victory, saying that the electoral commission had come under unbearable pressure from the government: "I do not know who won the election . . . We are culprits as a commission. We have to leave it to an independent group to investigate what actually went wrong."

But Kibaki is digging in, and innocent Kikuyus—many of whom did *not* vote for Kibaki, despite the announced results—are being attacked by furious people from other tribes. Meanwhile, the police and the army obey Kibaki's orders and attack non-Kikuyu protesters. It is not Odinga who needs to accept the "result" in order to save Kenya from calamity; it is Kibaki who needs to step down.

He probably won't, in which case violence may claim yet another African country. But don't blame it on "tribalism." Kenyans are not fools, and they know when they have been betrayed.

About 1,300 people were killed in the ethnic violence following the 2007 election, and several hundred thousand were burned out of their homes and wound up in refugee camps. Mediation by former UN secretary-general Kofi Annan led to a power-sharing deal in which Kibaki remained president, Odinga became prime minister (a post that was resurrected for the occasion), and the two parties joined in a "grand coalition" that left only a tiny opposition group in parliament. There has been little progress on the list of reforms that was agreed to, but many of the politicians from both parties who were appointed as ministers have done quite well. The popular verdict is that "they're eating together," and the decline of Kenya continues.

It has not fallen as far as Zimbabwe, however. Zimbabwe is much less complex ethnically than Kenya and it once had the best-educated population in English-speaking Africa, but the leader of the liberation war is still president thirty years later, and he just will not let go.

June 21, 2008
ZIMBABWE: CUTTING THE LOSSES

Opposition leader Morgan Tsvangirai was right to withdraw from the runoff presidential "election" in Zimbabwe on Sunday. Thousands of his supporters have been kidnapped and tortured by President Robert Mugabe's thugs since the campaign started, and eighty-six have been murdered already. Thousands more would probably have suffered the same fate if the election had gone ahead, and it would all have been for nothing. Mugabe was determined not to let the opposition win, regardless of what the voters did. He even said so.

"Only God can remove me," Mugabe has been saying in recent

speeches, vowing that he would refuse to give up the gains of the libera-tion war because of an 'x' on a ballot paper. He claims that the major opposition party, the Movement for Democratic Change (MDC), is part of a plot by the British government, Zimbabwe's former colonial ruler, to reimpose white rule on the country.

Whether this is genuine paranoia or merely low cunning, it lets the eighty-four-year-old president justify the reign of terror he has unleashed against opposition supporters since he lost the first round of the election to Tsvangirai as "a second liberation war." In wars, you can kill people who oppose you, and you are not obliged to count the enemy's votes.

So, many opposition party organizers have been killed, and in rural areas thousands of them have been driven from their homes in order to give Mugabe a clear run in the runoff election. And Mugabe's strategy was clearly going to succeed: either he would win a majority of the votes because enough MDC supporters had been terrorized into staying home, or else he would win the count later on.

He didn't win the count the first time, in late March, because he was overconfident. He let too many foreign observers in, and he allowed local vote tallies to be posted up at polling stations and didn't realize that oppo-sition activists would photograph them. Whatever the real vote count was, Mugabe's tame Zimbabwe Election Commission (ZEC) was unable to massage the outcome enough to give him a first-round victory: most of the local voting totals were too well documented.

After a month's delay, the ZEC released results showing Tsvangirai with about 48 percent of the vote to Mugabe's 43 percent. That was enough to force a second round of voting, since a candidate had to get more than 50 percent of the vote in the first round to avoid a runoff.

It was the best that the ZEC could do for Mugabe, but it was a huge humiliation for the liberation-war hero who has ruled Zimbabwe since independence in 1980. His advisers should have seen it coming, however: Mugabe has misgoverned Zimbabwe so badly that this once-prosperous country now has 2 million percent inflation.

One-quarter of the population have fled to South Africa to find work and support their families. Many more at home would be starving with-out the remittances from South Africa, as foreign food aid only gets through to supporters of Mugabe's ZANU-PF (Zimbabwe African National Union–Patriotic Front) Party. And public health has been neglected so badly that Zimbabweans now die, on average, at a younger age than any other nationality in the world.

Mugabe may not even know these statistics, but armed forces chief General Constantine Chiwenga, now the real power behind the throne, certainly does, and so do other regime members. They just don't care. If they lose power, they lose everything, for almost all their wealth was acquired illegally, and they have killed too many people.

In the past week, there have been reports of senior military and political figures showing up at torture sessions of MDC militants who were subsequently released. The message was clear: we do not fear prosecution for this because we will never relinquish power.

So Morgan Tsvangirai had to decide how many more lives he wanted to sacrifice in order to force Mugabe to steal the election openly. But how would that discredit Mugabe any more than the crimes he is committing right now? And what good does it do to "discredit" him?

Mugabe is a scoundrel and a tyrant, and the people who run his government and his army are brazen thieves, but there will be no effective intervention in Zimbabwe from outside. The only African leader who has enough clout to do that is South Africa's President Thabo Mbeki, and he will never act against his old friend Robert Mugabe.

Other African leaders will cluck ineffectually, but nothing will be done. Zimbabweans are on their own, as they always really were. Tsvangirai and a majority of the MDC have belatedly realized that there is no point in waiting for justice to prevail—but they have probably not yet thought beyond that. Basildon Peta, the head of the Zimbabwean Union of Journalists, certainly has. As he wrote after Tsvangirai announced his decision: "I hope it won't be another long round of Thabo Mbeki's timid mediation while Zimbabwe continues burning. The MDC must now do what it should do to rid Zimbabwe of this shameless criminal. The opposition party knows what that is, though I can't print it here."

Well, I can. It's called revolution in the streets.

Like Odinga in Kenya, Tsvangirai finally accepted a power-sharing deal brokered by foreign mediators in September 2008. Mugabe remained president and the opposition leader got the post of prime minister, but the all-important control of the security forces was retained by the ruling ZANU-PF party. There has been a slight recovery in Zimbabwe's devastated economy but foreign donors are still withholding aid on the assumption that ZANU-PF *will just steal it. Tsvangirai has no discernible influence on the government's conduct, but does not appear to have any better options. Mugabe will not leave power voluntarily—and revolution in the streets does not seem very likely either.*

September 1, 2009
ETHIOPIA: POPULATION, FAMINE AND FATE

A quarter-century after a million Ethiopians died in the great hunger of 1984–85, the country is heading into another famine. The spring rains failed entirely, and the summer rains were three weeks late. But why is famine stalking Ethiopia again?

The Ethiopian government is authoritarian, but it isn't incompetent. It gives fertilizer to farmers and teaches best practices. By the late 1990s, the country was self-sufficient in food in good years, and the government had created a strategic food reserve for the bad years.

So why are we back here again? Infant deaths are already over two per ten thousand per day in Somali, the worst-hit region of Ethiopia. (Double that number counts as full-scale famine.) Countrywide, 20 percent of the population already depends on the dwindling flow of foreign food aid, and it will get worse for many months yet. What have the Ethiopians done wrong?

The real answer (which everybody carefully avoids) is that they have had too many babies. Ethiopia's population at the time of the last famine was forty million. Twenty-five years later, it is eighty million. You can do everything else right—give your farmers new tools and skills, fight erosion, create food reserves—but if you don't control population growth you are just spitting into the wind.

It is so obvious that this should be the start of every conversation about the country. Even if the coming famine in Ethiopia kills a million people, the population will keep growing. So the next famine, ten or fifteen years from now, will hit a country of a hundred million people, trying to make a living from farming on land where only forty million faced starvation in the 1980s. It is going to get much uglier in Ethiopia.

Yet it's practically taboo to say that. The whole question of population, instead of being central to the international debate about development, food and climate change, has been put on ice. The reason, I think, is that the rich countries are secretly embarrassed, and the poor countries are deeply resentful.

Suppose that Ethiopia had been the first country to industrialize. Suppose some mechanical genius in Tigray invented the world's first steam engine in 1710, the first railways were spreading across the country by the 1830s, and, at the same time, Ethiopian entrepreneurs and impe-rialists spread all over Africa. By the end of the nineteenth century, Ethiopians would have controlled half of Europe, too. Never mind the improbabilities. The point is that an Ethiopia with such a history would easily be rich enough to support eighty million people now—and if it could not grow enough food for them all, it would import it. Just like Britain (where the industrial revolution actually started) imports food. Money makes everything easy.

In 1710, when Thomas Newcomen devised the first practical steam engine in Devonshire, the population of Britain was seven million. It is now sixty-one million, and they do not live in fear of famine. In fact, they eat very well, even though they currently import more than a third of their food. They got in first, so although they never worried in the slightest about population growth, they got away with it.

Ethiopia has more than four times the land surface of Britain. The rain is less reliable, but a rich Ethiopia would have no trouble feeding its people. The problem is that it got the population growth without the wealth. Stopping the population growth now is extremely difficult, but not doing so means that famine will be a permanent resident in another twenty years.

The problem is well understood. The population of the world's rich countries has grown about tenfold since the earliest days of the industrial revolution, but for the first half of that period, it grew quite slowly. Many babies died, and there were no cures for most epidemic diseases. Later the death rate dropped, but by then, with people feeling more secure in their lives, the birth rate was dropping, too. In most of the poor countries the population hardly grew at all until the start of the twentieth century. But once the population did start to grow, thanks to basic public-health measures that cut the death rate, it grew faster than it ever did in the rich countries.

Unfortunately, economies don't grow that fast, so these poorer coun-tries never achieved the level of comfort and security that allows most people to start reducing their family size spontaneously. At the current rate of growth, Ethiopia's population will double again, to 160 million people, in just thirty-two years.

You're thinking: that will never happen. Famine will become normal in Ethiopia well before that. No combination of wise domestic policies, and no amount of foreign aid, can stop it. And you are right.

What applies to Ethiopia applies to many other African countries, including some that do not currently have famines. Uganda, for example, had five million people at independence in 1960. It now has thirty-two million, and at the current growth rate, it will have 130 million by 2050. Uganda is only the size of Oregon.

History is unfair. Conversations between those who got lucky and those left holding the other end of the stick are awkward. But we cannot go on ignoring the elephant in the room. We have to start talking about population again.

Kenya, Zimbabwe and Ethiopia are all relatively well-run countries: the institutions of the state still exist, the roads are maintained, more or less, and the power is on in the cities for much of the day. There is another, quite numerous category of African countries that are run extremely badly, by extremely bad people. And for some reason that I simply don't understand, West Africa has the nastiest regimes and civil wars on the continent.

December 11, 2009
THE WEST AFRICAN CURSE

There have been political horrors in other parts of Africa—the genocidal former regime in Rwanda, the current regime in Zimbabwe, and any Congolese regime you care to name—but the worst regimes seem to arise along the stretch of tropical coastline between Ghana and Senegal.

Sierra Leone, Liberia and the Ivory Coast have all lived through nightmarish civil wars after long-ruling dictators died or were killed and junior officers seized power. Gambia has been ruled for the past fifteen years by a former army lieutenant, who now imports witch doctors from Guinea to hunt down witches who he believes are trying to kill him. And now Guinea has fallen into the hands of junior officers.

It's a classic pattern. For fifty years after independence, from 1958 to 2008, Guinea was ruled by just two "big men": Sékou Touré for twenty-six years and then Lansana Conté for another twenty-four. They and their cronies stole all the money, of course, while over 90 percent of the mineral-rich country's ten million people continued to live on less than a dollar a day. At least they lived in a relatively safe and orderly poverty.

Then Lansana Conté died late last year—and within hours, a group of young officers broke into the main television station to announce that they were taking over the country. Their leader was an army captain called Moussa "Dadis" Camara, who promised to hold free and fair elections by 2010, and that he would not run for the presidency himself.

Sensible promises, as before 2008 nobody except his own family and his junior officer friends had ever heard of "Dadis" (as he calls himself). He has no experience or qualifications relevant to running a government, but a presidential palace is a nicer place to live in than a barracks, and the pay and perks are much better, too. The experience kind of grows on you, and eventually you ask yourself: why leave?

If a general had taken power after Lansana Conté's death, he might have kept the promise to hand power over to a democratically elected civilian president, for generals already have comfortable houses, limos and lots of stolen money. However, generals usually don't have direct command of troops.

That's why it's so often the junior officers who seize power in West Africa: they have the troops, and they are not much constrained by traditional ideas of military discipline. They seize power because it's the only way to change their own lives for the better—and they generally start to quarrel among themselves after a while because they have already broken all the traditional bonds of hierarchy and discipline.

Guinea has now moved on to the next stage of the process. "Dadis" began talking about running for president himself last August. "I have been taken hostage by the people, a part of the people, with some saying that President Dadis cannot be a candidate and others saying President Dadis has to be a candidate," he told Radio France Internationale. In a burst of frankness, he added that if he did not stand for election another military officer would take over the country.

At that stage, Dadis probably had still had the backing of the other young officers. They were doing very nicely, too, and why would they complain as long as the supply of girls, drink and drugs kept flowing? But then the civilians got involved.

Various political groups that had opposed Lansana Conté for years now saw democracy being stolen from them again. They held a rally in Conakry's sports stadium in late September to protest against Dadis's presidential plans. Lieutenant Abubakar "Toumba" Diakité, another member of the military junta and the head of the presidential guard, was sent to deal with the situation.

He did so by massacring them. His soldiers slaughtered 157 people and raped dozens of women inside the stadium. Twenty women were kidnapped and videotaped for several days while they were being raped and tortured. It is possible that "Toumba" exceeded his instructions; the reaction certainly exceeded his expectations.

The junta denied it all, but the evidence was overwhelming. The African Union, United States, European Union, and the Economic Community of West African States all imposed sanctions on the junta, with ECOWAS president Mohamed Ibn Chambas saying bluntly that Guinea's military rulers were using state power "to repress the population . . . If the military junta has its way it will impose yet another dictatorship on them."

The United Nations sent a mission to investigate the massacre, raising the possibility that the International Criminal Court might bring charges against junta members for crimes against humanity. Dadis apparently concluded that it was time to throw Toumba to the wolves.

On December 4, Dadis went to the barracks where Toumba's troops are based in Conakry: not a wise move, as Toumba shot him in the head and went on the run. Dadis was flown to Morocco for emergency surgery, and the remaining junta members chose "General" Sékouba Konaté to act as front man in his absence.

If things run true to form, the final step in this tragedy will be for Toumba to start an insurgency in the interior of the country, plunging it into a long and horrible civil war of the kind that has ruined several of its neighbours.

This part of Africa seems cursed.

African intellectuals have given a great deal of thought to the question of why their states don't work as well (to put it mildly) as countries in most

other parts of the world. There is no consensus on the answer, but in the
past generation they have been moving towards one. Hence the proposal
discussed in the article below.

July 3, 2007
THE UNITED STATES OF AFRICA

"Before you put a roof on a house, you need to build the foundations,"
South African President Thabo Mbeki reportedly told diplomats at a
closed-door summit meeting of the African Union in Ghana last weekend. Some were quick to ridicule the summit's declared goal of creating
a unified African government by 2015; something that won't happen any
time soon—and may never happen—but it would be a very good idea.

"The emergence of such a mighty stabilising force in this strife-torn
world should be regarded . . . not as a shadowy dream of a visionary,"
declared Kwame Nkrumah, the first president of independent Ghana,
almost half a century ago, "but as a practical proposition which the
peoples of Africa can and should translate into reality . . . We must act
now. Tomorrow may be too late."

Nkrumah was pleading for a pan-African government instead of the
jigsaw-puzzle of ex-colonies that came into existence as the European
imperial powers left Africa. He was asking for the Moon: independence
struggles were waged within the borders of each colony, and the leaders
who emerged had their power bases within those borders. Wider unity
would have dethroned most of those leaders, so it did not happen. But
now the unity project is back.

The African Union was created five years ago out of the wreckage of
the discredited Organization of African Unity with the goal of making
Africa's rulers accountable. Now it is trying to revive the project for real
African unity, and there is no shortage of Africans who argue that it is
merely a distraction from urgent and concrete problems like Darfur and
Zimbabwe. Maybe they are right, but what if those crises are just symp-
toms of a deeper African problem?

At the time most African countries gained their independence in the
1960s, they had higher average incomes and better public services than
most Asian countries. Kenyans lived better than Malaysians; people in

the Ivory Coast were richer than South Koreans; Zimbabweans were healthier, lived longer and were better-educated than the Chinese. And there were more and worse wars in Asia than in Africa.

Now it's all dramatically the other way round, but why? Individual Africans are no less intelligent, hard-working or ambitious than individual Asians, so the answer must lie in the system. And the most striking characteristic of that system is the sheer number of independent states within Africa: fifty-three of them, in a continent that has fewer people than either India or China.

This is where the discussion usually veers off into a condemnation of the arbitrary borders drawn by the old colonial powers, which paid little heed to the ethnic ties of the people within them, but the point is that at least half of the fifty-three African countries have greater ethnic diversity within their borders than all of China, and a few, like Nigeria, approach India in the sheer range and diversity of their languages, religions and ethnic identities.

You *cannot* draw rational borders for Africa that give each ethnic group its own homeland. Even if you refused that privilege to groups of less than half a million people, you'd end up with over two hundred countries. So the old Organization of African Unity decreed that the colonial borders must remain untouchable, because the only alternative seemed to be several generations of separatist ethnic wars.

The problem is that quite a few of the separatist ethnic wars happened anyway, and many other African countries, to avoid that fate, became tyrannies where a "big man" from one of the dominant ethnic groups ruled over the rest by a combination of patronage and violence. Time was wasted, lives were lost and things went backwards. It was nobody's fault, but Africa needs to change this system.

There are more than two hundred ethnic groups in Africa that have over half a million people each, and *none* (except the Arabs of North Africa) that amount to even 5 percent of the continent's population. Only three languages—Mandarin Chinese, Hindi and Japanese—account for half the population of Asia. Even in Europe, eight languages account for 75 percent of the continent's population. Africa is different, and maybe the national state (or, rather, the pseudo-national state) is not the answer there.

The African federalists imagine a solution that jumps right over this problem: a single African Union modelled on the European Union, but where no ethnic group is even 5 percent of the population. Then politics stops being a zero-sum ethnic competition (at least in theory) and starts being about the general welfare. And also, in theory, the continent starts to fulfil its potential.

We will all be a good deal older before the United States of Africa, or whatever it will eventually be called, becomes more than a dream, but as Alpha Oumar Konaré, former president of Mali and head of the African Union, said at the start of the summit: "The battle for the United States of Africa is the only one worth fighting for this generation—the only one that can provide the answers to the thousand-and-one problems faced by the populations of Africa."

Let's face it, though: creating the United States of Africa will be a lot harder than founding the United States of America, and it will never work as smoothly, precisely because of that multitude of ethnic groups. There were still about five hundred different ethnic groups on the territory that would eventually be included in the U.S. when that country was created in the 1770s, but almost all of them except the English-speaking one had lost 90–99 percent of their numbers since the European invaders arrived two centuries before, mainly due to European diseases against which they had no immunity. The United States of America began as an ethnically homogeneous society—except for the slaves—that totally dominated its territory numerically, and it remains a culturally homogeneous society today. Africa, by contrast, is the most ethnically and culturally diverse part of the planet.

The linguistic problem in Africa is eased a bit because the elites everywhere have taken to using the language of whichever European empire conquered their area, but the sheer ethnic and tribal diversity of African countries is little less than it was at first contact with the Europeans. If you stand back far enough, this is cause for celebration, not lament. The five hundred cultural genocides that made the United States of America such a comparatively simple place to govern, and consequently so rich and powerful, did not happen in Africa.

Africans cannot take personal credit for that, but their immune systems can. Because there was constant north-south trade across the Sahara and down the East African coast for many centuries before the European empires arrived, Africans had already been exposed to all the lethal quick-killer diseases that had evolved in the mass civilizations of Eurasia.

Unlike the native inhabitants of the Americas and Australasia, the Africans survived.

As a result, Africa is the only continent that retains anything close to the ethnic diversity of early human populations. Some day that may be a source of great pride and strength, but in the present it is why African states are so weak, poor and corrupt.

13.

OIL

There's a bit of an arc to this section, because I was still quite conventional in my approach to the oil question at the start of the period. At the beginning, I'm pretty offhand in my treatment of the relationship between oil consumption and climate change, too—or maybe ignorant is the better word. Although, to be fair to myself, it was probably cutting-edge commentary at the time.

August 11, 2005
THE OIL GAME

"We ran out of $2 oil in 1973," said Henry Groppe of Groppe Long and Littel, at seventy-nine the oldest active oil consultant (and one of the most respected) in the business. "Then we ran out of $8 oil, then $15 oil. Now we're running out of $40 oil." It's a different way of looking at what is happening to the price of oil, and a much more useful one.

Last week the price of a barrel of oil reached sixty-five dollars. Oil has doubled in price in the past eighteen months, and oil-industry experts freely speculate that the price might hit eighty dollars, even one hundred dollars a barrel before year's end, hugely depressing world economic growth.

But here's an interesting fact: oil companies still decide whether a new field is worth developing by calculating whether they would turn a profit from it when the price per barrel falls to only twenty-five dollars. Do they know something that the rest of us don't?

Not really. They just know that prices always fluctuate, that swings in commodity prices tend to be much wider than in other goods—and therefore that "running out of forty-dollar oil" doesn't mean that the oil price will never fall below forty dollars again. It won't stay down there for good, but as John Maynard Keynes once remarked, "markets can remain irrational longer than you can remain solvent." You have to be able to make a profit from your new field when oil drops to thirty dollars per barrel (even if it is for the last time) and stays there for a couple of years.

The price of oil may hit eighty or even one hundred dollars this year, but if it does it will be due to an extreme market fluctuation, not a new average price. After all the current turmoil is past, the important thing is that the median oil price for the next half-decade—or until we run out of *all* the forty-dollar oil—will be in the mid-forties. That is good news in terms of the real crisis, climate change.

It's high enough to encourage energy conservation and drive people towards alternative, preferably non-carbon energy sources, but it doesn't actually paralyze the economy. We will need more pressure from a higher price later on to avoid a global climate disaster, but the economy can only respond so fast. Just the same, we are practically guaranteed a higher price later on—another doubling of the average price by 2010 or 2012, say—because we are probably at "peak oil" production right now.

Seventy percent of the world's oil comes from big fields that were discovered before 1970, and they are almost all in decline. The new discoveries are mostly smaller and more expensive to develop, and Henry Groppe recently predicted that oil production worldwide will decline by a million barrels a day each year from now on.

We can take no credit for it, but maybe we are on the best available glide path for a soft landing on climate change. Whether that will be good enough is, of course, another question.

Well, the price of oil did go back down for a while—but it touched $147 in mid-2008, and the new median seems to be in the high $70s or the low $80s. As a prophet, I'm not doing too well: as the Chinese say of Mao, seven parts good, three parts bad. (Although that's not really true of Mao, of course.)

What follows is a more serious attempt to understand what's actually happening.

November 2, 2007
TELLING THE TRUTH ABOUT OIL

If a diplomat is "an honest man sent abroad to lie for the good of his country" (Sir Henry Wotton, 1612), then oil-industry executives used to be the business world's equivalent of diplomats. The big international companies were chronically optimistic about the extent of their reserves, and state-controlled oil companies were even more prone to exaggeration. But now we have the spectacle of oil companies telling the truth about oil supplies—or at least more of the truth than usual.

The occasion was last week's Oil and Money conference in London, and the most spectacular truth teller was Christophe de Margerie, CEO of the French oil company Total, one of the international "big five." He said that "100 million barrels [per day] . . . is now in my view an optimistic case" for the maximum global output of oil that will ever be attained.

He was implicitly challenging the International Energy Agency's estimate that world oil output would reach 116 million barrels per day by 2030, and the slightly more optimistic U.S. government prediction that it will reach 118 million barrels per day by that date. Even these acts of faith are really a forecast of crisis, since calculations based on current trends (like a 15 percent annual growth in Chinese demand) suggest that 140 million barrels per day will be needed by 2030.

The implication of de Margerie's remarks is that the crisis is coming a lot sooner than that. World oil output is nearing ninety million barrels per day now, but it is never going to reach one hundred million barrels per day. Peak oil may be just a few years away, or it may be right now. (You will never know until after the fact, since it is the point at which global oil production goes into gradual but irreversible decline.)

Peak oil was first forecast by an American petroleum geologist, M. King Hubbert, who noticed that the curves for oil discoveries and oil production were a very close match, but with a lag of thirty to forty years between the discovery curve and the production curve. At that point, in 1956, Hubbert was the director of research for Shell Oil, and the focus of his research was American oil production, then still the biggest in the world.

At that time, American oil output was still rising rapidly, but Hubbert noticed that the shape of the rising output curve closely fitted the curve plotting the growth of American oil reserves during the years of the great discoveries in Texas, Oklahoma and California. However, there had been no other huge discoveries since then, so the annual amount added to American oil reserves had peaked and begun to decline in the late 1930s.

Hubbert simply assumed that the production curve would continue to match the discovery curve with a three- or four-decade lag, in which case, he predicted, U.S. oil production would peak and start to decline in 1970. That is exactly what happened, and American oil production is now down to about half of output in that peak year. So, "Hubbert's Curve" became famous in the industry, and was duly applied to global discovery and production rates as well.

Oil discoveries worldwide peaked in the 1960s, and Hubbert's forecast was that peak oil production worldwide would arrive in the 1990s. The discovery of two giant new oil fields in the 1970s (probably the last two) in the North Sea and the Alaskan North Slope pushed that date back a bit, however, and one of Hubbert's successors as chief of research at Shell, Colin J. Campbell, subsequently calculated that peak production globally would not arrive until 2007. Now, in other words.

It is still deeply unpopular in the oil industry to talk about peak oil, but essentially what de Margerie was saying, albeit in a cautious and coded way, is that it is here or nearly here. The same sort of talk is coming from Rex Tillerson, chairman and chief executive officer of Exxon Mobil Corporation, who told the *Financial Times* earlier this year that he believed oil production from sources outside the Organization of Petroleum Exporting Countries could see "a little more growth" but would soon level off. And OPEC is generally assumed to be pumping very close to maximum capacity.

It will get a lot worse if de Margerie is right, and he almost certainly is.

Nobody in the business actually believes that the reserves claimed by the members of OPEC *are accurate. During the years 1985–90, when* OPEC's *declared reserves grew by a massive three hundred billion barrels, no major new oil fields were brought into production. The "growth" was achieved by recalculating existing reserves, and the incentive for exaggeration was provided by* OPEC's *decision to set production quotas in proportion to the total size of each member's reserves. More than a quarter of the world's total "proven" oil reserves of 1.1 trillion barrels may be no more than an accounting fiction.*

And there's another thing to worry about: Hubbert's Curve may no longer describe our situation. He was using a symmetrical curve, where oil production rose gently before the peak, and fell gently afterwards. It matched the reality of the time, and we could probably deal with that. The problem is that the "enhanced oil recovery" methods they now use to prolong the life of aging oil fields extend the peak production—and are followed by a much steeper fall in production afterwards.

December 19, 2008
THE END OF OIL

Worried about peak oil? The International Energy Agency's annual report, the *World Energy Outlook 2008*, admits for the first time that "although global oil production in total is not expected to peak before 2030, production of conventional oil . . . is projected to level off towards the end of the projection period." When the *Guardian's* environmental columnist, George Monbiot, pressed IEA director Fatih Birol on that opaque phrase, the actual date turned out to be 2020.

The IEA's previous reports, which assured everyone that there would be plenty of oil until 2030, were based on what Birol called "a global assumption about the world's oil fields," and that the rate of decline in the output of existing oil fields was 3.7 percent a year. But this year some of the staff actually turned up for work occasionally and did a "very, very detailed" survey on the actual rate of decline. It turns out that production in the older fields is really falling at 6.7 percent a year.

There are still some new oil fields coming into production, but this number means that the production of conventional oil—oil that you pump out of the ground or the seabed in the good old-fashioned way—will peak in 2020, eleven years from now. Fatih Birol assumes, or rather pretends, that new production of "unconventional oil" will allow total production to match demand for another decade until 2030, but this is sheer fantasy.

So what are we to make of this news? Monbiot used Birol's admission to launch an impassioned appeal for the rapid development of non-oil alternative sources of energy. Doing so is obviously urgent if we are close to peak oil, but this may not be as great a crisis as it seems. It may not be a bonanza for the oil-producing countries, either.

The IEA presumes that demand for oil will rise indefinitely, so the price of oil only gets higher after peak oil, but in technology nothing is forever. Set into the front doorstep of my house (and most other nineteenth-century houses in London) is an iron contrivance called a boot scraper. It is a device for removing the horseshit from your boots before coming into the house, and the iron blade is worn into a shallow curve by a half-century of use.

Nineteenth-century cities depended on horses to move people and goods around. London in the 1890s had eleven thousand horse-drawn taxis and several thousand buses, each of which required twelve horses a day. Add all the private carriages and the tens of thousands of horse-drawn carts, wagons and drays delivering goods, and there were at least one hundred thousand horses on the streets of London every day—each producing an average of twenty pounds of manure.

Two thousand tons of manure a day. There were flies everywhere, and if you didn't shovel the manure up quickly, it dried up and blew into your eyes, hair, nose and clothes. As the cities grew, even more horses were needed and the problem grew steadily worse. In 1894 a *Times* writer estimated that in fifty years the streets of London would be buried under ten feet of manure.

In fact, within thirty-five years, the streets of London were almost completely free of horses, and filled with automobiles instead. They created a different kind of pollution, but at least you didn't step in it. The same fate is likely to overtake oil-fuelled vehicles in the next thirty-five years.

The shift will be driven by concerns about foreign-exchange costs and energy independence, and, increasingly, by the need to curb greenhouse-gas emissions. It is starting with ever-tightening standards for fuel efficiency, which will be followed by the first mass-market generation of electric vehicles, due in the next two or three years. The *coup de grâce* will be delivered by third-generation biofuels, probably produced from algae that do not use valuable agricultural land and that are fully competitive with oil in price and energy content.

We will never get back the eight wasted years of the Bush administration, and it may now be too late to avoid drastic climate change, but Barack Obama is clearly going to try. You do not appoint Steve Chu as your energy secretary, Carol Browner as your "climate tsarina," and John Holdren as your chief scientific adviser if you intend to evade the issue. So American oil consumption is going to start falling quite fast, quite soon.

The same is true elsewhere. Indeed, it is a safe bet that the demand for oil is going to fall faster than the supply over the next ten or fifteen years, even if we are already at or near peak oil. And if demand falls faster than supply, the price will collapse.

Ladies and gentlemen, place your bets . . .

Well, no, it is not a "safe bet." It is a "known unknown," one of Don Rumsfeld's much-derided but very useful categories.

The process of cutting oil demand begins with simple improvements in fuel efficiency. The Obama administration, for example, has issued regulations requiring an average of thirty-five miles per gallon across the new-car fleets of all the major US-based car producers by 2016, up from 21.5 miles per gallon at present. Since the total number of American vehicles is no longer expanding, this implies an ultimate drop of about 40 percent in the oil burned by U.S. cars. That will mean major cuts in U.S. oil imports and greenhouse-gas emissions—and this is before the electric vehicles and the "renewable fuel" vehicles hit the market. The game is afoot, and the outcome is not yet clear.

14.

CHINA

There is a poem by G. K. Chesterton called "The Secret People" that begins (and ends) this way:

Smile at us, pay us, pass us; but do not quite forget;
For we are the people of England that never have spoken yet.

The people of China have not spoken yet, either. But if the "Old Hundred Names" finally did speak one day, I wonder what they would say to their leaders.

August 24, 2006
THE REVOLUTIONARY MYTH

Arriving in Beijing on August 23 for his third visit to China in five years, Venezuelan President Hugo Chavez praised the country's Communist leaders to the skies for having rescued China from a "practically feudal" situation and for making it one of the world's largest economies in less than half a century. It was an entirely predictable remark by the firebrand Venezuelan leader. It was also entirely wrong.

According to Chavez, China's emergence as a leading economic power is "an example for Western leaders and governments that claim capitalism is the only alternative. We've been manipulated to believe that the first man on the Moon was the most important event of the twentieth century. But no, much more important things happened, and one of the greatest events of the twentieth century was the Chinese revolution."

Back in the late 1980s, when mocking the few remaining Communist believers had become popular sport in the former Soviet Union, one of my favourite gambits was to point out that Russia would have done far better economically if the Communist revolution of 1917 had never happened. No matter how pessimistic your assumptions about the way that a non-Communist Russia would have developed, it simply couldn't have done as badly as the Communists did.

To prove your point, all you had to do was pick some other country that had been at about the same stage of industrial development as Russia just before the First World War—Italy was the most obvious candidate—and compare the outcomes since.

Italy went through the Great Depression in the 1930s (which the Soviet Union escaped), and was on the losing side in the Second World War. Nobody would claim that post-1945 Italian administrations (all fifty-odd of them) have been models of good governance, and Italy is far poorer in natural resources than Russia. And yet by the late twentieth century Italians were four or five times richer than Russians, purely because they had avoided Communist rule. They were a lot freer, too.

The Soviet Communists always compared the circumstances before the revolution (which were pretty dreadful) with the situation seventy years later, and gave "the Revolution" full credit for all the changes for the better—as if other Russians, using less violent and oppressive means, could never have changed the country for the better. Even in the late 1980s, they effectively claimed that it would still be like 1917 in Russia if the Communist revolution had not happened.

So, here we are again, with the Chinese Communist regime taking credit for all the improvements in China since they won the civil war in 1949, and foreign leftists like Hugo Chavez holding out China as an example of what wonderful things can be accomplished under "socialism." But what would China be like now if the Communists had not won power in 1949? Much richer, much freer and not much less equal, either.

The right comparison is not between China in 1949 and China now. It is between China's economic progress since 1949 and that achieved by its neighbours that were in a roughly similar state of development at that time. The two closest parallels are South Korea and the "other China," Taiwan. Both had been Japanese colonies for decades before 1945, so they were a bit ahead of the mainland—but then Taiwan's population grew overnight by almost 40 percent in 1949, as nationalist refugees who had fought the Communist takeover of China flooded in, and Korea was devastated by the war of 1950–53.

Both Taiwan and South Korea were ruled for the next three decades by oppressive and ruthless military regimes. Neither country adopted raw free-market capitalism—the state protected infant industries and nourished them with low-interest capital—but at least they weren't tied to Marxist economics. By the 1980s, both countries had achieved economic takeoff, and democracy came soon afterwards.

Meanwhile China had the Great Leap Forward, the Cultural Revolution and various other man-made disasters, which meant that the per capita income did not even double between 1949 and 1979 (although misery was redistributed on a more equal basis). Then under Deng Xiaoping in the 1980s, China finally abandoned "socialist" economics and adopted the same style of state-assisted capitalism that its neighbours had been practicing for the past thirty years—at which point, finally, its economy began to grow significantly.

Today, the average Chinese income is about one-fifth of that in South Korea or Taiwan: slowly, they are starting to catch up. There is more freedom in China now, too, though the state is still above the law. There is still no democracy, of course. The Party constantly exhorts the people to be grateful for all that it has accomplished on their behalf, but they would probably have been much better off if it had never existed.

Chavez must know all this, and presumably thinks that it just doesn't matter: *his* socialist project is fuelled by oil revenues, so he doesn't have to observe the rules of normal economics. But he does need allies against the wrath of the United States, so he says the right things to his hosts, the Communist rulers of China. They may be closet capitalists these days, but if they don't have the myth that the revolution was beneficial, how can they justify their own monopoly of power?

Well, they can't, actually.

When it comes to ultra-ambitious projects of social engineering, the Chinese People's Republic has no equal. Mao's attempt to erase an entire culture during the Cultural Revolution left the Nazi dream of an Aryan master race and the Russian Communists' dream of New Soviet man in the shade. Only the Khmer Rouge even came close to Mao's ambitions, and they were acting on a very small stage. But the biggest social engineering project ever has left few visible bloodstains. It is the one-child policy that Deng Xiaoping imposed on China in 1979.

October 19, 2007
HOW MANY CHINESE ARE ENOUGH?

Even before the seventeenth congress of the Chinese Communist Party began last week in Beijing it was clear that at least one policy was not going to change: the proscription against more than one child per family. "Because China has worked hard over the last thirty years, we have four hundred million fewer people," said Zhang Weiqing, minister in charge of the National Population and Family Planning Commission, earlier this year.

In the eyes of the policy's supporters, the fact that China has only 1.3 billion people now justifies all the abuses of human rights that were committed to enforce it. True, a few women (or a few million women) were dragged off to have forced abortions in the bad old days, but now it's much more civilized. Besides, the end justifies the means, doesn't it?

Not having 1.7 billion people now (and not having over 2 billion in twenty years) is clearly a desirable outcome for China. Even with decades of high-speed economic growth there is a limit to how many people China can feed and clothe and house. But did the regime really have to impose such a draconian birth-control policy in order to stay within that limit?

The doubters point out that the Chinese government's "soft" birth-control policy in the 1970s—encouraging later marriage, fewer births and longer birth intervals—brought the total fertility rate (that is, lifetime babies per woman) down from 5.7 in 1970 to 2.9 by 1979. That is one of the fastest drops in the birth rate seen anywhere at any time—and it happened *before* the "hard" one-child policy was introduced in 1980.

Critics also point to the Indian experience, where an early experiment with enforced birth-control measures in the 1970s created such a backlash that nobody has dared to suggest it since—and yet, they argue, India's birth rate plummeted over the subsequent generation. From a total fertility rate of 6.3 in 1960, it has fallen to only 2.8 this year. The "demographic transition" from high birth-rate, high death-rate societies to longer-lived communities with lower birth rates still works its magic eventually. But it does take its time.

Compulsion does make a difference. India and China both started the 1960s with very similar fertility rates, and at that time China's population (648 million) was much bigger than India's (433 million). By 1980, China's fertility rate was already down (without compulsion) to the rate that prevails in India today; with compulsion, it has fallen even further, to little more than half the current Indian fertility rate. So China's population will level off at around 1.4 billion by 2020, while India's will go on growing to at least 1.7 billion.

How much difference does that make in practice? A lot. If China had taken India's approach, its population would probably reach two billion before it stopped growing. For every two Chinese in the country there would have been three. That could easily be the margin between success and disaster.

China's economic miracle (10 percent growth for the past two decades) skates permanently along the edge of environmental calamity. Just breathing the air in Beijing is the equivalent of smoking twenty cigarettes every day. The country has lost almost 7 percent of its farmland to development in the past ten years, and dozens of cities are experiencing severe water shortages. It's bad enough with the present population of 1.3 billion. What would it have been like without the one-child policy?

In many parts of the world it is politically unacceptable to suggest that the sheer number of people can be a problem. Population control is star-tlingly absent, for example, from discussions about how to minimize climate change. This is partly due to concerns about the religious sensibilities of some people, and partly because of the human-rights issues that it raises.

In addition to the human-rights abuses implicit in the one-child policy, there are grave demographic implications. One is the shrinking number of people in the working-age population who have to provide for a relatively large aged and retired population. Another, specific to societies where sons are seen as far more desirable than daughters, is a wave of selective abortions and female infanticide.

There have been relaxations in the one-child policy over the years—ethnic minorities are largely exempt from the rules, and rural families whose first child is female are allowed a second try—but almost two-thirds of Chinese families really do have only one child. And the fact that the government is determined to retain the policy suggests that it intends to bring the population down in the longer run, whatever the collateral social damage.

Most ecologists would say that China is well beyond its long-term "carrying capacity," even with its present population. Maybe the govern-ment is actually listening to them. Maybe it also knows that climate change will not be kind to China. There are things worse than a one-child policy. Famine, social disintegration and civil war, for example.

It's not entirely true that the price of this achievement was paid only by girls who were never born. There were also a great many boys who were not born. I don't belong to the "every sperm is sacred" brigade, so I don't know how to calculate what kind of loss this is. Should we mourn the five or ten million Canadian babies who were not born in the past fifty years because the birth rate fell precipitously after the 1950s? Just the same, there was a particular burden borne by the girls, especially in rural areas in the early years of the one-child policy, when the female babies were often born and then killed. And now there is another kind of price to be paid.

December 1, 2006
CHINA'S SURPLUS BOYS

We all know about the problem of China's missing girls: the tens of millions of female babies who were selectively aborted after their sex was determined by ultrasound, or were born and then just allowed to die, as families seeking sons took drastic measures to cope with the one-child-per-family rule. We pay less attention to the problem of the surplus boys, but it is very real.

By 2020, China will have about forty million more men of marriageable age than it has women for them to marry, and this is not just a social problem. It is a potentially catastrophic political problem as well. No sane government would want to rule over a country where there are forty million unattached males between the ages of twenty and forty rattling around with nobody to go home to in the evenings. This is a recipe for riots, even revolution. The solution? If China has not made enough girls, it will have to import them.

China is not a country that welcomes immigration for obvious demographic reasons but also for deeply rooted cultural reasons. There is great pride in the long history and the cultural and even racial homogeneity of the Han Chinese population, which often verges on a polite form of racism. Foreign brides often have a hard time fitting into Chinese families who are less than delighted by their son's choice. But China as a whole no longer has a choice in the matter.

There are already tens of millions of Chinese men condemned to lives of loneliness and celibacy, or at best furtive visits to prostitutes. They live in an economy that is rapidly growing richer, and out there, in the poorer countries of Asia, are millions of young women who would be happy to ease their loneliness and share their prosperity. The solution is obvious, and no government could stop it. No sane government would want to.

The implications of this impending huge influx of foreign brides are very large. China has never seen immigration on this scale before, and it is bound to resist the big cultural changes that come with it. Tens of millions of the next generation of children born in China will have foreign mothers and relatives abroad who expect to be visited or to come and visit once in a while. There will be some personal tragedies and a great deal of happiness, and, at the end of it all, China will be a changed place.

Changed for the better, for the most part. It's just a pity about all those Chinese girls, aborted, killed as infants or allowed to die of neglect, who won't be around to see it.

Here's an encouraging note, though. After eight years of really worrisome confrontation, relations between the People's Republic and Taiwan are on the mend.

November 4, 2008
TAIWAN AND CHINA: PORCUPINES ON A FIRST DATE

Mating is a notoriously tricky business for porcupines, but the first date is an especially awkward transaction. Likewise for prickly customers like China and Taiwan: when a high-level Chinese delegation arrived in Taiwan on Monday for landmark talks on closer relations, the Taiwan police prevented people on the roads into Taipei from waving Taiwan flags in order not to hurt the visitors' feelings.

The two countries (or one country, if you prefer) broke apart almost sixty years ago, and until this week, it was not even possible to travel directly between them: Taiwan-China flights had to go through Hong Kong, and ships had to stop off at the Japanese island of Okinawa. The 180-kilometre-wide Taiwan Strait remains one of the most heavily militarized regions in the world, with an estimated 1,300 Chinese missiles pointing at the island of Taiwan.

Even under the new government of President Ma Ying-jeou, which is committed to improving relations with the mainland, Taiwan keeps its defences up. Taipei recently signed its largest-ever arms deal with the U.S., agreeing on a $6.5 billion package of guided missiles, attack helicopters and other advanced weaponry. Beijing retaliated by cancelling a series of scheduled meetings between Chinese and U.S. generals—but it did not cancel the visit of Chen Yunlin, the most senior Communist official ever to set foot in Taiwan.

The first results of the encounter are already known: in future, cargo ships will be allowed to sail directly between Taiwanese and Chinese ports, and there will be over a hundred direct flights a week between cities in Taiwan and China. There are hopes, especially in Taiwan, that this will lead to greatly increased trade between the two states, and the next round of talks (which will be held every six months) will focus on closer financial ties as well.

But where is all this leading? Reunification? The opposition Democratic Progressive Party (DPP) in Taiwan fears so, and a million of its supporters across Taiwan demonstrated against the meeting last week. For his part, President Ma swears that he will make no moves that compromise Taiwan's sovereignty.

Well, then, could there be a permanent two-state solution in which Beijing and Taipei recognize each other as legitimate governments of independent countries? Beijing's leaders would rather die in a ditch, and so would many ordinary Chinese for whom the unity of the motherland is sacred. The truth is that neither side really knows the destination of this voyage, but they are nevertheless setting out on it together.

There have been great changes in China, where prosperity has soared and the ruling Communist Party has scrapped most of its ideology over the past quarter-century, but Taiwan has changed even more. Sixty years ago, after all, the Nationalist Party that ruled the island for so long was almost identical to the Communist Party in its structure, nationalism, and authoritarian style. Both parties were formed in the wave of nationalist fervour that swept China after the 1911 revolution overthrew the monarchy, and Chiang Kai-shek, who led the Nationalist Party for fifty years until his death in 1975, was just as autocratic as his great rival Mao Zedong, the leader of the Communist Party. But the Nationalists lost the civil war in 1949 and withdrew to Taiwan, where American sea power prevented the Communists from following, and so Taipei became the seat of the government-in-exile of the Republic of China.

That, at least, was how Chiang saw it, and he harshly suppressed any expressions of Taiwan separatism. His dream was to return to Beijing in triumph as the leader of a reunited China. But in the quarter-century after Chiang's death, the Nationalist Party in Taiwan, while remaining dedicated to a united China in principle, gradually moved towards a fully democratic system—and so lost power in 2000 to the DPP, a separatist party that wanted to declare an independent Taiwan.

There was genuine support for that goal in Taiwan, especially in the south, but it was never a real possibility: Beijing made it clear that a declaration of independence would trigger an invasion. So, after eight years of economic stagnation and growing corruption, the separatist DPP lost power in last March's elections, and the Nationalists returned to power under Ma. They remain committed in principle to the reunification of China, but not under a Communist dictatorship.

Improving trade with China is very important to Taiwan, which has not done well economically in recent years: the average Taiwanese still earns about five times as much as the average mainland Chinese, but the gap is narrowing. However, closer political ties are more problematic, and the military still stand ready on both sides of the straits. The two governments may be setting off on a voyage to nowhere, but at least it has started well.

15.

HOW WAR WORKS IN THE MIDDLE EAST

What follows is a more detailed examination of a single event than you'll find anywhere else in the book, and there's a reason for that. To paraphrase George W. Bush, a lot more shit goes on in a war than ever comes out in most of the media coverage, and I don't mean the atrocities. I mean the real motives of the players, and the way they measure success or failure, and just how much, or how little, people's lives count in those calculations. (Civilians generally don't count for very much.)

This is about the war that Israel and Hezbollah, the Shiite guerrilla fighters based in southern Lebanon, fought in the summer of 2006. It was obviously one-sided in the sense that Hezbollah has no air force, no navy and no tanks, but it did have rockets that could be fired from almost anywhere in southern Lebanon and reach somewhere in northern Israel. They were not very big or very accurate rockets, but the Israeli Defence Forces (IDF) could not ignore them.

The trigger for the war was a Hezbollah snatch operation: two IDF armoured Humvees patrolling the border were ambushed by anti-tank missiles while other Hezbollah militants fired rockets at an Israeli border town as a diversion. Three Israeli soldiers in the vehicles were killed and the other two were taken as captives. Five more Israeli soldiers were killed in a failed rescue attempt, while Israel launched a massive air and naval bombardment across Lebanon, striking not just Hezbollah but targets across the whole of Lebanon. After some delay, Hezbollah responded by launching hundreds of rockets at towns and cities across northern Israel.

Nothing was quite as it seemed, however, for both Israel and Hezbollah (though not the Lebanese government) had been planning and preparing for this war for several years. War is the continuation of politics by other means, as Karl von Clausewitz, the great military philosopher, almost said, and political strategies in the Middle East are particularly subtle, intricate and cynical. The wars, of course, have the same character.

July 17, 2006
ISRAEL: RE-ESTABLISHING THE DETERRENT

"What they really need to do is to get Syria to get Hezbollah to stop doing this shit, and it's over," said President George W. Bush over an unnoticed open microphone at the St. Petersburg summit on Sunday, but it isn't really that simple. There are two sides in every fight, and Israel is doing some shit, too.

Hezbollah certainly started the fight (by crossing Israel's border and taking two soldiers hostage), but it is not clear that either Syria or Iran is the mastermind behind the operation. Sheikh Hassan Nasrallah, the leader of Hezbollah, is perfectly capable of taking this initiative on his own.

True, the rockets that have been raining down on northern Israel (two thousand so far, leaving sixteen Israeli civilians dead) were made in Iran. But then the F-16s and Apache gunships that are pounding Lebanon (130 Lebanese civilians dead so far) were made in the United States, and that doesn't mean that Washington ordered the Israeli offensive against Lebanon.

Nasrallah knew that the Israeli retaliation for the kidnapping would fall mainly on innocent Lebanese (because they are much easier targets than his elusive guerrillas), but he doesn't care. He had a few surprises up his sleeve, like longer-range rockets that could strike deep into Israel and radar-guided Silkworm anti-ship missiles to attack the Israeli warships that used to shell the Lebanese coast with impunity. And if he manages to fight Israel to a draw, he will come out of this the most popular Arab leader since Gamal Abdel Nasser.

General Dan Halutz, the Israeli Chief of Staff, was also spoiling for a fight. His major concern has been that Israel's "deterrent power" has gone into decline, and he wanted to re-establish it. Some Israeli defence analysts, like Professor Gerald Steinberg of Bar Ilan University, believe that the plan for the massive strikes against Lebanon has been sitting on the shelf for several years, awaiting a provocation that would justify putting it into effect. But what does "deterrent power" actually mean?

Understand that, and you understand the remarkable savagery of the Israeli attacks on Lebanon. *Of course* they are a "disproportionate use of force," as French President Jacques Chirac called them the other day. That is the whole point. Israel's "deterrent power" lies in its demonstrated will and ability to kill and destroy on a vastly greater scale than anybody attacking it can manage. Its enemies must know that if one Israeli is killed, a dozen or even a hundred Arabs will die.

This has been a dominant concept of Israeli strategy from the very foundation of the state, and the "kill ratio" in all of Israel's wars, including its invasion of Lebanon in 1982 conformed to that pattern. The first time it didn't apply was in the struggle between Israeli troops and Hezbollah during Israel's prolonged occupation of southern Lebanon between 1982 and 2000, when the Israelis managed to kill only a few Hezbollah guerrillas for each of their own soldiers who died.

That steady drain of lives was the main reason the Israeli army pulled out of southern Lebanon six years ago, but many people in the Israeli defence establishment were concerned at the time that Israel's "deterrent power" had been gravely eroded by Hezbollah's victory. And subsequent clashes with the Palestinians did not see the old ratio restored: during the years of the so-called second intifada, only three Palestinians were killed for every Israeli.

Hence the perceived need within the Israeli armed forces to "re-establish deterrence," that is, to demonstrate that Israel can and may respond with massively disproportionate violence even to minor attacks. The IDF wasn't actually looking for a fight, but if a fight came along it intended to use the opportunity to make a demonstration of just how big an overreaction it was capable of.

After a week of mutual bombardment—Hezbollah rockets against Israeli artillery and aircraft—Hezbollah still has at least three-quarters of its rockets left. A large part of northern Israel will remain under attack from the skies—not very accurate attack, but about one rocket in a hundred kills someone—unless the Israeli army is willing to occupy all of southern Lebanon again.

Even more worrisome for Israel is the fact that deterrence is not really being re-established. This is not just a hiccup; it is evidence of a slow but inexorable shift in the terms of trade. Israel will remain unbeatable in war for the foreseeable future, but the good old days of cheap and easy victories will not come back again.

I was wrong about one thing: the IDF was actually looking for a fight, and had made its plans for the war clear to its American allies. More about that later, but as the war neared the three-week mark, things were not going well for the Israelis.

"Qana" refers to a bomb dropped by an Israeli aircraft on the town of that name during the 2006 war that caused a building to collapse on top of dozens of civilians, many of them children, who had taken cover in the basement. Some forty were killed. (This should not be confused with the Israeli shelling of a United Nations compound in Qana in 1996, in which more than a hundred civilians who had taken refuge there were killed.)

July 31, 2006
ISRAEL AND HEZBOLLAH: END GAME

The kill ratio is becoming a problem: Israel has been killing about forty Lebanese civilians for every Israel civilian who is killed. They are all being killed by accident, of course, but such a long chain of accidents begins to look like carelessness, and, even in Israel and in the United States, many people are getting uneasy about the slaughter. Elsewhere, the revulsion at what is happening is almost universal, and the death of so many women and children at Qana has greatly intensified the pressure on Israel and its de facto allies, the United States and Britain, to stop the war.

They are already making tactical concessions to lessen the pressure. Israel "partially suspended" its bombardment of Lebanon for forty-eight hours, and U.S. Secretary of State Condoleezza Rice promised to let the United Nations Security Council consider a resolution calling for a ceasefire this week. But Israel's generals still want another ten days to two weeks of war to batter Hezbollah into submission, and neither Israeli Prime Minister Ehud Olmert or his allies in Washington and London are really willing to override them just yet.

Israeli Defence Minister Amir Peretz told parliament on Monday that Israel cannot accept a ceasefire now, since if it did so then "the extremists [Hezbollah] will rear their heads again." In response, the U.S. and British governments have to dodge and weave a bit as doubts grow at home about the morality and feasibility of Israel's actions, but they can certainly arrange for the Security Council resolution to fail this week.

The real trick, in terms of keeping American and British public opinion on side, is to blur the sequence of events that led to the war and to present it as a desperate Israeli struggle against an unprovoked onslaught by thousands of terrorist rockets. As Prime Minister Tony Blair told the BBC, "It cannot be that Israel stops taking the action it's taking but Hezbollah continue to kill, kidnap, and launch rockets into the north of Israel at the civilian population there."

The website of the Israel Ministry of Foreign Affairs goes further, claiming that the operation in which Hezbollah captured two Israeli soldier and killed three others and the rain of Hezbollah rockets on Israeli cities were "simultaneous." Obviously, these are mad terrorists who must be removed from Israel's border at once and by any means possible. But unless "simultaneous" means "on the following day" in Hebrew, the website is deliberately distorting what happened.

There *was* an unprovoked Hezbollah attack on the Israeli army on July 12, seeking to kidnap soldiers who could be held as hostages and eventually exchanged for Lebanese prisoners who have been illegally held in Israel since the latter ended its eighteen-year military occupation of southern Lebanon in 2000. And no doubt the reason Israel held on to those prisoners in the first place was to have them as hostages in some future prisoner exchange with Hezbollah. That's how the game is played locally.

In the course of grabbing the Israeli hostages on July 12, Hezbollah fired rockets and mortars at the northern Israeli town of Shlomi as a diversion, but nobody was hurt there. And apart from that, *no* Hezbollah missiles struck Israel that day. Indeed, none had been fired at Israel for at least four years, although there were regular skirmishes between Israeli soldiers and Hezbollah fighters along the frontier. Hezbollah had the rockets, but they were not mad terrorists.

During the following twenty-four hours, however, Israel launched massive air strikes and artillery bombardments the length and breadth of Lebanon, striking Beirut airport, Lebanese air-force bases, the Beirut-Damascus highway, a power station, and all sorts of other non-Hezbollah targets and killing many civilians. It was only on July 13 that Hezbollah rockets begin to hit cities across northern Israel.

Nobody has clean hands here. Israel seized on the kidnap operation as the pretext for a massive onslaught aimed at destroying Hezbollah's resources and removing it from southern Lebanon—a goal also implicit in United Nations Security Council Resolution 1559, passed in 2004, which called for all Lebanese militias to be disbanded, but not one that the UN had envisaged as being accomplished by Israeli bombs. Hezbollah may just have been trying to raise its profile in Lebanon and the wider Arab world with a small but successful operation that humiliated the Israelis—or it may have foreseen the likelihood of a massive Israeli overreaction, and calculated that it could ride it out and win from it.

Whether that was its intention or not, it probably will ride it out and win. Having fired at least ninety missiles at Israeli cities on every day but two since the war began—though they only kill an average of one Israeli a day—Hezbollah launched only two rockets on Monday (probably a crew that didn't get the message to stop in time). If there should be a ceasefire in the next week, it will emerge the victor, since no international peace-keeping force is going to fight the kind of campaign that would be required to dig it and its weapons out of south Lebanon's hills and villages.

And if there is no ceasefire, then the Israeli Defence Force will be granted a further opportunity to demonstrate that it cannot do so either. At least, not at a cost in Israeli soldiers' lives that would be remotely acceptable to the Israeli public.

The war lasted thirty-four days but Israel made few ground advances into Lebanon. During the last few days before the ceasefire Hezbollah launched

twice as many rockets into northern Israel as its daily average in the first
week of the war. It would be hard to maintain that Israel had successfully
re-established deterrence.

August 7, 2006
SEEKING INVULNERABILITY

The three most ill-considered (and probably doomed) political enter-
prises on the international political scene today are the Israeli assault on
Lebanon, the U.S. campaign to force Iran to renounce its alleged nuclear-
weapons program, and the similar U.S. campaign that has been mounted
against North Korea. What common theme unites these three enter-
prises? The quest of invulnerability for one side, at the expense of total
vulnerability for the other.

Between 1945 and about 1970, the United States went through one of
the most difficult intellectual and emotional transitions in history. The
U.S. began that period as the home of almost half the world's surviving
industrial capacity and the sole possessor of the ultimate weapon, the
atomic bomb. It was unchallengeable and invulnerable. Yet by 1970, it
was ready to concede nuclear-weapons parity to the Soviet Union, an
openly hostile totalitarian state, and was negotiating arms-control agree-
ments that limited missile numbers but guaranteed the Soviets the ability
to destroy the United States.

That was logical and necessary, because you couldn't stop the Russians
from building more and bigger nuclear weapons. America's military thinkers had grasped the essential fact that no number of nuclear weapons on
their side, however large, could stop an enemy with the ability to deliver
even a few hundred nukes from effectively destroying their country.

The enemy would also be destroyed by U.S. retaliation, of course, so
let's work with that fact. Let us stabilize the U.S.-Soviet relationship by
accepting this unavoidable situation of mutual vulnerability—Mutual
Assured Destruction (MAD), as one critic of the policy named it—and
even enshrining it in international treaties. It made good strategic sense,
and it may well have saved the world from a nuclear war.

Accepting America's vulnerability was so emotionally repugnant that
many leading politicians and generals spent the rest of their careers

promoting new technologies like "Star Wars" that they hoped might restore U.S. invulnerability, but most of the U.S. political and military elite had the wisdom and maturity to support the policy. America could use their like today. So could Israel.

Israel's period of invulnerability began later, after the 1973 war, and has lasted far longer. No combination of Arab armies can defeat Israel in war, or even inflict major casualties on it. And should Israeli generals ever prove so incompetent that Arab armies did make a little headway, Israel still has its regional nuclear-weapons monopoly forty years after developing the things. (America lost its own nuclear monopoly after only four years in its confrontation with the Soviet Union.)

Israel faces a bigger "terrorist threat" than the U.S., but this is still a pretty marginal concern. Hezbollah's activities on Israel's northern borders were an occasional nuisance, but until Israel's quite deliberate overreaction to its hostage-seizure operation on July 12, it had not fired rockets at Israeli towns in years. Hezbollah had the capability to do so, and thus Israel was theoretically vulnerable (though not very, since the rockets hardly ever hit anyone), but it wasn't actually doing it.

In one sense, this war is an absurd attempt to eliminate this last little vulnerability by grossly disproportionate means. In a more serious sense, it is driven by the Israeli military's desire to re-establish deterrence: that is, to demonstrate anew that Israel can respond with grossly disproportionate violence to any provocation, spreading death and destruction far beyond the location of the original offence.

But that is another way of saying that Israel wants to show that everybody else in the region is completely vulnerable to its power, completely insecure. There is no stability in such a relationship, as the past forty years have amply demonstrated, and, in any case, this time deterrence will not be re-established. Israel is unable to eliminate Hezbollah, and its attack merely highlights the limitations of Israeli military power when deployed against non-state opponents.

The Lebanese government had no control of Hezbollah's forces in the south and no say in Hezbollah's operation to take Israeli troops hostage, which triggered the war. But Israel deliberately attacked Lebanese infrastructure and other targets not connected with Hezbollah in a deliberate attempt to make the non-Shia majority of Lebanon's population see

Hezbollah as a threat to their own security. It did not succeed; just as in the Second World War, bombing civilians tends to strengthen their support for the government or other organization that is the real target of the enemy's hostility.

Nor was "deterrence" re-established on the ground. Hezbollah's fighters were so well dug in that air power and artillery could not budge them. They were also so well trained that trying to dig them out with Israeli ground troops would be prohibitively expensive in terms of casualties, and the IDF wisely chose not to attempt it. Olmert's government did launch what amounted to an airborne public-relations stunt on the day the ceasefire was signed, in an attempt to present the appearance of a victory. But those whose opinions really mattered were not fooled.

August 15, 2006
THE NEW MIDDLE EAST

Common sense has prevailed. Most of the Israeli troops who were sent into south Lebanon last weekend have already retreated, and the last thousand or two will be back inside the Israeli frontier by next weekend. They are not waiting for the Lebanese army and the promised international peacekeeping force to come in and "disarm Hezbollah." They are getting the hell out.

The last-minute decision to airlift Israeli troops deep into the one thousand square kilometres of Lebanon south of the Litani river made good sense politically. That way, Israel didn't have to fight its way in and take the inevitable heavy casualties. Rather, it simply exploited its total control of the air to fly troops into areas not actively defended by Hezbollah just before the ceasefire. The goal was to create the impression that it had defeated the guerrilla organization and established control over southern Lebanon.

However, those isolated packets of troops actually controlled nothing of value, and they were surrounded by undefeated Hezbollah fighters on almost every side. Hezbollah could not have resisted for long the temptation to attack the more exposed Israeli units, perhaps even forcing some to surrender. So the Israeli troops are coming out now, in order to give Hezbollah no easy targets.

General Dan Halutz, the Israeli chief of staff, was right to make this decision, but it removes the last remote possibility that Israel can extract any political gains from the military stalemate in southern Lebanon. Hezbollah says it has no intention of disarming, and Lebanese defence minister Elias Murr says that his army will not try to disarm the militant organization. Hezbollah is staying put in southern Lebanon, and so are its weapons. At the end of this "war of choice," Israel has achieved none of its objectives.

Israel's assault on Hezbollah was as much a "war of choice" as the U.S. invasion of Iraq. Seymour Hersh claims in this week's *New Yorker* that the Bush administration approved it months ago, and the *San Francisco Chronicle* reported that a senior Israeli officer made PowerPoint presentations on the planned operation to selected Western audiences more than a year ago. "By 2004, the military campaign scheduled to last about three weeks that we're seeing now had already been blocked out," Professor Gerald Steinberg of Bar Ilan University told the *Chronicle*, "and in the last year or two it's been simulated and rehearsed across the board."

Israeli prime minister Ehud Olmert was seduced by this plan because, lacking military experience himself, he needed the credibility of having led a major military operation. Otherwise, he would lack support for his plan to impose unilateral borders in the occupied West Bank that would keep the major settlement blocks within Israel, while handing the rest to the Palestinians.

So Olmert seized on the kidnapping of two Israeli soldiers on July 12, the latest in an endless string of back-and-forth border violations, as the pretext for an all-out onslaught on Hezbollah. But it didn't work. The Israeli armed forces have effectively been fought to a standstill by a lightly armed but highly trained and disciplined guerrilla force, and there will be major repercussions at home and abroad.

The Israeli politician likeliest to benefit from this mess is Binyamin Netanyahu, the hardest of the hard-liners, who flamboyantly quit the Likud Party last year in protest over former prime minister Ariel Sharon's policy of pulling out of the occupied Gaza Strip. The last opinion poll in Israel gave Netanyahu an approval rating of 58 percent.

Much graver, in the long run, is the erosion of Israel's myth of military invincibility. It is always more economical to frighten your enemies into submission than to fight them, but Arabs have been losing their fear of Israel for some years now. This defeat will greatly accelerate the process, and there are a lot more Arabs than there are Israelis.

Syria's President Bashar al-Assad summed up the matter brutally but accurately when he said on Monday that Israel is at "an historic crossroads. Either it moves towards peace and gives back [the Israeli-occupied lands], or it faces chronic instability until [a new Arab] generation comes and puts an end to the problem."

Of course, he didn't mention that an Arab military victory over Israel, even far in the future, would also effectively put an end to the Arabs, since Israel already has hundreds of nuclear weapons.

16.

EUROPE

There is a North American view of Europe, especially popular on the right in the United States, in which the continent consists mainly of medieval city centres full of Gothic cathedrals and tourists, surrounded by festering slums full of feral Muslim immigrants. Ridiculous statistics are cited on Fox News, preposterous predictions of social cataclysm are bandied about even on the European right, and, occasionally, something happens that can be used by the ignorant media and politicians to reinforce that view.

November 4, 2005
NOT THE PARIS INTIFADA

"Scum," French Interior Minister Nicolas Sarkozy called the rioters who have seized control of many working-class "suburbs" around Paris every night since October 27, when two teenagers died in an accident that many blame on the police. Accused of pouring fuel on the flames, Sarkozy responded: "For too long politicians have not used the right words to describe reality."

Sarkozy plans to run for the presidency next year, and he wants to seem even tougher on crime and on immigrants (two separate issues that he regularly conflates) than his main rival, Prime Minister Dominique de Villepin. But his conviction that the policy of multiculturalism has failed has become the new popular wisdom in France, where right-wing commentators refer to the riots as the "Paris intifada"—as if the rioters were all Muslims.

Even William Pfaff, the best informed of American commentators, has stopped believing that people with different traditions can live side by side. Writing in the *Observer* after the terrorist bombs in London in July, he said: "A half-century of well-intentioned but catastrophically mistaken policy of multiculturalism, indifferent or even hostile to social and cultural integration, has produced in Britain and much of Europe a technologically educated but culturally and morally unassimilated immigrant demi-intelligentsia."

Pfaff was in effect arguing that the London bombs would not have happened if only British immigration policy over the past fifty years had worked to extinguish any sense of solidarity between the descendants of Muslim immigrants to Britain and Muslims elsewhere. That is no doubt true, so far as it goes, but not invading Iraq would have prevented the London bombs at a much lower cost.

The real problem with all this ranting about the failures of multiculturalism is that the Paris riots are actually a splendid demonstration of the successful integration of immigrants into French culture (which has, after all, a long tradition of insurrection and revolution). The riots in Paris are not a Muslim uprising. They are not even race riots. They are an outburst of resentment and frustration by the marginalized and the unemployed of every ethnic group.

The low-income housing estates that ring Paris and other big French cities are the dumping ground for people who haven't made it in the cool twenty-first-century France of the urban centres, and they include the old white working class as well as immigrants from France's former colonies in Arabic-speaking North Africa and sub-Saharan black Africa and from the poorer countries of Europe. Unemployment there is often twice the national average of 10 percent. Furthermore, they are not Muslim majority communities, or even non-white majority communities.

Every ethnic group lives jumbled together in the apartment towers, and the kid gangs that dominate the estates steal from strangers and residents alike and fight among themselves for control of the drug trade, but they are models of racial and cultural integration. This can be little consolation to the owners of the twenty-eight thousand vehicles that have been burned on those estates so far this year, but what we are seeing is an incoherent revolt by kids, many of them gang members, who would once have formed the next generation of the French working class.

The trouble is they are no longer needed in that role and they know that they have no future, so they are very angry. This said, they are not politically organized, and so, after a few more nights, the violence will die down again for a while.

In Britain, where unemployment is half the French level and the council estates are less grim and less isolated geographically, there is much less anger. There haven't been French-style riots in Germany either, although many Germans have deeply racist attitudes towards non-Christian and non-white immigrants. German cities also do not concentrate their poor people, immigrant and non-immigrant alike, in densely populated one-class "suburbs."

The French have little to be proud of in their immigration policy, but what has been happening there since late October is neither American-style race riots nor a Muslim rebellion. About half the kids burning the cars and the buildings are white, working-class, post-Christian French, and they get along with the black and Muslim kids just fine.

Europe has spent the last fifteen years tidying up after the great upheavals that first broke up the post-1945 Soviet empire in Central Europe, then the Soviet Union itself (which was really the old Russian empire under another name), and finally the Serbian mini-empire in Yugoslavia between 1989 and the mid-1990s. Apart from Yugoslavia and some parts of the Caucasus, the dismantling of the old empires was accomplished in a remarkably non-violent manner, but figuring out how to put the pieces back together in new patterns that made sense (and served the interests of the people concerned) was a long, hard slog. In Central Europe and the Balkans, what made it all work was the prospect of membership in the European Union.

April 28, 2006
THE UTILITY OF EUROSLAPS

"Sofia gets Euroslap," shrieked the headline in the Bulgarian newspaper *Trud* in early April, and it was true. Olli Rehn, the European Union's Commissioner for Enlargement, reporting to the European Parliament on Bulgaria's readiness to join the EU next January, had said that "the jury is still out," and that Sofia needs to do much more about fighting high-level corruption and organized crime if it hopes to get in next year.

This sort of foreign criticism provokes nationalist outrage in most countries, but the Bulgarians took it almost meekly. Prime Minister Sergei Stanishev promised to work hard to meet the EU's standards and deadlines, and, in his first eight months in office, his government has passed sixty new laws to that end. Euroslaps work.

Romania, also scheduled to become a full member of the EU next January, has done even better. Just two years ago, it was still seen as the more problematic of the two candidates, with high levels of corruption, an easily bought judiciary and rigged elections. But the combination of euro-sticks and euro-carrots worked so well in Romania that it is now no longer seen as a problem candidate.

Bulgaria still has some distance to go. There have been 157 contract killings in public places in Bulgaria since 2000, as gangsters battle it out over the proceeds of organized crime, and no high Bulgarian official has ever been convicted on corruption charges, but the threat to postpone its EU entry by a year is having the desired effect, and now Bulgaria is scrambling to fix things in time. "Enlargement," as the EU calls the process of bringing in new members, has been an amazingly effective tool for getting the former Communist countries of Europe to root out the corrupt systems and arbitrary habits that they inherited from their former rulers. Millions of people who served the Communist states are still serving their successors today in the government, the civil service and the judiciary, but the European Union has found a way to impose reform from outside without generating nationalist resentment and resistance.

"The heart of the EU's enlargement policy is conditionality," Olli Rehn wrote in the *Financial Times* recently. "The conditions for membership are clear and rigorous, and . . . require nothing less than a top-to-bottom reform of a would-be member's institutions and policies," and the benefits of membership are so attractive that the candidates jump through the hoops willingly. If Bulgaria doesn't fix its justice system in time, EU monitors will keep track of how many organized crime figures actually get prosecuted and how many corruption cases are brought against senior Bulgarian officials. It's undignified for a sovereign state to accept such supervision (which will last until the EU is satisfied that Bulgarian justice meets the EU standard), but the Bulgarians have decided that it's worth it.

The job is almost done: with the admission of thirty million Romanians and Bulgarians next January, all of the former Soviet satellites in Europe (plus the three Baltic states once part of the Soviet Union itself) will have been brought into the family. The EU will have grown from fifteen to twenty-seven members in less than five years, and all that remains to do to clear up the mess left over from the Communist era in Eastern Europe is to bring in the "Western Balkans": Albania and the now-independent countries of former Yugoslavia (except Slovenia, which is already an EU member).

The Western Balkans contains only twenty-five million people, but it now consists of six separate countries and will grow to eight when Montenegro and Kosovo get their formal independence from Serbia. Most of these countries are deeply scarred by the nationalist wars and massacres that ravaged the region in the 1990s, and nobody needs the EU process more than they do.

With the final goal almost in sight, however, "enlargement fatigue" is now sapping the will of some existing members (notably France and Germany) to continue with the process. Hence Olli Rehn's plea to the existing EU members last month: "Our conditionality works only if it is credible. Countries have to be sure that they have a realistic chance of joining the EU—even if it is many years away—if reformist leaders are to convince their public that it is worth making enormous efforts to meet the EU's conditions."

He's right, and with luck enlargement fatigue will turn out to be just a temporary phenomenon. But if it deprives the Western Balkans of hope at this point, all of Europe will regret it.

It is now clear that the European Union will not grow any farther east in this generation: the enlargement fatigue is real. Turkey, despite being an official candidate for membership, is unlikely ever to join, and the pipe dreams of Ukrainian or Georgian membership have blown away. But there is probably still enough will in Brussels to go through with the job of bringing in the Western Balkans, and the "halo effect" of the EU is still so attractive that those countries will actually reform themselves in order to be eligible for membership.

The hardest bit has been containing the misgivings of ordinary citizens in the older EU countries while this job is being done. The rapid expansion was stretching the EU's institutions to the limit, but any attempt to streamline the institutions drew people's attention to what was happening, usually with negative consequences. Getting the new constitution through was a four-year battle.

October 3, 2009
THE EUROPEAN UNION'S DEMOCRATIC DEFICIT

You can get the Irish to agree to anything, even a European superstate that forces abortion on them, conscripts their citizens for a European army, and compels Ireland to abandon its traditional neutrality. All you need is a severe recession (Ireland's economy is the hardest-hit of all the European Union members), and suddenly all those concerns fade away.

Sixteen months ago the Irish voted "no" to the Lisbon Treaty, a deal that streamlined decision making in the EU. For the first time, the twenty-seven-member union would have a president, a foreign minister, and voting rules that do not require unanimity on every single policy decision. Twenty-six members ratified the treaty in their parliaments, but Ireland's constitution required it to ratify treaties by referendum.

This led to a campaign in which Irish nationalists and leftists, backed by the right-wing anti-EU press in Britain (which circulates widely in Ireland), scared Irish voters into saying no. All the allegations about abortion, conscription, and the end of Irish neutrality in the first sentence of this article are untrue, but they all played a large part in that campaign.

The Irish "no" vote brought the process of European integration to a halt, but the EU then issued various statements promising the Irish government not to do what the Lisbon Treaty never gave it the right to do anyway. Last Friday, the Irish were sent back to the polls, and this time 67 percent of them voted yes.

This whole exercise became necessary, however, because the original proposal to create an EU constitution was voted down in Dutch and French referendums in 2005. Whenever you ask the actual people of European countries if they want to "strengthen" and "deepen" the European Union, they have this distressing tendency to say no.

So, after a "period of reflection," the proposed EU constitution was re-packaged as a mere treaty, which in most EU countries can be ratified by a parliamentary vote without a referendum. Party discipline ensured that most members of parliaments will vote the right way, and twenty-six out of twenty-seven parliaments did. Only Ireland required special treatment, and it was duly administered.

There is an obvious democratic deficit here. The grandees decide, and the people obey. Moreover, some of the grandees are very grand indeed. Take Jacques Chirac, president of France for twelve years until 2007.

Chirac has most recently been in the news when his pet Maltese terrier, Sumo, leaped up and bit his stomach—the dog was depressed by the move from the spacious grounds of the presidential palace to a private apartment on the Quai Voltaire—but the politician's real claim to fame is his ability to escape corruption charges.

The charges date back to when Chirac was mayor of Paris, from 1977 to 1995. Between 1992 and 1995 alone, he spent 2.5 million francs (about $500,000) in cash, mostly stuffed into brown envelopes in five-hundred-franc notes, to pay for lavish holidays for his family, his friends and their families. The money probably came from the almost one hundred million dollars in bribes and kickbacks that he'd received from companies seeking a share in a rebuilding program for schools in the Paris area.

Chirac avoided prosecution for twelve years by insisting that he could not be questioned about the affair while he was president. The legal machinery ground slowly into motion once he left office, but like banks that are too big to fail, Chirac is too grand to go to jail. It now appears that all legal proceedings against him will be quashed.

There are other current examples of this phenomenon—Italy's Prime Minister Silvio Berlusconi, for example—and many past ones. But the larger reality of which this is only one facet is that high politics in most

European countries is still an elite project. That is nowhere truer than in the project of the European Union.

If it had been left to the normal politics of European countries, the EU would never have happened. It was the post–Second World War elites of Europe, appalled by the wars that had devastated the continent, who conceived the goal of a European Union where the rival nationalisms would eventually wither away and Europe would live in peace.

From the European Coal and Steel Community in 1951 to the European Economic Community in 1957 to the European Union in 1993, they summoned into existence a political entity for which there was little popular demand. When local nationalism got in the way, they worked around it or waited it out — like in Ireland just now.

While the forms of democracy are always observed, the spirit that animates the EU is we-know-what's-good-for you, vote-again-till-you-get-it-right. If the result had not been a Europe that is prosperous, committed to protecting human rights and astonishingly peaceful, you'd condemn the whole project out of hand.

Chirac was bad enough; Berlusconi is ten times worse. The Italians go on voting for him anyway.

June 8, 2009
BERLUSCONI ON THE SLIDE?

When foreigners look at Italian Prime Minister Silvio Berlusconi, they see a ridiculous old goat with megalomaniacal tendencies and a history of white-collar crime, and wonder why so many Italians keep voting for him. Those who don't vote for him explain that he controls most of the country's television networks — and that his antics actually appeal to that considerable section of the population who dream of being rich and brazen enough to get away with blatant public misbehaviour.

Until recently, Berlusconi looked completely invulnerable, but in last weekend's elections for the parliament of the European Union, only 35 percent of Italians voted for his People of Freedom Party. He had predicted that 45 percent would. Is it possible that Italians are turning away from "Il Cavaliere" (The Knight) at last?

The source of the funds that let him become a major real-estate developer and then a multi-billionaire media magnate remains obscure. Accusations that he had links with the Mafia have never been properly refuted. Prosecutions against him for corruption and bribery were stalled by his lawyers until they expired because of the statute of limitations. (In some cases, he used his political power to move the expiry date up.) But having an affair with an eighteen-year-old girl may have been a step too far.

Silvio Berlusconi is seventy-two years old, but his hair transplant and perma-tan make him look younger. His habit of surrounding himself with attractive young women has long been indulged by Italian voters, although it clearly annoyed his wife, Veronica Lario. When he publicly told former showgirl (and now cabinet minister) Mara Carfagna that "I'd marry you like a shot if I wasn't married already" in 2007, Lario demanded and got a public apology. This time, however, she demanded a divorce.

As Berlusconi's sense of invulnerability has grown, he has thrown caution to the wind. In April, he drove to the outskirts of Naples to attend the birthday party of eighteen-year-old Noemi Letizia and gave her a gold necklace worth thousands of dollars. She calls him "Papi" (Daddy), which would be awkward enough if it were true (since he has been married to Veronica Lario for thirty years), but his relationship with Letizia may not be paternal.

It subsequently emerged that Berlusconi flew Letizia, then seventeen, to his private estate in Sardinia last Christmas. Her ex-boyfriend alleged that Berlusconi had phoned her out of the blue after seeing her photographs in a model agency's brochure. At this point Veronica Lario's patience finally snapped: she told the media that she was disgusted by his behaviour and that she would not remain the wife of "a man who consorts with underage girls."

As usual, Berlusconi tried to shrug it off, offering a series of increasingly implausible explanations for how he came to know the girl, but this time something was different. Despite the tight control he exercises over his own media and the state-owned channels, the story could not be contained, and many Italians who had tolerated his previous peccadilloes felt that this time he had gone too far. Hence the sharp drop in the Freedom Party's electoral fortunes.

But is this the start of a major shift in Italian politics, or only a blip on the graph? If I were a betting man, I'd bet on the blip.

The Italian "economic miracle" ended twenty-five years ago, and the state is all but broke. Fiscal irresponsibility has been the hallmark of almost all Italian governments since 1945, and the country has only avoided the dire consequences by continuously devaluing the lira and inflating its debts away. Since it swapped the lira for the euro, however, that escape hatch has been closed.

Few voters are willing to bear the intense and long-lasting pain that would be involved in putting Italy back on the fiscal straight-and-narrow, and no sane politician wants the responsibility of imposing that pain on the country. So the field is left clear for political conjurors like Berlusconi, magical thinkers who can persuade themselves and everyone else that everything will be all right.

The affair with the teenager is embarrassing, but it will be mostly forgotten by the time there is another national election, and Berlusconi has already discovered his next populist platform. He is going to become Italy's defender against the immigrant hordes.

"What immigrant hordes?" you could reasonably ask, for only 4 percent of Italy's residents are foreign-born. But Berlusconi knew exactly what he was doing when he said in an election speech: "When I walk down the streets of Milan and I see the large numbers of non-Italians, I feel like I'm no longer in an Italian or a European city but in an African one."

Up till now, openly racist talk has been the specialty of Berlusconi's coalition partner, the Northern League, but Il Cavaliere is going to steal their clothes. He will be around for quite a while yet, and the day of reckoning will be postponed once again.

Some days of reckoning, however, finally did arrive. Towards the end of the decade, the most wanted war criminals in the Balkans were being handed over or surrendering in rapid succession—and, in the Netherlands, they began coming to terms with the Dutch part in the tragedy.

June 19, 2008
THE GHOSTS OF SREBRENICA

Last week in The Hague, a Dutch court began hearing a case brought forward by the surviving relatives of the eight thousand Bosnian Muslim civilians who were murdered by Serb forces at Srebrenica in 1995, while supposedly under UN military protection. The survivors are claiming four billion dollars in damages from the Dutch state and the United Nations, which had created the "safe haven" at Srebrenica and sent the Dutch troops there to protect it. It's about time.

Good people make mistakes, and innocent people die; it happens all the time, especially in war. But Srebrenica was the worst mass killing in Europe since the Second World War, and it probably could have been avoided if the Dutch troops had shown a little more courage. If not, then they could have died fighting to stop it, because that was their duty.

Soldiers talk with understandable pride about the "unlimited liability" of their profession: the same phrase appears in many armies in many languages. Few other callings require that on some occasions you must die in order to do your duty, and the military profession is quite right in claiming that this sets soldiers apart. But you can't just talk the talk. You have to walk the walk, and the Dutch didn't.

The Dutch soldiers were sent to Srebrenica in 1995 to relieve the Canadian battalion that had been holding the UN-protected enclave. I happened to be in Canada at the time and a Dutch television crew asked me for advice on what their soldiers could expect in Srebrenica. I told them that the Canadians were very glad to be getting out because it was potentially a death trap.

I didn't mean a death trap for the tens of thousands of Bosnian Muslim civilians who were trapped there; that was obvious. I meant a death trap for the few hundred lightly armed Canadian soldiers who were protecting the Muslim civilians from the thousands of Serbs with artillery and tanks who had surrounded the enclave.

If the Serbs attacked, the Canadians would have to fight despite the odds—anything else would be a shameful betrayal of their duty—and they might lose dozens of people. They would probably save the enclave in the process because even the Serbian commander, General Ratko Mladic, would stop short of killing hundreds of UN troops. But it was a dreadful situation, and the Canadians were greatly relieved to be going home. Good luck to the Dutch.

The Dutch were unlucky. In July 1995, the Serbs began to make probing attacks on the enclave's perimeter, which was much too long to defend with only four hundred troops. The Dutch commander, Colonel

Ton Karremans, was in a difficult position, but his course was clear: protest loudly to Mladic and to the world, and call in NATO air strikes if the Serbian attacks continued. Meanwhile, the Muslim men within the enclave would be given back the weapons they had surrendered to the UN, and he would prepare to fall back to the town of Srebrenica, which could probably be held for a day or so—time enough for help to arrive, perhaps. But if the Serbs kept coming, Dutch soldiers would die.

So Karremans went to see Mladic, drank a toast with him, and agreed to hand over the Muslims in return for thirty Dutch soldiers who had been taken hostage. The Dutch commander didn't know that the Serbs were planning to exterminate all the men and boys in Srebrenica; the Serbs themselves only decided to do so after meeting with Karremans and realizing that they faced no opposition. But this was three years into the war, and he must have known that at the very least many hundreds of Muslims would be tortured, raped and murdered.

So the Dutch troops came home safely. In 1999, the UN admitted that it had failed to protect the Muslims of Srebrenica from mass murder, but said that none of its officials could be held responsible and invoked its legal immunity. In 2002, an official Dutch report blamed the Dutch government and senior military officials for the massacre, and Prime Minister Wim Kok's entire cabinet (which had been in power in 1995) resigned.

Then, in 2006, the Dutch government awarded those who had served in Srebrenica a special insignia "in recognition for their behaviour in difficult circumstances." They still didn't get it. Even if all the higher authorities had failed them, the soldiers' duty was clear, and they didn't do it.

I have talked to Canadian soldiers who served in Srebrenica before the Dutch, and they wonder if they would have behaved any better when the Serbs attacked. At least they know that they should have. Real soldiers are old-fashioned people who still believe in honour, and that is the most attractive thing about them.

17.

NUKES

Nuclear weapons have not actually gone away. However, they have become politically invisible, except of course for the ones that don't yet exist: for example, the ones that Iran might build one day. Even North Korea's few nuclear weapons actually fell off the international agenda after Pyongyang actually tested one or two. That is because the only conceivable use for an Iranian or North Korean nuclear weapon, assuming that the local government is sane, is as a deterrent: a guarantee that there will be terrible retaliation if somebody attacks either country with nuclear weapons. Only great powers ever threaten to use their nuclear weapons first—and even they'd have to be insane to actually do it.

September 22, 2005
THE NORTH KOREAN "THREAT"

If you want to understand why North Koreans are so worried you have to imagine the Doomsday scenario that haunts them.

Kim Jong Il wakes up early, because it's "The Day," but it takes him ages to get ready. His hairdresser fusses for half an hour to get his hair to stand up, then his corset is tightened to contain his bulging stomach, and finally he himself decides which shade of light tan Mao jacket he'll wear. Eventually he slips into his platform shoes and clops downstairs to meet his assembled generals.

"Are our nuclear missiles ready to fly?" he asks General Number One. "Yes, Dear Leader, they are both ready. One will strike Seoul, and the other will strike a large American base in Japan," the general replies. Then, mustering up all his courage, the general adds: "But are you sure this is a good idea? The Americans will know where they came from, and their retaliation will be terrible. By lunchtime our country will be destroyed and we will all be dead."

A single shot rings out and the impudent general falls to the floor. "Thus to all cowards and weaklings," cries Kim Jong Il, and then continues, in a more conversational tone: "We must destroy the nests of the capitalist imperialist vipers. It is our destiny, and we will dwell with Marx forever. Launch the missiles!" General Number Two salutes and says "Yes, sir! At once, sir!"

Having a little trouble with this scenario? Doesn't quite ring true? Good, because I have trouble with it, too. But this is roughly the scenario that panic-mongers have been asking us to believe in, and if it isn't true then there never was a crisis.

There wasn't. Last week was especially silly, with the members of the six-party talks on getting Pyongyang back within the nuclear non-proliferation regime (China, Japan, North Korea, South Korea, Russia and the United States) declaring a dramatic success on Monday, September 19, and North Korea apparently reneging on the deal on Tuesday. But there are reasons for this.

The North Korean negotiating style certainly leaves a good deal to be desired. They make dramatic announcements ("We have nuclear weapons!"), flounce out of treaties they have signed (like the Non-Proliferation

Treaty, in 2002), and try to change the meaning of deals they have signed before the ink is dry on the paper (like last week). It is the behaviour of people who have no experience of negotiations between equals—and, indeed, people raised in the authoritarian, almost Orwellian system that prevails in North Korea are very unlikely to have had that experience. But these are also shrewd negotiating tactics for people who are so weak that they have practically no cards in their hand. If you have no way to make other parties pay attention to your concerns, threatening to be unreasonable and cause a lot of damage is a good way to get them to listen. Even teenagers know that.

North Korea has no real cards in its hand. With half as many people as South Korea, it has an economy around one-tenth the size, and much of that goes to maintaining a military establishment that is more or less capable of matching the South Korean and American forces that confront it on the Korean Peninsula. Its people live on the brink of starvation (although Kim Jong Il clearly eats very well), and its ability to threaten the United States directly is precisely zero.

When the Bush administration designated North Korea as part of the "axis of evil," perhaps next for the treatment after Iraq, Pyongyang panicked. It had long been working on nuclear weapons secretly (and cheating on an earlier agreement to stop doing so), because it believed that they would deter an American attack, even if they could only reach nearby targets. Suddenly it pulled out of the Non-Proliferation Treaty and announced that it actually had operational nukes—though it may well have been bluffing.

That unleashed the so-called crisis of the past few years, but all North Korea was really looking for was a guarantee that it would not be attacked, and for some foreign aid. That was essentially what it got in the deal of November 19—North Korea agreed to abandon its nuclear-weapons program in exchange for economic aid, security assurances and improved ties with the United States—so the "crisis" should be over now.

It wasn't, unfortunately, because the U.S. Treasury Department suddenly imposed financial sanctions on North Korea on the (unproven) grounds that Pyongyang was counterfeiting U.S. dollars. It's still not clear whether this was a deliberate spoiling move by hard-liners within the Bush administration or just poor policy coordination, but the 2005 deal fell apart. A year later, North Korea tested its first nuclear weapon.

By 2007, inevitably, there was a new deal along much the same lines as the old one: North Korea promised to shut down the nuclear reactor that produced its fissile material, and was guaranteed a million tons of oil in return. By then, however, Pyongyang had at least two nuclear weapons (though nobody knows how well they work), and it looks like it gets to keep them.

The lesson? If you bribe somebody to be good, and that's your only leverage over them, then you should pay up.

February 18, 2009
A COLLISION AT SEA

A ship I once served in had a small brass plate on the bridge with a quotation from Thucydides, the Greek statesman, historian and seaman of the fourth century BC: "A collision at sea can ruin your whole day." It is still true.

It is harder to collide at sea than on land, since there are no blind curves and nothing moves much faster than a bicycle, so my normal reaction to a collision at sea is to think "How can they have been so stupid?" But here is a collision that beggars the imagination.

In the Atlantic Ocean, on the night of February 3–4, at an undisclosed depth, the British nuclear submarine *Vanguard* and the French nuclear submarine *Le Triomphant* ran into each other. Both boats were "boomers," missile-firing submarines carrying sixteen ballistic missiles, each of which can deliver several nuclear warheads at intercontinental range.

The Atlantic is the second biggest ocean in the world. The submarines are considerably smaller: around 145 metres long. So there they are, puttering along at six knots or less, with an entire ocean to play in, and freedom in three dimensions (they can go very deep if they want)— and they run into each other. The damage was slight, but it ruined the day for two whole navies. How could they have been so stupid?

All right, it's not quite that simple. The boomers—not just British and French missile-firing submarines but American and Russian ones, too— congregate in specific parts of the Atlantic that are called "nesting grounds." They need deep water that is relatively quiet, and they need to stay in range of their targets. In practice, then, they have only a quarter of the Atlantic to play with.

That still ought to be enough, but they are also deliberately running blind. If they operated their "active" sonar (the thing that goes "ping" in the war movies), they would detect everything on and below the surface for many kilometres around them—but everything they heard would also hear them.

They mustn't allow this to happen. Their job is to hide out in the depths of the ocean as a last-ditch nuclear deterrent that cannot be found and destroyed in a surprise attack. So they only run the "passive" sonar, which listens to all the noises in the water but does not give away their own position.

Unfortunately, passive sonar cannot hear vessels that are not making any noise—and modern submarines are designed to be ultra-quiet. In this case, they actually closed to touching distance without detecting each other's presence.

The subs were obviously on courses that converged slowly because the damage was minor and only in the bows. If one had gone straight into the side of the other, however, then both could have been destroyed. Down to the bottom go their nuclear reactors, plus anything up to a hundred or so nuclear warheads on their missiles.

Both crews would have been lost—more than two hundred men—but that would have been the end of it. None of the nukes would have exploded, and it really doesn't matter if there are a couple of tons of highly radioactive material scattered on the deep ocean floor hundreds of kilometres from the nearest land. Nevertheless, the incident reminds us that although the Cold War ended twenty years ago, the boomers of all the great powers are still out there on patrol, nuclear weapons at the ready, as if this were 1975. There is not a single good reason for them all to be doing this, but nobody has told them to stop. Why not?

Because we don't know what the future might bring? Perhaps, and as such I didn't say scrap the subs tomorrow, but tie them up in port and stop this nonsense. If we all end up in a new Cold War one day, then okay, you can have them back, but why are they cruising around out there now?

You have to keep the crews trained? Well, train them in other nuclear submarines—or if they really must train in these particular boats, then *take the missiles out.* It is not sane to keep deploying these instruments of mass death when no major power fears an attack by any other.

And, by the way, if you could all agree to stop these ridiculous patrols, it would be a useful step towards the more sweeping measures of nuclear disarmament that all the great powers say they want, and that President Barack Obama has adopted as a serious goal.

Obama is the first occupant of the White House since Ronald Reagan with the vision to imagine a future free of nuclear weapons, and unlike Reagan he's smart enough not to let the guardians of nuclear orthodoxy talk him out of it. He has a lot on his plate right now, but here's a step in the right direction that costs nothing: announce that the U.S. Navy will no longer run "combat patrols" with its nuclear-missile-firing submarines, and invite the world's other nuclear-weapons powers to follow suit.

After this little demonstration of folly, they'd all come along pretty promptly.

I suspect that Obama doesn't read my articles because he did not act on that perfectly sensible suggestion. On the other hand, he did cancel the preposterous Bush commitment to install Ballistic Missile Defence (BMD) radars and launchers in Eastern Europe, ostensibly to stop Iranian missiles with nuclear warheads from reaching the United States.

Ballistic missile defences sound less noxious than nuclear-tipped missiles, but in fact they are the other side of the same equation. If the BMD actually works, then deterrence doesn't work: the side with the BMD can nuke the other side and not worry about retaliation. This didn't matter much in the case of the Iranians, who had no nuclear weapons, but the prospect of American BMD in Eastern Europe drove the Russians crazy.

September 19, 2009
DEAD WALRUSES

"Some experts have doubts about the missile-shield concept," as the more cautious reporters put it. (That example comes from the BBC website.) A franker journalist would say that the ballistic-missile defence system that the Bush administration planned for Poland and the Czech Republic, and that President Barack Obama has just cancelled, has never worked and shows few signs of ever doing so.

Obama has done the right thing. It saves money that would have been wasted, and it repairs relations with Russia, which was paranoid about the system being so close to its borders. And the cancellation also signals a significant decline in the paranoia in Washington about Iran.

"Paranoia" is the right word in both cases. Iran doesn't have any missiles that could even come within range of the BMD system that was slated for Poland and the Czech Republic, let alone nuclear warheads to put on them. According to U.S. intelligence assessments, Iran is not working on nuclear weapons, nor on missiles that could reach Europe, let alone the United States. Washington's decision to deploy the system anyway was so irrational that it made the Russians paranoid as well.

Their intelligence services told them the same thing that the U.S. intelligence community told the Bush administration: that Iran had no nuclear weapons or long-range ballistic missiles, nor any possibility of getting them for five to ten years. So what was the U.S. really doing in setting up the system so close to Russia's borders?

The intelligence people in Moscow also told Russian leaders that the U.S. system was useless junk that had never managed to intercept an incoming missile in an honest operational test. (All the tests were shamelessly rigged to make it easy for the intercepting missiles to strike their targets, and still they failed most of the time.) Besides, although the planned BMD base in Poland was close to Russia, it was in the wrong place to intercept Russian missiles.

So why did the Russians get paranoid about it? Because although they knew how the American military-industrial complex worked—they have similar problems with their own domestic version—they simply could not believe that the United States would spend so much money on something so stupid and pointless. Surely there was something they were missing; some secret American strategy that would put them at a disadvantage.

No, there wasn't, and almost everybody (except some Poles and Czechs who want U.S. troops on their soil as a guarantee against Russian misbehaviour, and some people on the American right) was pleased by Obama's decision to pull the plug on the project. But why did the Bush administration choose to deploy this non-functioning weapons system in Eastern Europe in the first place?

The answer lies in another weapons project that began in 1946: the nuclear-powered airplane. It could stay airborne for months and fly around the world without refuelling, its boosters promised, and that would give America a huge strategic advantage. There was only one problem. The nuclear reactor needed a lot of shielding, as the aircrew would be only feet away. The shields had to be made of lead. And lead-filled airplanes cannot fly.

Fifteen years and about ten billion dollars later (in today's money), there was still no viable design for a nuclear-powered bomber, let alone a flyable prototype. Ballistic missiles were taking over the job of delivering nuclear warheads anyway, and so, when Robert McNamara became defence secretary in the Kennedy administration in 1961, he was astonished to discover that the nuclear-powered aircraft was still in the defence budget. It was, he said, "as if I came down to breakfast in the morning and found a dead walrus on the dining-room table." It took McNamara two years to kill the program, against fierce opposition from the air force and defence industry, and the fact that the nuclear-powered aircraft did not and could not work was irrelevant.

Former general Dwight D. Eisenhower's presidency is perhaps best remembered for his warning against what he called the "military-industrial complex" in his farewell speech in 1960, but he actually gave two warnings. The other was that "public policy could become the captive of a scientific-technological elite." These were the lobbies that kept the nuclear airplane going for seventeen years, and they have kept the BMD system going for more than a quarter-century.

President Obama has killed the most pointlessly provocative of the Ballistic Missile Defence deployments, but he still cannot take the political risk of admitting that the system doesn't work (though he twice explained in his speech that the United States needed missile defence systems that were "proven and cost-effective"). It is the grandchild of Star Wars, a sacred relic blessed by Saint Ronald Reagan himself, and it will keep appearing at dining-room tables for years to come.

18.

OF TIME AND HUMAN NATURE

November 28, 2004
HUMAN MONSTERS

"He could be very entertaining," Stalin's niece Kira Alliluyeva told biographer Robert Service in 1998. The dictator had her jailed in his last round of purges, after the Second World War, but she still remembered how kind he had been to her when she was a little girl, how he took her on his knee and sang songs to her—and that he had a fine singing voice. Not only that, he wrote limpid poetry in Georgian as a youth, read Dostoevsky and his subordinates saw him as a considerate boss.

He also had millions of people killed, which is why, until Service's recent book, *Stalin: A Biography*, people were reluctant to write about his human side. Yet a moment's thought will tell you that the "great" dictators could never have achieved such power over other people if there were not something attractive about their personalities.

Maybe it's the fact that most of their victims are no longer with us that now makes it possible to see the mass murderers of the mid-twentieth century as complex human beings rather than mere one-dimensional monsters. It will be quite a while before some brave Cambodian makes the first film that shows the human side of Pol Pot, and in China they haven't gotten around yet to admitting officially that Mao Zedong was a monster. But in Europe, where the horrors are a bit more distant in time, it's all the rage.

The current wave of books and films about human monsters began with a couple of ground-breaking Italian biographies that showed the human side of Benito Mussolini, but he wasn't really on the first team of mass murderers. Service's biography of Stalin is different—and so is Bernd Eichinger's groundbreaking film on the last days of Hitler, *Der Untergang (Downfall)*.

Released in Germany to generally positive reviews in September, *Downfall* is the first German film to tackle Hitler directly—fifty-nine years after the man's death. Set in the last twelve days of Hitler's life, as the Soviet army fought its way towards his deep, multi-storey bunker in central Berlin in April 1945, it documents his rages and his self-pity, and depicts him as an ordinary human being.

Hitler says "please" and "thank you." He eats pasta. He is kind to the terrified women who continue to carry out their secretarial duties as the apocalypse rages overhead. When he finally marries his mistress Eva Braun (which he always refrained from doing because, he said, he was wedded to the German people), he is implicitly accepting that his life is over, and that they will have to die in a little while—but he kisses her gently on the lips.

It's all true, based on the accounts of people who were in the bunker and survived, but the film stirred up a storm in Germany. Most of the criticisms echoed the words of Golo Mann, one of Hitler's first biographers, who warned thirty years ago that the more biographers explored Hitler's origins and psychology, the more inclined people would be to understand him. From there, Mann said, "it is only a small step towards forgiving and then admiring." But that is not true.

Admitting that Hitler and the other great murderers were human is painful, but to deny it is to absolve ourselves of any moral connection to what happened. Whatever the risks involved in acknowledging our common humanity, they are outweighed by the need to understand that it is human beings, not instantly recognizable as moral monsters, who commit great atrocities.

Consider Ernesto "Che" Guevara, the revolutionary hero whose iconic image, taken from a 1960 photo, once graced millions of students' walls. There is no doubt that injustice inspired genuine rage in him. Since he never got to rule anywhere, however, his image is unsullied by any knowledge of what he would have done if he actually had power.

There has been a film out about Che, too. Called *The Motorcycle Diaries*, it follows the epic trip he and a friend made up the length of Latin America on an old Norton 500 in 1952. It documents how these young Argentine sons of privilege had their eyes opened to the realities of poverty and exploitation in Latin America—and leaves them just before Che joined Fidel Castro in his Mexican exile and began his own meteoric revolutionary career.

Che comes across as an attractive human being, and his dedication to the poor is clearly genuine. But the ideology he espoused in order to change the human sorrow he saw was Marxism, and he did not water it down. He used to prostrate himself before portraits of Stalin, and advocated "relentless hatred of the enemy that . . . [transforms] us into effective, violent, selective and cold killing machines." If Che Guevara had led a successful revolution in Bolivia, instead of dying in the attempt in 1967, there would certainly have been mass killing.

Mass murder in the name of a principle is as human as apple pie, borsht and steamed rice. Treating the perpetrators as space aliens simply disguises the nature of the problem. The potential mass killers live among us, as they always have. They often have perfectly good manners; some even have high ideals. And the only way the rest of us have to keep them from power is to remember always that the end does not justify the means.

I know. It's trite. But the reason things are trite is often because they are true, and they are no less true because they are said a lot. The problem is that time passes, and eventually we forget to say them.

April 25, 2005
HITLER ANNIVERSARY

Adolf Hitler has now been dead slightly longer than he was alive, and he is about to stop being real. So long as the generation whose lives he terrorized is still with us, he remains a live issue, but the sixtieth anniversary of his death on April 30 is the last big one that will be marked by those who survived his evil and remember his victims. By the time the seventy-fifth anniversary comes around, the survivors and witnesses will almost all be gone. And then Hitler will slip away into history.

It's a process that is nearly impossible to avert because basic human psychology is at work here. Once enough time has passed and all the people involved in a given set of events are dead, we forget to think of them as real people whose triumphs and tragedies matter. Only the loving attention of a filmmaker, a dramatist or a novelist can bring them to life again for us even briefly.

Federico Fellini made the point in his 1969 film *Satyricon*, a story set in the ancient Mediterranean world that has its characters emerge from classical myths and come to life. For about a hundred minutes, we really care about them, in a strange way. The last shot shows the hero coming out of a labyrinth into fresh air and sunlight—and then, with no warning, in the middle of a sentence, the frame freezes and morphs into a time-worn fresco of the same scene. Fade to black.

It's shocking because Fellini makes us understand the true nature of our relationship with the past. Its people have been dust for hundreds or thousands of years, and for all that we try to give them the respect and the weight that we give to the living and recently dead people, the fact is that we can't. The point when historical characters, good or bad, make the transition from flesh-and-blood heroes and villains to mere frescoes on a wall is the point where living people no longer remember them with love or hate. With Hitler, we are nearing that point.

You don't think that could happen? Consider the way we now treat the "Corsican ogre," Napoleon Bonaparte. He has become a veritable industry for military historians, and is revered by half the population of France because he ruled the country at the height of its power and led the French to several dozen great military victories before his boundless ambition finally plunged the country into total defeat. Nobody seems particularly perturbed by the fact that his wars caused the deaths of about four million people.

That is a far smaller number than the thirty million or so deaths that Hitler was responsible for, but Europe's population was a great deal smaller in Napoleon's heyday. Europeans actually stood about the same chance of dying as a result of Napoleon's actions at the height of his power in 1808 as they did from Hitler's actions in 1943 — and Napoleon has been forgiven by history. So, if all of those who died in Hitler's war are soon to enter the same weightless category of the long-dead, what is to keep history from forgiving him, too?

There is one profound difference between Napoleon and Hitler, however: both were tyrants and conquerors, but only Hitler committed deliberate genocide. Most of the people who fought and died in the Second World War didn't even know about the Nazi death camps at the time. Nonetheless, in retrospect, it is the Holocaust, the six million Jews who died not in the war but in the camps, which has come to define our attitudes towards Hitler, and has transformed him into the personification of absolute evil.

So he should remain, but history is mostly about forgetting and not very much survives the winnowing of the generations. Jews are right to want this piece of history not to be forgotten, and the rest of us need it too because remembering the astonishing amount of pain and loss that a man like Hitler could cause by manipulating hatreds is an essential part of our defences against a recurrence. But the bitter truth is that from now on maintaining this level of awareness will be increasingly uphill work.

I would not raise this issue at Passover if the anniversary of Hitler's suicide did not make it the one right time to do so. I also understand why most Jews have zealously defended the unique status of the calamity that befell their people and resisted any link with other, smaller but not utterly dissimilar tragedies that have befallen other peoples: the Armenian massacres, the Cambodian genocide, Rwanda and the rest.

We cannot afford to let Hitler fade into the past because we need him to remind us of our duty to the present and the future. If the memory of the Holocaust is to stay alive not just for Jews but for the whole world, it may be time to start rethinking how to present it to twenty-first-century audiences for whom the Second World War and the Second Punic War seem equally lost in the unremembered past. Was it only about the Jews, or should we see the Holocaust as a warning to us all?

What happened to the Carthaginians at the end of the Second Punic War gives us a clear answer to that question. History gives us lessons, but the world is full of distractions and it's hard to remember.

July 25, 2009
TURN THE PAGE

Two years ago this month, there were twenty-four left. Now they are all gone, and there is nobody alive who fought in the First World War. Well, there is still Jack Babcock, who joined the Royal Canadian Regiment in 1917 but got no closer to the fighting than England, and American veteran Frank Buckles, who drove an ambulance in France as a seventeen-year-old in 1918. But the last real combatant, Harry Patch, who was wounded at the Battle of Passchensdaele in 1917, died on Saturday.

They've been going fast. Erich Kaestner, the last German veteran, died in January 2008. Tony Pierro, who fought with the American Expeditionary Force in France in 1918, died in February. Lazare Ponticelli, the last of the generation of French men who fought in the trenches, died a month later. (One-third of all French males between thirteen and thirty years old in 1914 did not survive the war.)

Yakup Satar, who joined the Turkish army in 1915 and fought in Iraq, died in April 2008. Delfino Borroni, the last Italian WWI veteran, died in October. Australia's Jack Ross died last month, and Britain's Henry Allingham, the grandest old man of all, died a week ago.

Henry Allingham was almost twenty in 1916 when he took part in the Battle of Jutland, the greatest clash of armoured steel battleships in history. (He saw the giant shells "skipping off the water.") As a mechanic in the Royal Naval Air Service, he flew missions over the freezing North Sea in 1917 in seaplanes that he described as "motorised kites." And he spent 1918 in France trying to recover British planes that came down in No Man's Land.

"We were moving forward at night," he recalled about the Western Front. "It was dark . . . I fell into a shell hole. It was full of arms, legs, ears, dead rats—a lot of dead, rotten flesh . . . I lay there in the dark, not daring to move, cold and with my uniform stinking. I was frightened." Sixty million men had the same memories, but they are no longer with us.

Harry Patch was an apprentice plumber when he was conscripted in 1916, and nineteen years old when he arrived at the Western Front in 1917. He lasted four months before a German shell burst overhead, killing three close friends and wounding him in the groin. He was evacuated to England, and never saw the war again.

He married in 1918, had children, followed his trade of plumbing, and served as a volunteer fireman during the bombing raids on Bristol during the Second World War. He died on Saturday, at the age of 111. So what have Harry Patch of Somerset and his sixty million comrades (for it no longer matters which side they were on) left behind for us?

One thing they were very clear about: we can't do this anymore. In the First World War, we crossed a threshold. All the advances in science and technology came together and created a kind of industrialized warfare that is simply unsustainable in human terms. It consumes soldiers, civilians, whole cities at a rate that endangers civilization itself. All the technological innovations that have been added since the First World War—armoured divisions, bomber fleets, nuclear weapons—only deepen the lesson, they don't change it. Human beings have fought wars since we were all hunter-gatherers, and those who were good at it tended to prosper. Now, if you are really good at war, you will be destroyed.

Europe is where industrialized total war first appeared. We can still send expeditionary forces into the weaker parts of what we used to call the Third World and bash them to our heart's content, but if we get into a serious fight with another fully industrialized country we will both be destroyed. (This is a lesson that emerging industrial countries like India, China and Brazil can learn cheaply from history, or very expensively from experience.)

What else did the sixty million leave us? Inscribed on the wall of the chapel at the Royal Military Academy Sandhurst, where I taught War Studies as a much younger man, is the first line of Horace's ode: "Dulce et decorum est pro patria mori" (How sweet and fitting it is to die for one's country).

Wilfred Owen was killed crossing the Sambre canal a week before the First World War ended. He never got any older than twenty-five, but he put the wisdom that the millions bought with their lives into his poem "Dulce et Decorum Est." It's about a poison gas attack, and the last lines run: "If you could hear . . . the blood / Come gargling from the froth-corrupted lungs . . . / My friend, you would not tell with such high zest / To children ardent for some desperate glory, / The old Lie; Dulce et Decorum est / Pro patria mori."

It's almost a century now since anybody but fascists and fools saw war as glorious. The government may tell us that our "glorious dead" have "fallen," but we know that they were only teenagers, and that they died in agony and lost the rest of their lives. Sometimes we even worry that we sent them to kill people for us.

In 1917, during the Third Battle of Ypres, Harry Patch was manning his machine gun when a German got close enough that he looked like a real person—and suddenly Harry realized that he didn't want to kill him. Shouldn't kill him, in fact. He shot the German in the shoulder, which made him drop his rifle, but he kept coming.

So Harry shot him again, first above the knee and then in the ankle. God knows if the German survived all this, but at least Harry was trying. So are the rest of us. Most of the time.

The most interesting thing—the best thing—about being trained as an historian is that you end up inhabiting a much deeper chunk of time. What you get out of that is perspective: the present no longer seems so all-encompassing and all-important, but just another station along the line between the past and the future. What happens in this present can be important, but most of it isn't.

I write all the time about events that I know will be utterly forgotten in five years' time and that don't really matter that much even now. Still, they are interesting to me and, besides, writing about them is my job. But I also try to figure out which trends and developments are really important: what will the high-school students of 2060 have to write essays about? Fortunately, I have lots of time to work on this problem, as change happens a lot slower than people think.

August 13, 2007
SLOW FORWARD

William Gibson invented the word "cyberspace" (in his debut novel *Neuromancer* in 1984), and this gives him the right to pontificate about the future. He has been right about bits of the future, too, in the way that science-fiction writers often are, especially about the ways that new technologies interact with human beings. But he can be very wrong about the present.

In a recent interview with Tim Adams, published in the *Observer*, Gibson confessed that he had stopped writing about the future because new technologies were happening too fast. "What I grew up with as science fiction is now a historical category," he said. "Previous practitioners, H. P. Lovecraft, say, or H. G. Wells, had these huge, leisurely 'here and nows' from which to contemplate what might happen. Wells knew exactly where he was and knew he was at the centre of things."

Whereas we, poor orphans, are adrift on a heaving ocean of constant change, living our jump-cut lives in a state of constant uncertainty. If you haven't heard this line of argument before you are presumably a cave-dwelling hermit. Every generation dramatizes its own experience of the world, and talking about how hard it is to live with endless, unpredictable, high-speed change is one of the favourite occupations of the Western intelligentsia. It is, of course, nonsense.

We do not live in an era of major change, neither in the technologies that shape our environment nor in the social values that shape our lives. That kind of experience is still available in the developing world, when villagers move to the cities, but in the rich countries change has slowed to a crawl.

Between 1825 and 1875, people had to get used to railways, steamships and the telegraph: the average speed of land travel increased fivefold, and information quite suddenly passed between continents in minutes, not weeks. Cities of over a million people proliferated, and the deferential social order of the countryside began to give way before the onslaught of egalitarian values. Revolutionary ideas like Darwinism and Marxism changed the whole way that people looked at the world. That really was high-speed change.

In 1875, gas lighting was the big new thing that made the streets safe and the evenings at home several hours longer. By 1925, gaslight was gone and electricity was everywhere. Horses were replaced by cars, aircraft were becoming commonplace, and the richer homes had radios, telephones and fridges. These were genuine mass societies, complete with their own new forms of education, entertainment and politics, and they also developed mass warfare on an unprecedented scale.

H. G. Wells didn't inhabit a huge, leisurely "here and now" from which to contemplate what might happen when he wrote *The War of the Worlds* in 1898. He was recently divorced, living with a former student in a rented flat less than a kilometre from where I am now sitting, in the midst of a London that had grown tenfold in population in less than a century. What made the book sell was that it echoed all the secret fears of a society shocked and dazed by the speed of change.

Between 1925 and 1975, the pace of change was still high, but it was slowing. Major new technologies like electronics and nuclear fission provided better radio (it's called television) and bigger explosions, but the pace of change was mostly incremental and did not transform people's experience of the world. Antibiotics revolutionized medicine, however, and the gender revolution fundamentally changed relations between the sexes. If you were born in 1925, the world you lived in when you turned fifty in 1975 was a very different place.

Whereas if you were born in the developed parts of the world in 1975—or even in 1955—you have seen very little fundamental change in your lifetime. You travel in basically the same cars and trains and planes as your parents and even your grandparents did. You have the same domestic appliances and roughly the same social values as the previous generation, and modern medicine has not extended your predicted lifespan by even five years. Even popular music is an unbroken continuum since the 1950s. The only truly major new technology that has permeated the entire society in this whole period is computers.

Which, of course, was precisely the technology that William Gibson fixed on as the basis for his dystopian futures, but despite all the hype, the "Information Technology Revolution" really isn't enough to redefine the way we live. We inhabit a period that has seen no more by way of fundamental technological change, and considerably less intellectual and social upheaval, than the latter half of the eighteenth century.

We should probably be grateful for that, because high-speed change, however exhilarating at the start, really is disorienting and exhausting if it lasts over a whole lifetime. But it's probably coming back to destabilize the lives of our children and grandchildren, who will likely face drastic changes in the climate that will affect everything right down to the availability of food for their families.

The cause of those changes, ironically, will not be the high-tech innovations of the twentieth century but the dirty nineteenth-century technologies with which we built our industrial civilization. In other words, we are going to get two waves of disruptive change for the price of one. This has just been the island of tranquillity and prosperity in between. Lucky us.

19.

TERRORISM II

We are awash in deliberate lies and subtler distortions of reality that are meant to justify mistaken and counter-productive military strategies, and people are dying as a result. Some of them are our soldiers, and many more of them are the people our soldiers kill. The "terrorist threat," grotesquely inflated by both official sources and the media, is the ultimate justification for these strategies.

Ridiculous though it sounds to outsiders, Americans are regularly told that their survival as a free society depends on beating the "terrorists." They should treat those who say such things as fools or deliberate liars not worthy of a moment's attention, but they don't. If you control the terminology you control the debate, so the U.S. government puts a huge effort into controlling the definition of "terrorism."

May 2, 2008
TWO TAKES ON TERRORISM

"Terrorism," like "fascism," is one of those words that people routinely apply to almost any behaviour they disapprove of. We had a particularly impressive spread of meanings on display last week.

At one extreme, the U.S. State Department released its annual *Country Reports on Terrorism*, a congressionally mandated survey of all the incidents that the United States officially regards as terrorism. There were, it said, 14,499 such attacks last year. (That's seventy-one fewer than the previous year, so there is hope.)

At the other extreme, the Reverend Jeremiah Wright, Barack Obama's former pastor and current nemesis, when asked to justify his earlier remark that the 9/11 attacks on the United States were "America's chickens coming home to roost," helpfully explained that the U.S. had dropped atomic bombs on Japan and "supported state terrorism against the Palestinians and black South Africans," so what did Americans expect?

"You cannot do terrorism on other people and expect it never to come back on you," Wright elucidated. "These are Biblical principles, not Jeremiah Wright bombastic divisive principles." Are we to believe then that it was God who selected a bunch of Saudi Arabians and Egyptians to punish the United States for its misdeeds against the Japanese, Palestinians and South Africans?

Mass slaughter of the innocent as a tool of divine justice is a familiar concept in the Bible (Jericho, Sodom and Gomorrah, the Ten Plagues of Egypt), and it would have held equal appeal for the nineteen Arab fanatics aboard those hijacked aircrafts on 9/11. But divine terrorism doesn't really qualify under the State Department's definition, since God, even when he perpetrates "premeditated, politically motivated violence . . . against non-combatant targets," is not acting as a "sub-national group or clandestine agent."

God is more of a sovereign power in his own right. This puts him in the same category as sovereign states, whose actions, however violent and even illegal, cannot by definition be described as "terrorism." If you don't believe me, ask the State Department.

So much for Jeremiah Wright's attempt to define the American use of nuclear weapons against Japan as terrorism. It was terrible and terrifying, and it was intended to terrorize the Japanese people into surrender, but it was not terrorism. Neither are Israeli actions against the Palestinians, even if a hundred Palestinians are dying for every Israel victim of Palestinian terrorism, and a high proportion of the dead Palestinians are innocent civilians. Israel is a state, and as such, by definition, what it does cannot be called terrorism.

Now that that's clear, let's move on to what the U.S. State Department does define as terrorism. The first thing that strikes you, reading the *Country Reports on Terrorism,* is that 6,212 of the "terrorist attacks," over two-fifths of all the 14,499 that it records for last year, were in Iraq. Might that be connected in some way to the fact that Iraq was invaded by the United States five years ago, and for all practical purposes remains under U.S. military occupation?

Algerian rebels used similar tactics against French imperial rule, including numerous brutal attacks on innocent civilians. So did the Mau Mau guerrillas against their British colonial masters in Kenya, and the Viet Cong against the American presence in South Vietnam, as did other people fighting against foreign occupation or domestic oppression in dozens of other countries. Their tactics were regularly condemned by their targets, but nobody tried to pretend that the world was facing a wave of irrational and inexplicable violence called "terrorism."

Yet that is precisely the assumption that underlies the State Department's annual reports on "terrorism," and indeed the Bush administration's entire "war on terror." Or rather, it is the perspective through which the report's authors want the rest of the world to see the troubles in Iraq, Afghanistan and so on, for they cannot be so naïve that they truly believe the link between the presence of U.S. occupation troops and a high level of terrorist attacks is purely coincidental.

You can see the same perspective at work in the distinction that is made between Israeli attacks on Palestinians (the legitimate actions of a sovereign state) and Palestinian attacks on Israelis (terrorism). Thus U.S. support for Israel is also legitimate, while Iranian support for Palestinian militants makes Iran the "most active state sponsor of terrorism."

Others play this game, too—notably the Russians in Chechnya—but it is really an American innovation. Terrorism is turned into a uniquely wicked and inexplicable phenomenon, while legitimate states and armies can get on with the business of killing people in legitimate wars.

The pollution of the language by tendentious definitions has also infected
the military. The U.S. armed forces (like most others) used to give their
operations code names like "Anvil" and "Overlord." By the twenty-first
century, however, it gave the invasion of Iraq the code name "Operation
Iraqi Freedom," while the Afghan invasion was retrospectively renamed
"Operation Enduring Freedom"(after the original code name, "Operation
Infinite Justice," was judged potentially offensive to Muslims).

Doesn't the U.S. military realize that this is Soviet-style propaganda-
speak, and that it demeans their dignity as soldiers? Apparently not, or,
more simply, they just lack the guts to do anything about it. Lack of guts
has become a more general problem in this decade, actually.

June 26, 2008
BLACK'S FAUX PAS

A "faux pas" is not a lie or an error. It is a truthful statement which, for
political or social reasons, the speaker should not have made. But since
he did make it, let us discuss it.

In an interview published in the July issue of *Fortune* magazine,
Charlie Black, chief strategist to John McCain, observed that the
Republican presidential candidate would benefit from a surge of support
if there were a terrorist attack on the United States before the election.
You could hardly make a more obvious statement, but in today's United
States, you are not supposed to say it out loud.

It's easy to see how Black was led into this faux pas. In the interview,
he had mentioned the assassination of Pakistani opposition leader Benazir
Bhutto last December as an example of an emergency in which McCain's
experience would trump Barack Obama's lack of same. "[McCain's]
knowledge and ability to talk about it re-emphasized that this is the guy
who's ready to be commander-in-chief," said Black, "and it helped us [in
the polls]." So the interviewer asked the obvious next question: would the
public also see McCain as the better man to deal with another terrorist
attack on the United States?

What was Black supposed to say? "No, I'm sure that Senator Obama
would deal with it every bit as well as my candidate"? This was a live interview, and he had inadvertently created an opening for the interviewer

to ask the taboo question, and then Black put his foot in it: "Certainly it would be a big advantage to McCain." Cue fake shock and synthetic horror as everybody on the Democratic side pretends that Black is playing the "politics of fear."

This is "Gotcha" politics of the lowest order. It is why debate on certain key subjects in the United States since 9/11 has been reduced to bland and mindless slogans on both sides of the political divide. Obama cannot say that the terrorist threat to the United States has been inflated past bursting point for the past seven years, and that it is high time to shrink it to its real, rather modest dimensions and get on with the country's other long-neglected agendas. He would be crucified by the Republicans as "soft on terrorism," and the U.S. media would uncritically echo the charge.

Instead, various Obama spokespersons condemned Black's candid remark and, by extension, McCain's tactics. "It is critical that the candidates debate national security . . . in an atmosphere free from fear tactics and political bluster," intoned Richard Ben-Veniste, a former member of the bipartisan September 11 commission whom the Obama campaign trotted out for the media. What Black said involved neither fear tactics nor political bluster, but at this level, hypocrisy rules.

Black himself, of course, had to make a grovelling apology, and McCain had to distance himself from his chief strategist as far as possible: "I cannot imagine why [Black] would say it. It isn't true. I've worked tirelessly since 9/11 to prevent another attack on the United States." But it *is* true: a terrorist attack would obviously drive millions of American voters back into the arms of Mr. Security, because a great many people assume that ex-fighter pilots are just better than first-term senators at dealing with that sort of thing.

Nobody said that John McCain was hoping for a terrorist attack on the United States, although that is the implicit accusation he is denying when he talks about "working tirelessly" to prevent such an attack. And that superficial and pathetic exchange of views is probably the closest that the United States is going to come to a genuine debate on security issues during this entire election campaign.

So let us move on to something more interesting. What would "the terrorists" really like to do to the U.S. between now and November, assuming that they have the ability to do something? Attack now, or wait until later?

We are not talking about confused juveniles with dreams of seventy-two virgins here. We are talking about senior leaders who think in strategic terms and plan years ahead. So, if they want a McCain presidency, they attack the U.S. in a way that Charlie Black quite accurately said would boost the Republican vote. If they want an Obama presidency, they do nothing.

I cannot read their minds, but I do know what would swing their decision one way or the other. If they want to collect their winnings now, they will favour an Obama presidency and an early U.S. military withdrawal from the Middle East, after which they could reasonably hope to overthrow one or two regimes in the region and come to power themselves. If they would rather keep the U.S. mired in the region for longer, inflicting casualties on American troops and building up their own prestige with radical youth in the area, in the expectation of greater political gains later on, then they would back McCain. So, they would try to help his election by blowing something up in the United States.

The bottom line, however, is that they probably lack the ability to blow anything up in the U.S., which makes it a rather moot point.

The truly remarkable thing about the al-Megrahi case (below) is not the likelihood that he was framed by the Western intelligence services, but the radically different responses of the American and British relatives of the victims to the same evidence. The British almost all concluded that the spooks were lying; most of the Americans never questioned their word, even for a moment.

August 21, 2009
AL-MEGRAHI: WHATEVER WORKS

Abdelbaset Ali al-Megrahi was an intelligence agent, and since he worked for the Libyan government he probably did some bad things. But he probably did not do the specific bad thing for which he was sentenced to twenty-seven years in prison in Scotland.

He only served eight years. He was released on compassionate grounds last Thursday by the Scottish Justice Secretary, Kenny MacAskill, and then flew home to Libya. He is dying of cancer, but his release outraged the Americans whose relatives died aboard Pan Am Flight 103 in December 1988. They believe that al-Megrahi is a mass murderer who should die in jail.

There were also British victims of the attack, and almost none of their relatives think that al-Megrahi should have been in jail at all. As their spokesman, Jim Swire, put it, "I don't believe for a moment that this man was involved [in the bombing]."

THE PRIME SUSPECT

Back in 1988–89, Western intelligence services saw the bombing of Pan Am 103 as an act of revenge. The U.S. warship *Vincennes* had shot down an Iranian Airbus five months before, killing all 290 passengers, and the Iranians were getting even. (The U.S. was then secretly backing Saddam Hussein's war against Iran, and the *Vincennes*, operating illegally in Iranian territorial waters, shot down the airliner thinking that it was an Iranian fighter.)

There was some evidence for this "Iranian revenge" theory. In 1989, German police found the same kind of bomb that brought down Pan Am 103 in a house in Frankfurt used by the Popular Front for the Liberation of Palestine–General Command. The PFLP-GC was based in Syria, and Syria and Iran were allies, so maybe . . .

THE SWITCHEROO

But then, in 1990, Saddam Hussein invaded Kuwait. Washington needed Arab countries like Syria to join the war against Saddam so that the liberation of Kuwait looked like a truly international effort. Syria's price for sending troops was removal from America's Most Wanted list. Suddenly Syria was no longer the prime suspect in the Pan Am case—and if Syria was out, so was Iran. Still, more Americans died on Pan Am 103 than in any other terrorist attack before 9/11, and somebody had to take the fall. Libya was the obvious candidate because it had supported various terrorist attacks in the past.

Soon new evidence began to appear. It pointed to Abdelbaset al-Megrahi, who had been working as a security officer for Libyan Arab Airlines in Malta in 1988. A Maltese shopkeeper identified him as the man who bought children's clothing like that found in the suitcase containing the bomb that brought down Pan Am 103.

It was pretty flimsy evidence, but Colonel Gaddafy, Libya's ruler, was desperate to end the Western trade embargo against his country. He never admitted blame in the Pan Am affair, but he handed al-Megrahi and a colleague over for trial in a Western court anyway.

THE KANGAROO COURT

Al-Megrahi's trial took place in 2001. His colleague was freed, but he was sentenced to twenty-seven years (in a Scottish prison, as Pan Am 103 came down in Lockerbie). As time passed, however, the case began to unravel.

The Maltese shopkeeper who had identified al-Megrahi, Tony Gauci, turned out to be living in Australia, supported by several million dollars the Americans had paid him for his evidence.

The allegation that the timer for the bomb had been supplied to Libya by the Swiss manufacturer Mebo Telecommunications turned out to be false. The owner of Mebo, Edwin Bollier, revealed that he had turned down an offer of four million dollars from the Federal Bureau of Investigation in 1991 to testify that he had sold his MST-13 timing devices to Libya. One of Bollier's former employees, Ulrich Lumpert, testified at al-Megrahi's trial that MST-13 timers had been supplied to Libya—but, in 2007, he admitted that he had lied at the trial.

And this year it was revealed that Pan Am's baggage area at London's Heathrow airport was broken into seventeen hours before Pan Am 103 took off on its last flight. (The police knew that twelve years ago but kept it secret at al-Megrahi's trial.) The theory that the fatal bag was put on a feeder flight from Malta became even less likely.

All of which explains why the Scottish Criminal Cases Review Commission announced in 2007 that it would refer al-Megrahi's case to the Court of Criminal Appeal in Edinburgh. Their reason: he "may have suffered a miscarriage of justice."

THE DEAL

The Review Commission's decision caused a crisis because a new court hearing would reveal how shoddy the evidence at the first one was. Happily for London and Washington, al-Megrahi was dying of cancer and this made a deal possible: he would give up his plea for a retrial, no dirty linen about the original trial would be aired in public, and he would be set free.

A miserable story, but hardly a unique one. A man who was probably innocent of the charges against him, a loyal servant of the Libyan state who was framed by the West and hung out to dry by his own government, has been sent home to die.

And then we have homegrown terrorism, near the village where my wife's family has had a house since the 1950s, in deepest France.

August 18, 2009
BASQUE TERRORISM: AS GOOD AS IT GETS

It's still a nest of terrorists around here, but nobody worries about it much. These days, when you hear a helicopter at night it's only the medevac chopper bringing some urgent case down to the main hospital at Bayonne on the coast.

In the bad old days, the helicopter you heard would have been using infrared detectors to spot Basque terrorists heading across the mountains at night into Spain. This southwestern corner of France is just as Basque as the much larger Basque-speaking provinces of Spain, but ETA (Euskadi Ta Askatasuna [Basque Land and Liberty]) always used France as a safe rear area and did its actual killing across the frontier.

The terrorists are still around, and they enjoy a certain amount of local support. Last Saturday was the summer festival in our local town, Saint-Jean-Pied-de-Port (or Donibane Garazi, in Basque), and everybody for miles around was drinking and dancing in the square below the citadel, waiting for it to get dark enough for the fireworks to begin. Suddenly banners were unfurled on the city walls: "Kidnapped? Tortured? Murdered? Where is Jon?"

So I ask around, and it turns out that everybody knows who Jon is. He's a local man, universally believed to be an ETA member, who got on a train to Toulouse but never arrived. Everybody also believes that he was carrying a large sum of money for ETA, which leads nasty cynics like myself to contemplate several alternative possible reasons for his disappearance, but local opinion is convinced that it was the state that got him.

Yet local opinion is not really very upset about it. Most people don't care much whether the French police seized or killed Jon, or if somebody else robbed and killed him, or even if he just decided to disappear and live on the proceeds. It's all part of the game that some play on the fringes of society, and they're welcome to play it as long as they don't frighten the horses.

Across the border in Spain, where the killing happens, people take ETA much more seriously, and there is less sympathy for the killers among Spanish Basques than among French Basques. But there is also an irreducible hard core of support for the extreme nationalist option. Spain does not let political parties that openly support terrorism run in national elections, but when a radical Basque party was allowed to run in the June elections for the European Parliament, it got 140,000 votes. That's only 5 percent of the population in those provinces—the terrorist struggle for Basque independence has so few supporters because the Basque provinces of Spain already have almost complete control over their own affairs. But that tiny minority of hard-liners is enough to sustain the armed struggle forever.

The "struggle" has killed 825 people over the past forty years, including three police officers killed by ETA bombs and sixty people injured by a truck bomb in Burgos this summer. There have been three ceasefires over the years, the last in 2006, but they never lead to a final deal because there is a small but steady supply of young people who cannot resist the lure of extremism. It gives meaning to their little lives.

But even on the Spanish side of the frontier, where there are deaths from terrorism every year, few people see it as a dominant factor in their lives. It's just background noise, like the daily toll from traffic accidents.

The French police now cooperate closely with their Spanish counterparts in trying to catch the ETA militants who shelter in the French Basque provinces, but even when they didn't, nobody in Spain suggested invading France to stamp out the terrorist sanctuaries. Doing so would be grotesquely disproportionate, like invading Afghanistan to protect Americans from Arab terrorists.

The ETA story, like that of the Irish Republican Army in Northern Ireland, teaches us three things. The first is that you don't need a territorial "base" to carry out terrorist attacks; an isolated farmhouse or an anonymous city apartment will do. The second is that you should treat terrorism like any other crime: use the police to track the perpetrators down, and don't inflate the whole problem enormously by getting the army involved. The third is that you must not expect a decisive victory.

Eight years of the "war on terror" have created a huge military, corporate and bureaucratic lobby in the United States whose livelihood depends on a highly militarized approach to terrorism, so it will be a long time before a saner strategy prevails in Washington. Britain's learning curve in Northern Ireland was thirty years long, and Russia has learned nothing yet in Chechnya. But people generally do the right thing in the end—after they have exhausted all the alternatives.

There's not really a lot more to be said about terrorism, but you cannot ignore the role of the media. Here's a recent example of just how bad they can be.

November 6, 2009
MYSTERIOUS MOTIVES

Earlier this year, the Pentagon committed fifty million dollars to a study investigating why the suicide rate in the military is rising: it used to be below the suicide rate in comparable civilian groups, but now it's four times higher. Thirteen American soldiers were killed by a gunman at Fort Hood in Texas last Thursday, but since the invasion of Iraq in 2003, seventy-five others have died by their own hand at the same army base. Why?

To most people, the answer is obvious. The wars in Iraq and Afghanistan have been frustrating, exhausting and seemingly endless, and some people just can't take it anymore. But the Pentagon is spending fifty million dollars to search for other possible causes, because it doesn't like that answer.

The U.S. military budget tops half a trillion dollars, so the military can splash out on diversionary studies that draw attention away from the main problems of combat fatigue and loss of faith in the mission. And we are seeing exactly the same pattern in the response to the killings at Fort Hood, although in this case the military are also getting the services of the U.S. media for free.

Let's see, now. A devout Muslim officer serving in the U.S. Army, born in the United States but of Palestinian ancestry, is scheduled to deploy to Afghanistan in the near future. He opens fire on his fellow soldiers, shouting "Allahu akbar" (God is great). What can his motive have been? Hard to guess, isn't it? Was he unhappy about his promotion prospects? Hmm.

There is something comic in the contortions that the U.S. media engage in to avoid the obvious fact that, if the United States invades Muslim countries, some Muslim Americans are bound to think that America has declared war on Islam. It has not, but, from Pakistan to Somalia, the U.S. is killing Muslims in the name of a "war on terror."

Some of them are enemies of the U.S. government, and some of them are innocent civilians. Some of them are even "friendly-fire casualties" among soldiers collaborating with the United States, like the Afghan soldiers killed recently by a U.S. air strike. But every single day since 2003, U.S. soldiers have killed Muslims, and every day those deaths have been reported in the media.

So is it possible that the shooter in Fort Hood, Major Nidal Malik Hasan, who was waiting to ship out to Afghanistan, did not want to take a personal part in that enterprise? Might he belong to that large majority of Muslims (though probably a minority among American Muslims) who, unable to discover any rational basis for U.S. strategy since 9/11, have drifted towards the conclusion that the United States is indeed waging a war on Islam?

Perish the thought! Rather than entertain such a subversive idea, official spokespersons and media pundits in the United States have been trying to come up with some other motive for Major Hasan's actions. Maybe he was a coward who couldn't face the prospect of combat in Afghanistan. Maybe he was a nutcase whose actions had no meaning at all. Or maybe he was unhappy at the alleged abuse he had suffered because he was Muslim/Arab/Palestinian.

After a few days, while the commentariat hesitated before competing narratives, the media are settling on the explanation that it was ethnic/racial/religious abuse that drove Nidal crazy. Bad people doing un-American things were ultimately responsible for the tragedy, and that's the end of it.

The one explanation that is excluded is that America's wars in Muslim lands overseas are radicalizing Muslims at home. Never mind that the homegrown Muslim terrorists who attacked the London transport system in 2005, or the various Muslim plotters who have been caught in other Western countries before their plans came to fruition, have almost all blamed the Western invasions of Muslim countries for radicalizing them. Never mind, above all, that what really radicalized them was the fact that those invasions made no sense in terms of Western security. No Afghan has ever attacked the United States, although Arabs living in Afghanistan were involved in the planning of 9/11. There were no terrorists in Iraq, no weapons of mass destruction, and no contacts between Saddam Hussein and al-Qaeda. So why did the U.S. invade those countries?

The real reasons are panic and ignorance, reinforced by militaristic reflexes and laced with liberal amounts of racism. But people find it hard to believe that big, powerful governments like those of the United States, Britain and the other Western powers involved in these foolish adventures could really be so stupid, so the conspiracy theories proliferate.

It is a testimony to the moderation and loyalty of Muslim communities in the West that so few of their members have succumbed to these conspiracy theories. It is evidence of the profound denial that still reigns in the majority community in the United States that the most obvious explanation for Major Nidal's actions didn't even make the media's short list.

I cannot know for sure what moved Major Nidal to do the terrible things he did: each individual is a mystery even to himself. But I do see the U.S. media careening all over the road to avoid the huge and obvious fact that obscures half the horizon. Time to grow up.

20.

THE OLD DOMINIONS

It is a curious category, although fifty years ago it would have seemed more natural: these are the countries, heavily influenced but not entirely defined by immigration from Britain, that used to be known as the Dominions. The Big Three are Canada, South Africa and Australia, although New Zealand and even Newfoundland also used to get honourable mention on the war memorials.

The links are fainter now, but they are still there. My mother, for example, a Newfoundlander of Irish origin, found it strange that two of her five children ended up married to South Africans—until I pointed out that it was all due to the British empire. In fact, there are people I love in all the "Dominions," not to mention in Britain itself.

But here's a question. How come Canada didn't send troops to Iraq and Australia did?

February 12, 2006
THE DEPUTY SHERIFF SPEAKS

Some people are born with so great a talent for brazen effrontery that they have no choice but to become politicians. One such person is Australia's prime minister, John Howard, who intervened in the U.S. presidential race this week to warn Americans not to vote for the Democrats in general, and Barack Obama in particular.

Obama, declaring his candidacy for the Democratic presidential nomination, said that U.S. troops should be out of Iraq by March 2008. John Howard, who faces an election campaign himself later this year, seized on these remarks to restate his own fervent support for the Bush administration strategy that created the Iraq quagmire in the first place.

He said that Obama's Iraq policy "will just encourage those who want to completely destabilize and destroy Iraq, and create chaos and a victory for the terrorists in Iraq to hang on and hope for an Obama victory." (Even in his mangled syntax, he sounds much like President George W. Bush.)

Thus far, however, Howard's remarks remained within the bounds of normal political discourse. If some Australian voters believe that the invasion of 2003 did not already "completely destabilize and destroy Iraq and create chaos," and that only a U.S. withdrawal would bring about that outcome, then they are free to vote for Howard, and he is free to solicit their votes. He even stands a decent chance of winning, since the average Australian knows no more about the realities of the Middle East than the average Iraqi knows about Australian politics.

But then Howard continued: "If I were running al-Qaeda in Iraq, I would put a circle around March 2008 and be praying as many times as possible for a victory not only for Obama but also for the Democrats."

Never mind the usual guff about "al-Qaeda in Iraq," as if that particular strand of Arab radicalism dominated the resistance to foreign occupation in Iraq—indeed, as if the "terrorists in Iraq" were a cause rather than a consequence of the U.S.-U.K.-Australian invasion of the country. The point is that Howard was telling Americans how to vote, and foreign leaders are not supposed to do that.

Nobody in the United States will lose much sleep over Howard's intervention. Indeed, most Americans are probably unaware that Australia still has a token troop contingent in Iraq, and don't even know

John Howard's name. The White House will certainly not rebuke him for urging Americans not to vote Democratic. Nonetheless, what is truly interesting is Obama's response to Howard's rant, and what it reveals about Australian defence policy. "I think it's flattering that one of George Bush's allies on the other side of the world started attacking me the day after I announced," Obama said. "I would also note that we have close to 140,000 troops on the ground now, and my understanding is that Mr. Howard has deployed 1,400, so if he is to fight the good fight in Iraq, I would suggest that he calls up another 20,000 Australians and sends them to Iraq. Otherwise it's just a bunch of empty rhetoric."

Howard replied that the Australian deployment was a "very significant and appropriate contribution," given the country's small population. Really? The United States has about three hundred million people; Australia about twenty million, or one-fifteenth as many. So a "very significant and appropriate contribution" by Australia would be one-fifteenth of 140,000 troops or 12,100 Australian troops, not 1,400. It's all gesture politics and political posturing—but then, so is Australian defence policy in general.

The key turning point in modern Australian foreign policy was the realization, sometime in 1942 or 1943, that the British empire could no longer defend the country, and that the only big country that might be willing to assume that role was the U.S. So the question became, and has remained, how to guarantee that the United States will come to Australia's aid in an emergency, even if America's own vital interests are not directly involved.

There is no good answer to this question, but it would obviously help if Australian troops show up to help whenever the United States gets involved in a war anywhere in Asia—and that includes the Middle East. However, this policy is too demeaning to national pride to explain clearly to Australians, so the various Australian military ventures abroad have to be explained in other terms—the "Communist threat" in Vietnam, the "terrorist threat" in Iraq. And the actual troop commitment is kept as small as possible, in order not to rouse public opinion against it.

Australians have fortunately never had the occasion to find out whether volunteering to be America's "deputy sheriff" in Asia would really produce the desired U.S. response if Australia's own interests were threatened, but this notion remains at the heart of Australian defence policy.

If the United States invaded Mars, Australia would send a battalion along to guard the supply depot.

Australia is basically a huge island with easily controlled sea frontiers. Canada is a strategic island, in the sense that its frontiers are either with oceans or with the United States. Only South Africa has a direct land frontier with what we used to call the Third World, and it is an enormously attractive destination for impoverished would-be immigrants from the rest of the African continent. Yet it does not really make a serious effort to control its own frontiers.

This may end in tears.

May 20, 2008
SOUTH AFRICA AND THE IMMIGRANTS

It was looking ugly there for a few days, with mobs of South Africans in townships around Johannesburg randomly murdering several dozen "foreigners" (migrants from other African countries) and injuring several hundred. But now President Thabo Mbeki has acted decisively: he has announced the establishment of a panel of inquiry into the violence. That should fix it.

Just in case he gets impatient while waiting for the panel's report, however, I can tell him what it will say—or at least, what it should say. It should say that the root problem is his government's "non-interventionist" policy on immigration: its refusal to control or even count the number of people arriving in South Africa from other African countries.

The mere fact that the commonly used estimate is "three to five million" illegal immigrants says it all: the authorities really have no idea how many foreigners are in South Africa. Furthermore, the higher estimate is probably closer to the truth, for some four million people have left Zimbabwe alone to seek work abroad, and almost all of them have gone to South Africa.

This "open borders" non-policy has worthy motives. Many of South Africa's current leaders are men and women who spent decades in exile during the fight against apartheid, and the migrants come mostly from the countries that gave them shelter at that time. How can they turn away people from those countries—from Zimbabwe, above all—now that the shoe is on the other foot?

Such openness is an honourable sentiment, but more easily experienced if, like South Africa's current leaders, you lead a secure and comfortable life in one of the nicer northern suburbs of Johannesburg. If you happen to live in Alexandra township (not all that far from those pleasant suburbs) amidst garbage and violence and chronic poverty, and you don't have a job, it's a little harder to access such noble emotions—because one-tenth of the people in the country are illegal immigrants, and lots of them do have jobs.

Miserable, underpaid jobs, for the most part, but in a country where the true unemployment rate is somewhere near half there are bound to be a great many people who resent foreigners getting any jobs at all. Especially because there is some truth in the complaint of poor and uneducated South Africans that the illegal immigrants get the unskilled jobs because employers can pay them less and they won't dare complain.

None of this justifies murder, but it does begin to explain it. Thabo Mbeki was incredibly foolish to assume that he could just let foreigners flood into the country and not expose them to a popular backlash. The South African media are filled with self-flagellating editorials that all basically ask: "What kind of people are we if we can behave like this?" The answer is: not saintly inhabitants of some imagined "rainbow nation" that has risen above the normal human plane, just ordinary people under pressure and behaving badly.

Last week in Italy, other ordinary people threw Molotov cocktails into Gypsy camps and burned them down. Most of those people have jobs, live in comfortable surroundings, and eat quite well, and they *still* behaved badly. There are only about 150,000 Gypsies in Italy, half of whom are distant descendants of people who have been there since the fifteenth century. They are less than a quarter of 1 percent of the population, and yet 68 percent of Italians want them all expelled.

The South African poor have been amazingly patient as year after year has gone by—fourteen years now since the end of apartheid—and little has changed for the better in their lives. The black poor still loyally vote for the African National Congress (ANC), but their anger was going to burst out somewhere or other, sooner or later. By holding the door open to so many illegal immigrants, the government has guaranteed that they would be the primary target.

Maybe this is some Machiavellian plan to divert popular anger from the government itself, but probably not. More likely, it's just that the leaders don't see what has been happening to ordinary people. How else could Thabo Mbeki go on defending Robert Mugabe, the destroyer of Zimbabwe, year after year, when Mugabe's misdeeds were the main reason that this enormous wave of illegal immigrants struck South Africa?

Justice Malala, whose column appears in the *Times* (the online version of South Africa's *Sunday Times*), nailed it on Monday when he wrote: "[Our] people are behaving like barbarians because the ANC has failed—despite numerous warnings—to act on burning issues that are well known for having sparked similar eruptions across the globe . . .

"The Mbeki government's refusal to even acknowledge the crisis in Zimbabwe has resulted in as many as 3 million Zimbabweans walking the streets of South Africa . . .

"Mbeki's resolute refusal to address the crisis in Zimbabwe—and his friendship with President Robert Mugabe—has brought them here. His block-headedness is directly responsible for the eruption of xenophobia."

Such plain talk is not "blaming the victim." It is recognizing realities, which is the first step towards addressing them. And where the despairing poor of South Africa should be addressing their anger is not at helpless Zimbabweans but at their president, who let this human catastrophe happen.

Mbeki finally left power, in the most humiliating of circumstances, in late 2009. The man who took his place, after the 2009 election, was the same man Mbeki had spent the previous few years trying to have jailed on corruption charges: Jacob Zuma. It is not yet clear what he is going to do about South Africa's borders.

Canada has only one disputed frontier, in the Arctic. But the dispute is not with the Russians, as Prime Minister Harper likes to pretend; it is with the Americans. Worse yet (for those with dreams of the Canadian North as a new source of wealth) the Northwest Passage will never be a useful commercial route regardless of whether Canada controls it or not.

September 15, 2009
THE NORTHERN PASSAGES

Early next week two German-owned container ships will arrive in Rotterdam from Vladivostok in the Russian Far East, having taken only one month to make the voyage. That's much faster than usual — but then, they didn't take the usual route down through the South China Sea, past Singapore, round the bottom of India, through the Suez Canal (pay toll here), across the Mediterranean and up the west coast of Europe. They just went around the top of Russia.

It's the first-ever commercial transit through the Northeast Passage by non-Russian ships, and it shortens the sea trip between East Asia and Europe by almost a third. The melting of the Arctic sea ice made it possible, although for the moment it's only possible for a couple of months at the end of the summer melt season, when the Arctic Ocean's ice cover shrinks dramatically. But it is a sign of things to come.

The voyage is more evidence that climate change is well underway and will strike the Arctic region hard. But it also shows that all the recent fuss about the Northwest Passage is irrelevant.

The Northwest Passage, another potential shortcut between Europe and East Asia, goes through the Canadian Arctic archipelago. Although icebreakers have traversed it from time to time, no ordinary commercial ship has ever carried cargo through it. But when the Russians put on their little propaganda show at the North Pole two years ago, the Canadian government had kittens.

In 2007, Artur Chilingarov, a Russian scientist famous for his work in the polar regions and Arctic adviser to then-president Vladimir Putin, took a mini-sub to the North Pole and planted a Russian flag on the seabed. Canada's prime minister, Stephen Harper, immediately flew to Iqaluit in the high Arctic and responded with a rabble-rousing speech.

"Canada has a choice when it comes to defending our sovereignty in the Arctic," he said. "We either use it or lose it. And make no mistake: this government intends to use it." He then announced a program to build six to eight armed Arctic patrol vessels to assert Canadian control over the Northwest Passage and a deepwater naval base on Baffin Island to support them.

"I don't know why the Canadians reacted as they did," Chilingarov told me a few months later in Moscow, and on the face of it, he had a case. After all, Russia has no claims over any land or water that might conceivably belong to Canada, and Canada makes no claim on the North Pole. But Chilingarov actually understood the game that Harper was playing quite well.

Canada's dispute over sovereignty of the Northwest Passage is actually with the United States, not Russia. The Russians have absolutely no interest in the Northwest Passage, since they have their own rival, the Northeast Passage (which they call the Northern Sea Route). Still, the U.S. has long maintained that the Northwest Passage could be very useful if it were ice-free, so Washington insists that it is an international waterway which Canada has no right to control.

Canada disputes that position, pointing out that all six potential routes for a commercially viable Northwest Passage wind between islands that are close together and indisputably Canadian. But Ottawa has never asserted *military* control over the Northwest Passage until now, because to do so would risk an awkward confrontation with the United States. However, if you can pretend that you are building those warships and that naval base to hold the wicked Russians at bay, not to defy the Americans . . .

That is Harper's game, and he now visits the high north every summer to reassert Canada's sovereignty claims. In the end, however, it will make no difference, as the Northwest Passage will never become a major shipping route. The Northeast Passage is just too much easier.

The problem for Canada is that all the routes for a Northwest Passage involve shallow and/or narrow straits between various islands in the country's Arctic archipelago, and the prevailing winds and currents in the Arctic Ocean tend to push whatever loose sea ice there is into those straits. It is unlikely that cargo ships that are not double-hulled and strengthened against ice will ever get insurance for the passage at an affordable price.

On the other hand, the Northeast Passage is mostly open water (once the ice retreats from the Russian coast), and there is already a major infrastructure of ports and nuclear-powered ice-breakers in the region. If the distances are roughly comparable, shippers will prefer the Northeast Passage every time—and the distances *are* comparable.

Just look at the Arctic Ocean on a globe, rather than in the familiar flat-Earth Mercator projection. It is instantly obvious that the distance is the same whether shipping between Europe and East Asia crosses the Arctic Ocean by running along the Russia's Arctic coast (the Northeast Passage) or weaving between Canada's Arctic islands (the Northwest Passage). The same is true for cargo travelling between Europe and the west coast of North America, and the consequence is that the Northwest Passage will never become commercially viable.

21.

IRAQ II

By mid-2006, the war in Iraq was rarely front-page news. It was actually the worst time of all for the Iraqis, with the Sunni-Shia civil war killing many thousands each month and creating refugees in the millions, but for most North Americans, it had become just a familiar noise in the background, like bad plumbing. For the families who actually had sons and daughters there it was very different, but they were mostly working-class Americans who were blinded by "patriotism" and unused to protest.

That's really why Bush and Blair got away with it, despite some amazing displays of ignorance.

May 26, 2006
MISSING THE POINT

U.S. President George W. Bush and British Prime Minister Tony Blair, giving their umpteenth joint press conference at the White House on Thursday, showed the amateurs how to deal with the media. Wry, humble, funny, rueful, always upbeat—they were a polished double act that could have put a positive spin on the Black Death. Iraq has allegedly "turned the corner" again after five months of bitter deadlock. A new government has taken office in Baghdad that only lacks a defence minister and an interior minister, and Bush and Blair were there to sell it as a success.

The press always likes to have its tummy tickled, so all the questions were basically friendly. The answers to the last question, however, were very revealing. A journalist recalled that both men have admitted to missteps and mistakes in Iraq, and asked them which ones they regretted most.

President Bush did public penance for his macho remarks about the emerging Iraq resistance movement—"bring 'em on"—back in the hyper-confident "Mission Accomplished" days of 2003. It was charming, vintage Bush: "I learned some lessons about expressing myself maybe in a little more sophisticated manner, you know." And he avowed that "the biggest mistake that's happened so far, at least from [in terms of] our country's involvement in Iraq, is Abu Ghraib."

Tony Blair aimed for a more reflective tone: "I think that probably . . . we could have done de-Baathification in a more differentiated manner than we did . . . But the biggest reason why Iraq has been difficult is the determination by our opponents to defeat us."

Now there's a novel concept: our opponents are determined to defeat us. No wonder that Blair added: "Maybe in retrospect, when we look back, it should have been very obvious to us." But the resentful whine in Blair's voice was entirely genuine: how was he to know they would fight back? Maybe he could have done de-Baathification a bit better, but apart from that, it's not his fault.

Tony Blair is a fairly bright man, and George W. Bush is not as dim as he seems, so how can they be so obtuse about Iraq? De-Baathification, re-Baathification, retro-Baathification—nothing can change the basic fact that the Baath Party that had ruled Iraq since the 1960s was deeply nationalist and profoundly hostile to the United States (because it is

Israel's closest ally) and to Britain (because it is the former imperial ruler of Iraq).

Fire all the Baathists, and they will go underground and join the resistance. Leave them in their jobs, and they will be a fifth column of spies and saboteurs for the resistance. Likewise for the empty debate about whether U.S. proconsul Paul Bremer made a fatal mistake by disbanding the entire Iraqi army in the spring of 2003. Disband the army, and several hundred thousand trained men will take their skills and their weapons and join the resistance. Leave the existing army in place and its officers will sell the foreign-occupation troops out to the resistance at every opportunity, while awaiting the right moment for a national uprising against the foreigners.

The original decision to invade Iraq was the fatal mistake; the rest is just consequences. Iraq's government was crueller and less loved than most regimes in the Arab world, but the United States and Britain would be facing the same kind of resistance movement today if they had invaded Morocco, Egypt or Yemen in 2003. There is no country of over two million people in the Arab world where an invading American army would not soon be confronted by the kind of resistance it is facing in Iraq.

History matters, and for Arabs all recent history is bad. Britain lured the Arabs into revolt against their Turkish overlords in the First World War with a promise of independence, then carved them up into the familiar Middle Eastern states of the present and bound them all in colonial servitude. It also promised Jews a national homeland in Palestine, the state of Israel—which America has unstintingly supported, regardless of Israel's policies towards its Arab neighbours, for over forty years. Why would any Arab country welcome an invasion by the United States and Britain?

The Anglo-American invasion of Iraq was doomed from the first, and Bush and Blair had dozens of experts on call who could have told them why. Either they didn't listen, or they chose not to ask.

By early 2007, it was clear that the United States was on its way out of Iraq as fast as possible, so the major objective for most of the players became saving face and avoiding blame. All those wasted deaths had to be somebody else's fault.

February 26, 2007
BLAME THE IRAQIS

As the people who talked the United States into the Iraq War try to talk their way out of the blame for the mess they made, one dominant theme has emerged: blame the Iraqis. Our intentions were good; we did our best to help; but the Iraqis are vicious, incompetent ingrates who would prefer to kill one another rather than seize the freedom we brought them. It's not our fault that it turned out so badly.

And it has turned out rather badly, hasn't it? President George W. Bush will go no further than to say that he is "disappointed by the pace of success," and his British sidekick, Prime Minister Tony Blair, still insists, "We will beat them [the Iraqi resistance] when we realize that it's not our fault that they're doing this." But practically everybody else in the U.S. and Britain knows that the invasion of Iraq was a huge disaster.

Somebody must be to blame, and it cannot be us, so it must be those brutal, stupid Iraqis. There was no surprise last November when arch neo-conservative Richard Perle, ex-chairman of the Pentagon's Defense Policy Board Advisory Committee, said that he had "underestimated the depravity" in Iraq. He has a lot of blame to shift, so he would say that, wouldn't he?

It was no surprise, either, when right-wing columnist Charles Krauthammer of the *Washington Post*, once an eager supporter of the war, elaborated on the same theme less than a month ago: "Thousands of brave American soldiers have died trying to counter, put down and prevent civil strife. But when Arabs kill Arabs and Shias kill Shias and Sunnis kill all in a spasm of violence that is blind and furious and has roots in hatreds born long before America was even a republic, to place the blame on [America] is simply perverse . . . Iraq is their country. We midwifed their freedom. They chose civil war."

Brazen, self-serving distortions of the truth by people who have a lot of explaining to do, are not in the least bit surprising, because if the ghastly mess in Iraq wasn't the fault of Iraqis, then it would have to be the fault of Americans. Perle and Krauthammer would figure quite prominently among the Americans in question.

But what is one to make of Gary Trudeau peddling the same line in his comic strip *Doonesbury*? The strip runs daily in 1,400 newspapers around the world, and often serves as the vehicle for political or social commentary from a liberal perspective. It never supported the invasion of Iraq, but this Monday's strip was a classic exercise in stereotyping and blame-shifting.

An American colonel, planning the day's operation in the streets of Baghdad, notices that his Iraq army opposite number has not shown up yet and sends a soldier to find him. Cut to the Iraqi army officer: still behind his desk, coffee cup in hand, ashtray full of cigarettes. He says to the young American soldier: "It's not in my book. Are you sure it's today?" The U.S. solder wearily replies "Yes, sir. You'll recall we fight every day."

Unravelling the message doesn't take a Marshall MacLuhan: U.S. troops are carrying the burden of the war while lazy, cowardly Iraqis shun their duty. They don't deserve us.

The strip the weekend before last was even more blatant in blaming the failure on the Iraqis. An American soldier gets behind the wheel of a Humvee and says "Ready to do this, partner?" to the same Iraqi officer, sitting beside him in the front seat. The Iraqi officer is asleep.

As they approach the target house, the Iraqi officer, now awake, says "I know this house. The owner is Sunni scum." "Well, intel wants us to capture the guy alive," says the American. "That will not be possible. I am sworn to revenge," replies the Iraqi.

"Why," asks the American. "What'd he ever do to you?"

"A member of his family killed a member of mine," replies the Iraqi officer, cigarette dangling from his lips. "What? When did this happen?" asks the shocked American.

"1387," replies the Iraqi officer. "What is the MATTER with you people?" screams the American.

Get the message? These Ay-rabs are not only lazy, they are so savage that they harbour murderous grudges over six centuries; even Americans cannot bring these people to their senses; let's get the hell out of here; it isn't our fault that it all went wrong.

Getting out of Iraq is the least bad thing the United States can do now, and the sooner the better. If Americans must manufacture racist fantasies about the victims in order to salve their pride on the way out, then so be it. But it is a shameful, childish lie.

So, if they are on their way out, what happens next? I wrote the following piece three years ago but I don't think I would change a word of it today.

June 23, 2007
THE MIDDLE EAST AFTER IRAQ

The war in Iraq is clearly lost, both on the ground and in the court of American public opinion, and the pullout will probably begin about ten minutes after the new U.S. president is inaugurated in January 2009. That's only eighteen months from now, so it's time to think about what happens next.

The American withdrawal will not stop with Iraq. Iran is going to be the new great power in the region, and the little Arab oil sheikh-doms on the opposite side of the Gulf will probably close down the U.S. bases on their soil in order to keep Iran sweet. There will be no Iranian troops in Iraq, however, and Iran lacks the military capability for adventures in the further reaches of the Arab world even if it had the desire.

After Iraq, there will be huge resistance in the United States to any more military commitments in the Middle East, so for the first time in forty years the status quo in the region will not be backed by a U.S. military guarantee. Beyond forecasts of civil war in Iraq, however, there has been little effort to discern what the Middle East will actually look like after the U.S. troops go home.

There is already a civil war in Iraq, and it might even get worse for a time after American troops leave, but these things always sputter out in the end. There will still be an Iraqi state, plus or minus Kurdistan, and regardless of whether or not the central government in Baghdad exercises real control over the Sunni-majority areas between Baghdad, Mosul and the Syrian border.

The Sunni Arab parts of Iraq have been turned into a training ground for Islamist extremists from all parts of the Arab world by the American invasion. Once the American troops are gone, however, the action will soon move elsewhere, for the U.S. defeat in Iraq has dramatically raised the prestige of Islamist revolutionaries throughout the Arab world and beyond.

The real price of America's Middle Eastern adventure will be paid not in Iraq itself, but in the Arab states that still have secular and/or pro-Western regimes. The main (and generally outlawed) political opposition in Saudi Arabia, Syria, Jordan, Egypt, Libya, Algeria and half a dozen others has been Islamist revolutionaries for many years already, and now some of them are going to win.

It's not possible to predict *which* Arab states will fall under Islamist control, and they certainly aren't all going to: the pipe dream of a world-spanning Islamic empire remains precisely that. But it will be astonishing if one or more of the existing Arab regimes does not fall to an Islamist revolution in the next few years.

For the citizens of the country or countries in question, this could be a big problem, since it would probably mean not democracy and pros-perity but just more decades of poverty and a different kind of tyranny. For people living outside the Middle East, however, it would probably make little difference.

Islamist-ruled *states* are not the same as bands of freelance fanatics. If they have oil to export, then they will go on exporting it, because no major oil producer can now do without the income that those exports provide; they need it to feed their people. And they would have little incentive to sponsor terrorist attacks outside the region, for they would have fixed addresses, and interests to protect.

For Israel, however, the situation has changed fundamentally. For the first twenty years of its existence, Israel was a state under siege. For the past forty years, since the conquests of 1967, it has had the luxury of debating with itself how much of those conquered lands it should return to the Arabs in return for a permanent peace settlement. (The answer was always "all of them," but that was not an answer many Israelis would hear.)

Now the window of opportunity is closing. Before long, some of the Arab states that Israel needs to make peace with are likely to fall to Islamist regimes that have an ideological commitment to its destruction. (Hamas's capture of the Gaza Strip is a foretaste of what is to come.) Israelis trying to evade hard choices have long complained that they had "nobody to negotiate with." This is about to become true.

The invasion of Iraq was America's biggest foreign-policy blunder since Vietnam, and the Middle East will be a very different place as a result. But, as with Vietnam, the consequences for the West of U.S. mili-tary defeat in Iraq are likely to be smaller than people expect. Five years from now, the oil will still be flowing, terrorism will be a minor nuisance, and America's reputation will have recovered.

Unless, of course, the Bush administration decides to attack Iran before it leaves office. Then the heavens really would fall.

The famous "surge," by itself, could not have created the interval of calm that has allowed the United States to make a relatively dignified exit from Iraq. By 2007, the Sunnis, once the core of the resistance, had lost the civil war against the Shias decisively and disastrously, and most formerly mixed neighbourhoods of Baghdad had been entirely cleansed of their Sunni residents. It was the Islamist fanatics of "al-Qaeda in Mesopotamia" and their local extremist allies who had dragged the Sunnis into that civil war, and it was now a matter of survival for the Sunni community to get rid of them and end that war.

The traditional Sunni authorities and the non-Islamist leaders of the resistance had been pushed aside (and sometimes assassinated) by the extremists, and the survivors were ready for a temporary truce with the Americans while they dealt with this more urgent problem. In fact, they were willing to collaborate with the occupation forces in destroying the power of al-Qaeda and its allies, and so, by 2008, the daily toll of violent deaths in Iraq was dropping fast.

The irony was that in this safer and more stable environment, the Iraqi government that had emerged from the 2005 elections, an alliance of Shia and Kurdish parties, no longer depended so heavily on American troops to protect it—and was thus much more able to resist American demands. Throughout 2008 the Bush administration persistently tried to get Baghdad to grant the United States permanent military bases in Iraq as part of the withdrawal agreement, but to no avail. The final deal required all American troops to be off the streets of Iraqi cities by mid-2009, and gone from the country entirely by the end of 2011. So what did the whole bloody exercise achieve, if anything?

June 19, 2009
WAS IT WORTH IT?

By the end of this month all U.S. military forces will have withdrawn from Iraqi cities. Effectively, the U.S. war in Iraq is over. Was it worth it?

There are two quite separate balance sheets of costs and benefits, one for Iraqis and the other for Americans. It's too early to give a final answer for the Iraqis, but, for the United States, the answer is definitely no.

No matter what happens in Iraq now, the Obama administration will not recommit U.S. troops to a combat role in the country, so we can calculate approximately how much the Iraq adventure cost the United States with some confidence. The total cost will work out to well over a trillion dollars, if we count the long-term cost of caring for the veterans.

Random attacks may kill a few hundred more American soldiers in Iraq before all the troops go home, but the final death toll will certainly be less than five thousand. That is only one-tenth of the fatalities that U.S. troops suffered in the Korean War or the Vietnam War, so the cost in lives was relatively low for Americans. But what did the United States gain in return for that investment?

Not a subservient ally, certainly. When Iraqi Prime Minister Nouri al-Maliki held a meeting with three hundred top Iraqi military commanders early this month, an American general showed up to monitor the proceedings as usual. He was politely asked to leave. Washington's ability to influence decisions in Iraq is dwindling by the day.

So the balance sheet for the United States is in the red, but not catastrophically so. The investment did not produce any worthwhile returns, but the negative consequences were not great either, and the investment was not all that big. More money has been thrown at failing American banks in the past eight months than was thrown at Iraq in six years.

What about the Iraqis, then? For them, the price in lives was at least a hundred times higher, and maybe more. They also suffered the almost complete collapse of an economy that was already severely damaged by Saddam's wars and the subsequent trade embargo. The level of violence has dropped sharply from its peak in 2006–07, but the monthly death toll from political killings (including sectarian ones) is still higher than it was during the last decade of Saddam's rule.

For the 80 percent of Iraqis who speak Arabic, the greatest costs have been the destruction of the old secular society, which, even under Saddam, allowed women more freedom than most other Arab regimes, and the brutal ethnic cleansing that resulted in an almost complete physical separation of the Shia and Sunni populations. At least three million people are still afraid to return to their homes, and most never will.

That was a direct result of the American invasion, for without it the al-Qaeda fanatics would never have gained such a foothold in the Sunni community. Nevertheless, it was the senseless al-Qaeda terrorist attacks on the Shias that unleashed the civil war of 2006–07, which the Sunnis, being outnumbered three-to-one, were bound to lose. It will take at least a generation to heal this wound.

The other 20 percent of the population, the Kurds of northern Iraq, got a semi-independent state out of the invasion, though they still go along with the fiction of a united Iraq. This is not a stable arrangement, however, and the risk of an Arab-Kurdish war in Iraq over the ownership of the Kirkuk oil fields cannot be discounted.

On the other hand, Iraqis now have a more or less democratic system, with more or less free media. They have a government that is more corrupt and significantly less competent than the old Baathist regime, but at least it will not waste the country's wealth on foreign wars. Given ten or fifteen years of good luck and high oil prices, Iraq could climb back to the level of prosperity it enjoyed in the 1970s.

So was it all worth it? There is no consensus on this question even among the Iraqis themselves. We may know the answer by 2020.

22.

CLIMATE II

Most people, not just in the United States but everywhere in the West, are still unwilling to accept that people in the poor countries have the same right to consume at industrial levels as people in the rich countries do. As witness: Western media treatment of the Nano car.

January 11, 2008
NANO HYPOCRISY

The jokes about the Nano, Tata Motors' new affordable car for the Indian middle class, were harmless, although very old. They told the same jokes about the Fiat 500 and the Citroen 2CV in the 1950s, when mass car ownership first came to Europe. "How do you double the value of a Nano?" "Fill the tank." "How many engineers does it take to make a Nano?" "Two. One to fold and one to apply the glue." But the hypocrisy wasn't funny at all.

The typical story in the Western media began by marvelling that Tata has managed to build a car that will sell for only 100,000 rupees ($2,500). Everybody agrees that it's "cute" and that it can hold five people, provided they don't all inhale at the same time. It has no radio, no air conditioning, and only one big windshield wiper, but such economies mean that it really is within reach of tens of millions of Indians who could only afford a scooter up to now. And that is where the hypocrisy kicks in.

What will become of us when all these Indians start driving around in cars? There's over a billion of them, and the world just can't take any more emissions. It's not the "People's Car," as Tata bills it, but rather the "People's Polluter," moaned Canada's *National Post*, adding that "a few dozen million new cars pumping out pollution in a state of semi-permanent gridlock is hardly what the Kyoto Protocol had in mind."

But hang on a minute. Aren't there more than a dozen million cars in Canada already, even though it only has one-thirtieth of India's population? Aren't they, on average, twice the size of the Nano (or, in the case of the larger sport utility vehicles, five times the size)? Does the phrase "double standard" come to mind?

"India's vehicles spewed 219 million tons of carbon dioxide into the atmosphere in 2005," fretted the *Guardian* in London. "Experts say that figure will jump almost sevenfold to 1,470 million tons by 2035 if car travel remains unchecked." And the *Washington Post* wrote: "If millions of Indians and Chinese get to have their own cars, the planet is doomed. Suddenly, the cute little Nano starts to look a lot less winning."

But practically every family in the United States and Britain already has its own car (or two). Don't they realize how ugly such commentary sounds? Don't they understand that everybody on the planet has an equal right to own a car, if they can afford it?

If the total number of people who can afford cars exceeds the number of cars that the planet can tolerate, then we will just have to work out a rationing system that everybody finds fair, or live with the consequences of exceeding the limits.

"Contraction and convergence" is the phrase they need to learn. It was coined almost twenty years ago by South African-born activist Aubrey Meyer, founder of the Global Commons Institute, and it is still the only plausible way that we might get global agreement on curbing greenhouse-gas emissions worldwide. The notion is simple: we must agree on a figure for total global emissions that cannot be exceeded, rather as we set fishing quotas in order to preserve fish stocks. Then we divide that amount by six and a half billion people, and that gives us the per capita emission limit for everyone on Earth.

Of course, some people (in the developed countries mostly) are currently emitting ten or twenty times as much as other people (mainly in the developing countries), and eventually this will have to stop. The big emitters will gradually have to "contract" their per capita emissions, while the poor countries may continue to grow theirs, until, at an agreed date some decades in the future, the two groups "converge" at the same level of per capita emissions. And that level, by prior agreement, must be low enough that global emissions remain below the danger point.

If you don't like that idea, then you can go with the alternative: a free-for-all world in which everybody moves towards the level of per capita emissions that now prevails in the developed countries. No negotiations or treaties required: it will happen of its own accord. So will runaway climate change, with average global temperatures climbing as much as six degrees Celsius higher by the end of the century, and a future of famine, war and mass death.

Clucking disapprovingly about mass car ownership in India or China misses the point entirely. At the moment, there are only eleven private cars for every thousand Indians. There are 477 private cars for every thousand Americans. By mid-century, there will have to be the same number of cars per thousand people for both Indians and Americans—and that number will have to be a lot lower than 477, unless somebody comes up with cars that emit no greenhouse gases. Otherwise, everybody loses.

June 29, 2008
LAST EXIT FOR THE HOLOCENE

"Damn! I think we just passed the last exit for the Holocene!"
"I'm sorry, honey, I wasn't looking."
"We have to get off this highway. What's the next exit?"
"It's a long way ahead. Goes to somewhere called Perdition."
(Ragged chorus from the back seat) "Are we there yet, Daddy?"

The Holocene era is that blessed time of stable, warm climate (but not too hot) and unchanging sea levels, in which human civilization was born and grew to its present size. In ten thousand years, our numbers have increased about a thousandfold—but we may be about to leave the Holocene, and that would be too bad. No other climatic state would let us maintain our current numbers, and mass diebacks are no fun at all.

James Hansen, the director of NASA's Goddard Institute for Space Studies in New York, is one of the most respected scientists working in the field of climate studies. It was his famous speech to the U.S. Congress twenty years ago that put climate change on the U.S. political agenda, and led indirectly to the Earth Summit and the Framework Convention on Climate Change of 1992 and to the Kyoto Protocol of 1997. Now, he has something else to say.

For most of the past decade, Hansen adhered to the emerging consensus among climate scientists that the maximum permissible concentration of carbon dioxide in the atmosphere is 450 parts per million. That was believed to give us a 50 percent chance of getting away with an average global temperature only two degrees Celsius hotter than it was at the beginning of the 1990s. Now Hansen doesn't believe in the 450 parts per million barometer anymore.

Four hundred and fifty parts per million was chosen partly because it seemed impossible to stop the rise in carbon dioxide before reaching that point—we're already at 387 parts per million, and going up almost 3 parts per million per year—and partly because it seemed relatively safe. Two degrees Celsius hotter would turn a lot of subtropical land into desert, cause bigger hurricanes, and turn most of Asia's big rivers into seasonal watercourses that are empty in summer, but it would not melt the ice caps. At least that's what scientists thought, although everybody knew that the numbers were soft.

You can do a lot with climate models, but the Earth hasn't actually seen a carbon dioxide concentration as high as 450 parts per million since about thirty-five million years ago. So Hansen and some colleagues went to work on exactly that period, and came back with some bad news. If you leave the world at even 425 parts per million for very long, all the ice will probably melt: Greenland, Antarctica, the lot. And the sea level will rise seventy to eighty metres.

How do they know this? The world was very hot and completely ice-free for a long time before thirty-five million years ago, but the amount of carbon dioxide in the atmosphere was falling gradually. When it reached 425 parts per million, Antarctica began to freeze over, and if that's where the first permanent ice appeared while carbon dioxide was on the way down, it's probably where the last permanent ice will disappear when carbon dioxide is on its way back up.

Now, there's a big margin of error when you are dealing with thirty-five million years ago: plus or minus 75 parts per million, in this case. That means that the fatal number, when all the ice disappears, could really be as high as 500 parts per million—or it could be as low as 350 parts per million. If that is the range within which *all* the world's ice will eventually melt, and you like living in the Holocene, then you probably should not put all your money on a 450 parts per million ceiling for carbon dioxide.

So Jim Hansen is now spearheading a campaign to get 350 parts per million recognized as the real long-term target we should be aiming for. Tricky, since we are already at 387 parts per million and rising fast. But last week, when I spoke to him at the Tällberg Forum's annual conference in Sweden, he explained: "To figure out the optimum is going to take a while, but the fundamental thing about the 350 [parts per million target], and the reason that it completely changes the ball game, is precisely the fact that it's less than we have now.

"It means that we really have to start to act almost immediately. Even if we cut off coal emissions entirely, carbon dioxide would still get up to at least 400, maybe 425, and then we're going to have to draw it down, and we're almost certainly going to have to do it within decades."

But there is time. The oceans and the ice sheets react so slowly to changes in the air temperature that you can overshoot the limit for a while, so long as you get the temperature back down before irreversible changes set in. Stop at 450 parts per million in twenty-five years' time, then get back below 400 in another twenty-five, and down to 350 by, say, 2075. It could be done: there is still one last exit for the Holocene.

By late 2008, I was fully up to speed on climate issues. I had interviewed many of the key scientists, read a lot of the research, and come to some conclusions. I had even produced a radio series and written a book about it, Climate Wars, *whose second edition I warmly recommend to you. And it seemed absolutely clear to me that we were not going to make it through the crisis without huge losses unless we resorted, at least for a time, to geo-engineering.*

September 26, 2008
TIME FOR GEO-ENGINEERING?

Scientists have their own way of phrasing things, and this is how Dr. Oerjan Gustafsson of Stockholm University announced the approach of a climate apocalypse in an email, sent last week from the Russian research ship *Jacob Smirnitskyi* in the Arctic Ocean:

"We had a hectic finishing of the sampling program yesterday and this past night. An extensive area of intense methane release was found. At earlier sites we had found elevated levels of dissolved methane. Yesterday, for the first time, we documented a field where the release was so intense that the methane did not have time to dissolve into the seawater but was rising as methane bubbles to the sea surface."

Molecule for molecule, methane gas is twenty times more potent than carbon dioxide as a warming agent. However, since methane doesn't stay in the atmosphere as long—around twelve years, on average, compared to a hundred years for carbon dioxide—and human activities do not produce all that much of it, concerns about climate change have mostly been focused on carbon dioxide. The only big worry was that warmer temperatures might cause massive releases of methane from natural sources.

There are thousands of megatons of methane stored underground in the Arctic region, trapped there by the permafrost (permanently frozen ground) that covers much of northern Russia, Alaska and Canada, and that extends far out under the seabed of the Arctic Ocean. If the permafrost melts and methane escapes into the atmosphere on a large scale, it would cause a rapid rise in temperature—which would melt more permafrost, releasing more methane, which would cause more warming, and so on.

Climate scientists call this a positive feedback mechanism. So long as it is our emissions that are causing the warming, we can stop the warming if we reduce the emissions fast enough. But once positive feedbacks like methane release are in play, and start to drive the warming, it's out of our hands: we could cut our emissions to zero only to find that the temperature is still rising.

Fear of this runaway feedback is why most climate scientists see a rise of two degrees Celsius in the average global temperature as the limit that we must never exceed. Somewhere between two and three degrees Celsius, they fear, means massive positive feedbacks such as methane release would kick in and take the situation out of our hands.

Unfortunately, the heating is much more intense in the Arctic region. So far, the average global temperate has risen only 0.8 degrees Celsius in the last century and a half, but the average temperature in the Arctic is up by four degrees Celsius. The result? The permafrost is starting to melt and the trapped methane is escaping.

That is what the research ship *Jacob Smirnitskiy* has just found: areas of the Arctic Ocean off the Russian coast where "chimneys" of methane gas are bubbling to the surface. What this may mean is that we have no time left, if we hope to avoid runaway global warming—and yet it will obviously take many years to get our own greenhouse-gas emissions down. So what can we do?

There is a way to cheat, for a while. Several techniques have been proposed for holding the global temperature down temporarily in order to avoid running into the feedbacks. They do not release us from the duty of getting our emissions down, but they could win us some time to work on that task without running into disaster.

The leading candidate, suggested by Nobel Prize–winning atmospheric chemist Paul Crutzen in 2006, is to inject sulphur dioxide into the stratosphere in order to reflect some incoming sunlight. (This mimics the action of large volcanic eruptions, which also lower the global temperature temporarily by putting huge amounts of sulphur dioxide into the upper atmosphere.)

Another, less intrusive approach, proposed by John Latham of the National Center for Atmospheric Research in Boulder, Colorado, and Stephen Salter of Edinburgh University, is to launch fleets of unmanned, wind-powered vessels, controlled by satellite, that would spray a fine mist of seawater up into low-lying marine clouds in order to increase the amount of sunlight that they reflect. The great attraction of this technique is that if there are unwelcome side effects, you can turn it off right away.

These techniques are known as "geo-engineering" and, until recently, discussing them has been taboo in most scientific circles because of the "moral hazard": the fear that if the public knows you can hold the global temperature down by direct intervention, people will not do the harder job of cutting their emissions. But if large-scale methane releases are getting underway, the time for such subtle calculations is past.

Starting now, we need a crash program to investigate the feasibility of these and other techniques for geo-engineering the climate. Once the thawing starts, it is hard to stop, and we may need such techniques very soon.

And what does all this mean for "The True North Strong and Free"?

December 11, 2009
CANADA'S FUTURE CLIMATE

The Copenhagen talks on climate change are going badly, which doubtless pleases the federal government. It thinks a weak agreement, or none at all, will serve Canada's economic interests. It is wrong.

There are only two likely scenarios, really. In one, the rich countries make big emissions cuts in the next ten or fifteen years, and the developing countries at least cap their emissions. That better future is still ugly in many places—but not in Canada. The other is the "business-as-usual" scenario, in which the developed countries do not reduce their greenhouse-gas emissions fast enough and the developing countries just let them rip.

Nobody gets away unscathed in the "business-as-usual" scenario. When British Foreign Secretary David Miliband revealed the latest numbers from the Met Office's Hadley Centre last October, predicting that a world in which emissions go unchecked may see a four degree Celsius rise in average global temperature by 2060, he simply said: "We cannot cope with a four-degree world."

Actually, Britain probably could cope. As an island, cooled by the surrounding ocean, it would only be three degrees warmer, which means that it would probably still be able to grow enough food to feed itself. That is vital in a four-degrees-warmer world, because almost nobody will be exporting food anymore.

Oceans cover two-thirds of the planet's surface and are cooler than the land, so the average temperature over most land areas is higher than the "average global temperature." The Hadley Centre predicts that a global average of plus four degrees means that average temperatures will be five to six degrees higher in China, India, Southeast Asia and most of Africa, and up to eight degrees higher in the Amazon (which would burn, of course).

The result would be a 40 percent fall in world wheat and corn production and a 30 percent fall in rice production by 2060—in a world that would, by then, have to feed two billion more people. So there would be mass starvation, and waves of desperate refugees trying to move to a country where they could still feed their kids.

Canada's only land border, fortunately, is with the United States, and the Americans would certainly seal the Mexican border against refugees from farther south. They would want Canadian water, though—and yet we would probably be short of water ourselves, because the farther inland and the farther north you go, the higher the temperature rises.

The Hadley Centre predicts that the thickly populated parts of Quebec, Ontario and the eastern Prairies would be an average of seven degrees hotter than they are today. Alberta, British Columbia and New Brunswick would be six degrees hotter; while Newfoundland, Nova Scotia and Prince Edward Island, surrounded by the sea, might be only four or five degrees hotter.

Would Canada still be a grain exporter at those temperatures? Would it even be able to feed itself? It depends on what happens to the rainfall, not just the temperature, but the answer might be no, and not being self-sufficient in food in a starving world would be a very unpleasant experience.

You get big problems closer to the equator at plus two degrees, but Canada would still be safe. At plus four, Canada faces catastrophe, too. That is the difference, for Canadians, between an effective climate-change treaty and a botched one—or none at all.

Canadians, including the government, assume that we will be okay no matter what happens on the climate front, so we can afford to put our other interests (like protecting the income from the tar sands) first. It is not true.

All the countries of the Earth sent their representatives to Copenhagen in December 2009 to negotiate a treaty that would keep the climate within its familiar bounds. They didn't expect to get it finished there in every detail, but many people hoped that the Copenhagen conference could at least settle the big, contentious issues, leaving only the fine print for later. But the major powers present didn't have agreement in principle when they arrived, and they didn't have it when they left either.

December 19, 2009
COPENHAGEN AFTERMATH

"The city of Copenhagen is a crime scene tonight, with the guilty men and women fleeing to the airport," said John Sauven, executive director of Greenpeace U.K., on Friday night. "There are no targets for carbon cuts and no agreement on a legally binding treaty."

The guilty men included U.S. President Barack Obama and Brazilian President Luiz Inácio "Lula" da Silva, who took the first planes out. Xie Zhenhua, the head of China's delegation, lingered behind to declare that "The meeting has had a positive result, everyone should be happy." But many people are unhappy, including most of the 130 presidents and prime ministers who showed up for the Copenhagen conference.

Their countries spent two weeks struggling unsuccessfully to bridge the gulf between the rich and poor nations over who pays to fix the eminently fixable problem of global warming, but at least they were clear on the goal. They wanted a treaty that would hold the warming to a safe level (although they could not agree on what that level was). Most of them even wanted to make it legally enforceable.

Yet the result, the Copenhagen Accord, was essentially a drive-by shooting, negotiated in a few hours by the U.S., China, Brazil, India and South Africa. It contains no hard numbers for emissions cuts and no deadlines. Nonetheless, Barack Obama insisted that it was a "meaningful result" because they had "agreed to set a mitigation target to limit warming to no more than two degrees Celsius and, importantly, to take action to meet this objective."

It's easy to make fun of this stuff. Those wise and powerful men set a target of no more than two degrees Celsius of warming—which is exactly the same target they declared at the G8/G20 summit last July. "Importantly," they also agreed "to take action to meet this objective"—though they could not agree on what the action would be, or when they would decide on it.

For this, 192 countries spent two weeks negotiating at Copenhagen? Why bother? It was an utter waste of time. But why is anybody surprised? Even I knew that it was bound to end up like that.

Two weeks ago, I wrote: "The Copenhagen summit will certainly fail to deliver the right deal. The danger is that it will lock us into the wrong deal, and leave no political space for countries to go back and try to get it right later. Public opinion is climbing a steep learning curve, and the asymmetrical deal that cannot be sold politically today might be quite saleable in as little as a year or two."

Well, Copenhagen certainly didn't lock us into the wrong deal. The reason no deal was possible is that public opinion in the developed countries is still in denial about the fact that the final climate deal must be asymmetrical. Until the general public grasps that idea, especially in the United States, there will be no real progress.

Most Western leaders understand the history. For two centuries, the countries that are now "developed" got rich by burning fossil fuels. In the process, they filled the atmosphere with their greenhouse-gas emissions to the point where the atmosphere now has little remaining capacity to absorb carbon dioxide without tipping us into disastrous heating.

This means that rapidly developing countries like China, India and Brazil will push the whole world into runaway warming if they follow the same historical path in growing their economies. As they are relatively poor, they have been investing mainly in fossil fuels, just as the West did when it was starting to industrialize. A wide variety of alternatives is now available, but only at a higher price.

So how do we deal with this unfair history? The developed countries must cut their emissions deeply and fast, and they must give the developing countries enough money to cover the extra cost of growing their economies with clean sources of energy instead of fossil fuels. That's the deal, but most voters in the U.S. don't understand it yet.

That's why Barack Obama couldn't promise to cut American emissions to 20 or 25 percent below 1990 levels by 2020, as most other industrial countries were offering to do. Instead, he could only offer a paltry 4 percent cut—and he couldn't even guarantee that.

His most visible problem is the U.S. Senate, a body whose constitutional role is to delay change. The Senate has become more corrupt in recent decades because of the almost unlimited spending power of special-interest groups, but an uncorrupted Senate would not pass drastic climate legislation either. Like Obama himself, it cannot risk getting too far ahead of the American public.

Until Americans start to take climate change seriously, Obama will not be able to move. And it is politically impossible for the Chinese to make concrete commitments until the Americans do. We will just have to wait until the Americans get there.

Each year in which we don't reach an adequate global climate deal means higher global average temperatures. Each lost year probably implies around fifty million extra premature deaths from famine, disease and war between now and the end of the century, because a higher end temperature means more of all those things. But that's just the current tariff: by 2015, the annual cost in lives of further delay will rise steeply. Time is not on our side.

23.

DEMOGRAPHY IN ACTION

People care hugely about demography, even if they sometimes don't know that that's the word they want. No political debate in Quebec, for example, is complete without a discussion of the dangerous rise (or catastrophic fall—take your pick) in the proportion of non-francophones in the population. It's fundamentally about how one tribe is doing vis-à-vis other tribes, and you can't blame people for caring about that.

January 29, 2007
MAKING BABIES FOR FUN AND PROFIT

"The number of women aged between 15 and 50 is fixed," explained Japanese Health Minister Hakuo Yanagisawa in a speech in Matsue City last Friday. "Because the number of birth-giving machines and devices is fixed, all we can ask for is for them to do their best per head." Then he paused a moment and hastily added: "Although it may not be so appropriate to call them machines."

Too late. Even in Japan, a government minister calling women "birth-giving machines" is bound to raise a fuss, even if he has the excuse of being old (seventy-one) and stupid. Yanagisawa spent the weekend making abject apologies, and the debate about the plunging Japanese birth rate moved on. But he wasn't just rude; he was also wrong. Governments *can* affect the birth rate.

Last week, France revealed that more babies were born there in 2006 than in any other year for the past quarter-century—830,000 of them, in fact. The fertility rate, which has been rising for years, is now up to 2 babies per woman and, at the rate it is currently rising, will reach the "replacement rate" of 2.1 next year. Compared to Japan's incredibly low 1.26 babies per woman, it is a veritable baby boom, but within Europe the French birth rate is exceeded only by the Irish.

Japan and France had roughly similar demographic trends after the Second World War. First came the baby boom, as a result of which Japan's population grew from 75 million to the current 127 million and France's went from 40 million to 63 million. By the 1990s, however, both countries' birth rates had dropped below replacement level. In the long run, that means the actual population is beginning to shrink. Japan's population started to decline again in 2004, and by 2050 it is predicted to be only ninety million.

This is quite normal in the developed world, where among the larger countries only the United States still has a growing population (and that mostly thanks to immigration). Japan's population is falling faster than most, but Italy's and Russia's are falling just as fast.

Yet the French birth rate, which was following the same pattern, suddenly turned around in 1996 and started going up again. What are they doing right? "The deciding factor [is] that it is easier to reconcile professional activity and a family life here than in most other European countries," suggested Jean-Michel Charpin, director of the National Institute of Statistics and Economic Studies.

The dates do more or less match up. France's unusually family-friendly policies, like universally affordable day care and generous parental leave, were launched in the early 1990s under then Families Minister Ségolène Royal (now the Socialist candidate for the presidency), and only a few years later the birth rate started to recover.

Even the racists in the National Front do not oppose such policies because every ethnic group has responded in the same way to these incentives: the fertility rate among France's immigrant population is only slightly higher than that of the population at large. If current trends persist—that is, a declining population in Germany and a slowly rising population in France—by 2050 France will have the second-largest population in Europe, behind only Russia.

Others are beginning to notice the French success, and Russia most of all. Russia had 150 million people when the Soviet Union broke up in 1991; it's already down to 143 million and it is shrinking by 700,000 people every year. This has been causing something close to panic in the Kremlin, where they see the increasingly empty spaces of Siberia and the Russian Far East as a standing temptation to an overcrowded China. (That sentiment may be paranoid but you hear it expressed in Moscow all the time.)

"The most acute problem in modern-day Russia is demography," said President Vladimir Putin last May, and announced measures to increase the birth rate even more sweeping than those in France. Starting this month, Russian women who give birth to a second child will get an immediate cash bonus of 250,000 roubles ($9,500). That's a small fortune in an economy where the minimum wage is just over $300 a month.

At the same time, Putin doubled the state benefit for a first child to $55 a month, while women who have a second child will get an extra $110 a month, plus financial help with child care. Have three children, and you will get close to the minimum wage without working at all. That should be enough to stabilize the population. Get the alcohol problem under control—one third of male deaths in Russia are alcohol-related, and life expectancy for men is only fifty-nine—and Russia's population might even start growing again.

Not that the world actually needs more Russians or French or Japanese, of course. There are already ten times as many of them as there were five hundred years ago, and that's probably already more than the planet can bear over the long run.

The first time I went to Russia—back in the early eighties, when it was still the Soviet Union—I knew something was wrong beyond the obvious things like no commercial advertising and a pervasive glumness, but it took me three or four days to figure it out. And then, suddenly, I realized what it was: with the exception of a few conscript soldiers from the Central Asian republics absolutely everybody on the streets was white.

All the Soviet-bloc countries were like that. They simply hadn't had any immigration because who in their right mind would have wanted to move there? Even today they are still the most ethnically homogeneous societies in the West (on the assumption that they are all really part of the greater "West," which I think is fair). That's probably why they are the most racist part of the West, too. The ethnically more complex societies are also the more tolerant ones.

January 29, 2009

MULTIRACIAL BRITAIN

If you are the head of something called the Equality and Human Rights Commission, your job is to complain about the racism, gender discrimination and general unfairness of the society you live in. So Trevor Phillips, chairman of Britain's EHRC, broke with tradition when he said last week that Britain is "by far—and I mean by far—the best place in Europe to live if you are not white."

Phillips, whose own heritage is black Caribbean, made his remarks on the tenth anniversary of a report on the murder of a young black Londoner, Stephen Lawrence, that condemned the British police as "institutionally racist." So they were, at the time—but having lived in London half my life, I think Phillips is right. Things have changed.

Lucinda Platt of the Institute of Social and Economic Research at Essex University thinks so, too. She has just published a report revealing that one in five children in Britain now belongs to an ethnic minority— and one in ten lives in a mixed-race family. The first statistic might merely confirm Enoch Powell's fears of forty years ago. The second proves that he was utterly wrong.

Enoch Powell was the Conservative politician who made a famous speech in 1968 predicting a race war if the United Kingdom did not stop non-white immigration from the former empire. He dressed it up with quotes from the classics, but the message was plain: "As I look ahead, I am filled with foreboding. Like the Roman, I seem to see 'the River Tiber foaming with much blood.'"

"That tragic and intractable phenomenon which we watch with horror on the other side of the Atlantic," Powell went on, referring to the race riots that devastated many large American cities after the assassination of Dr. Martin Luther King, " . . . is coming upon us here by our own volition and our own neglect. Indeed, it has all but come. In numerical terms, [the non-white part of the British population] will be of American proportions long before the end of the century. Only resolute and urgent action will avert it even now."

Powell was promptly expelled from the shadow cabinet, but an opinion poll soon afterwards showed that 74 percent of the British population shared his fears. The general opinion at the time in Europe, based mainly on observation of the American experience, was that different races could not live comfortably together.

Fast-forward forty years, and Britain is more or less as Powell predicted: the proportion of non-whites among its citizens is almost the same as it is in the United States. But the next generation of British are not fighting each other, as Powell predicted; they are marrying each other.

Among British children who have an Indian heritage, 11 percent live in families with one white parent. Among kids with a Chinese heritage, 35 percent have one white parent. Among children with a black Caribbean heritage, 49 percent do. Including my next-door neighbours.

Among Muslim Britons, the rate is much lower (only 4 percent for kids of Pakistani heritage), but the younger generation of British people is largely blind to ethnicity and religious differences, all the old shibboleths. And apart from some former mill towns where unskilled immigrants from a single ethnic group confront the old white working class, both of them now unemployed, there are few racially segregated ghettoes in Britain.

Of London's thirty-two boroughs, none is less than 10 percent non-white. On the other hand, only three reach 50 percent non-white, and those just barely. Despite the happy-ever-after inauguration of Barack Obama, the urban scene in New York, Los Angeles or Chicago is dramatically different.

This does not prove that British people are more virtuous than Americans. It just shows that people of different races can live comfortably together, can even come to see race as essentially irrelevant to their choice of mate, *provided that there is no heritage of race-based slavery*.

The French "race riots" of 2005 and 2007 occasioned much discussion of France's failure to integrate its immigrants, but lots of angry white kids took part in those riots, too. The same was true of the Brixton "race riots" in London in 1981. They were actually anti-police riots, and whites were welcome to join. Many did.

Eastern Europe is different: it has far fewer non-whites, and so it is far more racist. But Britain, and to a lesser extent France, is rather like Canada, another country that was 98 percent white only fifty years ago, but now has a racial diversity that equals or exceeds that of the United States. Yet it simply isn't an issue for most of the young. Indeed, London and Toronto are probably the two best cities in the world in which to bring up mixed-race kids.

None of this detracts from the historic achievement of Americans in electing a black (well, all right, mixed-race) president. It's just to say that it was much harder to do that in the United States because of the malign influence of history.

All the more credit to Americans for doing it anyway; and full marks to the British and the Canadians for showing that race really doesn't matter when history doesn't get in the way.

The biggest demographic change of the current era, by now visible in every continent except Africa, is the greying of the planet. People are living longer and the birth rate is dropping, so the old will soon outnumber the young. This has an intriguing implication: an older population is probably also a more peaceful one.

December 27, 2004
GENERATION CHANGE

"The disasters of the world are due to its inhabitants not being able to grow old simultaneously. There is always a new and intolerant nation eager to destroy the tolerant and mellow."
—Cyril Connolly, *The Unquiet Grave*, 1945

That's history for you. King Lear was an exception, but most of Shakespeare's kings and princes were under thirty, many under twenty. Their hormones were still raging, so of course they committed murders, massacres and the like. In a world where the average life expectancy was thirty and most people didn't even survive childhood, politics was bound to be pretty turbulent. It was always the same, in every part of the planet—but what if all the nations grew up together?

At the end of a discouraging year, here is an encouraging thought: the world *is* growing up. The average age in the world today is twenty-eight. (In Shakespeare's time, it was around fifteen.) By 2050, it will be forty. At the age of forty, calculations of long-term self-interest have largely prevailed over hormones. Aging doesn't necessarily make people nicer, but it certainly makes them more careful.

When experts play around with population growth statistics they are mostly concerned about overpopulation, pressure on resources and the environment, all the usual worries—and they are right to worry about those things. They pay less attention to the political effects because they are less easy to trace, but they are there, and they are very important.

There has been a steady run of good news on the population front in the past few decades. In 1968, the United Nations Population Division predicted that the world population would grow to twelve billion by 2050. By 1992, the same office was predicting ten billion people by 2050. Last month, it predicted that the world's population would peak at 8.9 billion, and not until 2300—although it will already be pretty close to that figure by 2050.

In reality, even this is probably a pessimistic prediction. All these projections have been based on an assumption that birth rates will continue to fall—a straightforward projection of the world's population based even on today's birth rate would yield a total of around fifteen billion people by 2050—but the assumptions about how fast they will fall have consistently been too conservative.

You can see why the forecasters tended towards pessimism: the recent history of human-population growth has resembled an avalanche. It took almost all of human history to reach a total of two billion people, around 1927. It took less than fifty years to add the next two billion, by 1974. It took less than twenty-five years to add another two billion, by 1999. And we're still growing at seventy-six million a year: an extra two Canadas every year.

In 1950, there was not a single country where the population was not growing rapidly, the average woman had more than five children in her lifetime, and the birth rate was not dropping significantly anywhere. Then came the new birth-control technologies and the rise of women's liberation ideologies, and in many Western countries the birth rate dropped by half in ten years. As recently as 1974, however, the median birth rate worldwide was still 5.4 children per woman, so the pessimists were still winning the arguments.

They believed that only literacy could spread the ideas and techniques that made birth rates fall, and that literacy would not grow fast enough. Well, literacy has grown a lot faster than they expected—between 1980 and 2000, literacy rose from 18 percent to 47 percent in Afghanistan; from 33 percent to 64 percent in Nigeria; from 66 percent to 85 percent in China; and from 69 percent to 87 percent in Indonesia. But birth rates have dropped even faster than literacy has risen: the global average is now 2.7 children per woman.

Some of the most startling recent drops have been in places where women's illiteracy is still quite high—Bangladesh and parts of India, for example—so we clearly need a broader criterion than mere literacy. In fact, *any* form of mass media, including broadcast media that do not require literacy, seems to have the same effect on the birth rate. (Though purely local cultural factors also play a role: Pakistan and Bangladesh both had a birth rate of 6.3 in 1981; now Bangladesh's is 3.3, while Pakistan's is still 5.6.)

The global birth rate may be no more than a decade away from dropping to replacement level, 2.2 children per woman. Most developed countries have already dropped well below that rate. This does not immediately stop population growth, since all the children who have already been born will have a child or two themselves, and then live for another fifty years afterwards. It does not solve the environmental crisis either, since all of these seven or eight billion human beings will aspire to the kind of lifestyle now enjoyed only by the privileged billion or so.

But it does mean that populations almost everywhere will start greying within the next decade, and in due course, the old will come to outnumber the young. (The exceptions are almost all in African and Arab countries which together amount to only a tenth of the world's population.) Based on historical precedent, countries where the average age is rising are unlikely to become aggressor nations. Peace through exhaustion, perhaps?

24.

RELIGION II

I ended the first bunch of articles on religion by saying that we shouldn't even get into the relationship between religion and war, but you knew I wouldn't be able to resist, didn't you? So here it is. Or one little corner of it, anyway.

May 13, 2007
BLAIR: WHY DID HE DO IT?

It has been the longest goodbye in modern politics, and there are still another six weeks to go before Tony Blair finally hands the prime minister-ship over to Gordon Brown on June 27. After he finally leaves office, most people in Britain assume Blair will go off and make a living on the lecture circuit in the United States (where he is far more popular than he is at home). He won't be much missed.

It is strange that a prime minister who has presided over an unprecedented surge of prosperity in Britain should be so deeply unpopular, but the reason why lies in a single word: Iraq. Support for that war in Britain is even lower than it is in the United States, and the popular conviction that the public was misled into invading Iraq by a leader who ruthlessly manipulated the "evidence" to get his way is even stronger. The argument is only about why he did it—and the consensus answer is that it was religion.

In "post-Christian Britain"—the phrase dates from the 1970s but is even truer today—Blair is what was once known as a "muscular Christian": a person who believes that his faith requires him to act, and justifies his actions. Only a minority of British prime ministers in the past century have been Christian believers—Winston Churchill, for example, was a completely irreligious agnostic—and even the ones who were personally devout felt that religion should remain a private matter.

In terms of spin control, this phenomenon extended even into Blair's government, as the prime minister was under strict instructions not to speak about his faith in public. "We don't do God," as spin master Alastair Campbell once put it. But in fact Blair did "do God," and that is what led him into Iraq.

Columnist Geoffrey Wheatcroft got it exactly right in the *Independent* last Sunday: "In some ways [Blair] is more innately American than British. Blair may not have prayed with the born-again George Bush, but their shared faith was certainly a bond, and [Blair's] wearing his faith on his sleeve would not have seemed too odd or embarrassing in the U.S., where more than half the population goes to church and where supposedly grown-up politicians can say they approach difficult problems by asking: 'What would Jesus do?'"

The problem was that it *would* seem odd and embarrassing in Britain, where only 7 percent of the population regularly attend church or its equivalent. The notion that British foreign policy was being driven by one man's faith would have inspired mass revolt if Blair's motives had been made plain. But they weren't: the spin machine did its job well.

From the time he took office in 1997 Blair talked about having a "moral" foreign policy, but it wasn't clear at the time that this meant he believed in doing good by force. Then came a series of more or less legal military interventions abroad in which British troops did do some good: stopping the genocide against Muslims in Kosovo in 1999; ending the civil war in Sierra Leone in 2000; and overthrowing the Taliban in Afghanistan after the terrorist atrocities of September 11, 2001.

These uses of military force all succeeded at a relatively low cost—the flare-up of guerrilla warfare in Afghanistan today is due to the neglect of the country *after* 2001—and it was flowers and champagne for Tony Blair each time. He was doing good by force, and he was doing very well by it politically, too. But the lesson Blair learned was that this sort of thing comes cheap and easy, and it was getting to be a habit. Then along came the Bush administration's plan to invade Iraq.

It is clear, in retrospect, that Blair had agreed to commit British troops to the invasion by the spring of 2002, and it is hard to believe that he was so ignorant and ill-advised as to believe the nonsense about Saddam Hussein's weapons of mass destruction and his alleged links to the al-Qaeda terrorists. But it is very easy to believe that he leapt at another chance to do good—that is, rid the world of a wicked dictator—by force.

Blair's perennial claim that "I have always done what I believe to be right" is no defence for his decision to join in the invasion of Iraq—do the rest of us usually do what we believe to be wrong?—but he firmly believes that his good intentions absolve him of responsibility for the outcome. The United Nations is a wreck, the reputations of the United States and the United Kingdom have never been lower, and Iraq is an almost measureless disaster, but no higher authority will ever officially hold Blair responsible for any of this, and so, in practical terms, he is quite right.

Enjoy the lecture circuit, Tony.

Recent research suggests that the word "sanctimonious" may have been invented specifically to describe Tony Blair (although certain questions about the temporal sequence remain to be resolved). Whereas you would never call Joseph Ratzinger "sanctimonious." Arrogant, narrow-minded and rude, certainly, but not "sanctimonious."

January 15, 2008
EPPURE SI MUOVE

The Pope's words have come back to haunt him, and so they should. The authorities at La Sapienza University in Rome had invited him to come and speak this week at the inauguration of the new academic year, but the physics department mobilized in protest. It was at La Sapienza seventeen years ago that Pope Benedict XVI, then Cardinal Joseph Ratzinger, declared that the trial and conviction of the Italian astronomer Galileo by the Inquisition in 1633 for asserting that the Earth goes around the Sun, was "rational and just."

The scientists took this to mean that Ratzinger sees religious authority as superior to scientific inquiry, and seized the occasion of his return visit to make a fuss about it. Radical students then took up the cause, festooning the campus with anti-Pope messages, and on Tuesday the Vatican announced that the visit was off. It's a tempest in a rather small teapot, but Ratzinger has stirred up a series of such tempests over the years.

Last year, during a visit to Brazil, Pope Benedict declared that the native populations of the Americas had been "silently longing" for the Christian faith that arrived with their conquerors and colonizers, and that it in no way represented the imposition of a foreign culture. Indigenous groups protested bitterly, but he stood his ground.

In 2006, speaking at the University of Regensburg, he quoted, with seeming approval, a fourteenth-century Byzantine emperor's comment: "Show me just what Muhammad brought that was new and there you will find things only evil and inhuman, such as his command to spread by the sword the faith he preached."

When Muslims protested, Pope Benedict took refuge in the claim that he was just quoting somebody else, not saying it himself. (You know how those quotes from Byzantine emperors just pop into your mind unbidden.) His defence of the Church's treatment of Galileo all those years ago was done in just the same style: an outrageous proposition delivered in what he seemed to think was a deniable way.

Galileo was the first man in Italy to build a telescope, through which he discovered the moons of Jupiter—and the sight of them rotating around a much larger planet set him to thinking about the relationship between the Earth and the Sun. Copernicus had published his book asserting that the Earth rotated about the Sun more than half a century before, and a "Copernican" had been burned at the stake for his heretical views in 1600, so Galileo approached the matter carefully. On the other hand, unlike Copernicus, he had a telescope, so he could *see* what was going on.

Galileo was summoned to Rome in 1616 and ordered not to write about the Copernican theory any more, but, in 1623, a man he saw as a patron and sympathizer, Cardinal Maffeo Barberini, was chosen as Pope Urban VIII. He travelled to Rome again, and believed that he had been given permission by Pope Urban to discuss the Copernican theory in public, provided he presented it as only a hypothesis. Unfortunately, either the political balance in the Vatican subsequently changed, or else Galileo simply misunderstood what he had been told.

When he published his book in 1632 it was banned. In 1633, he was interrogated in Rome under threat of torture, and condemned for "following the position of Copernicus, which is contrary to the true sense and authority of Holy Scripture." He recanted his views to save his skin, but they sentenced him to life imprisonment anyway.

But there is a story, perhaps untrue, that as Galileo was led away he muttered defiantly under his breath "Eppure si muove" (And yet the Earth moves). True or not, scientists continue to view this scene as the great defining moment in the conflict between authority and truth—or, if you like, between faith and reason. Clearly, so does Joseph Ratzinger, which is presumably why he felt compelled, back in 1990, to take one more kick at Galileo.

Speaking at La Sapienza, Rome's most prestigious university, he declared that the Church had been quite right to try and punish Galileo. Or rather, in a typical Ratzinger ploy, he quoted the maverick Austrian philosopher Paul Feyerabend, who said: "At the time of Galileo the Church remained much more faithful to reason than Galileo himself. The process against Galileo was reasonable and just." God knows what Feyerabend actually meant by that, but that was the quote that Ratzinger chose to use.

If you pay attention to what Pope Benedict has been saying all these years, it's clear that he does see Catholicism as superior to other religions and faith as superior to reason. There is nothing surprising about this. After all, he is the head of the Catholic Church, and many, if not most, committed Catholics do believe these things.

But he does go a little further than most. In the circumstances, you can see why the scientists at La Sapienza University were not all that keen on a return visit.

There are certain things that you can't do in a column that is read by people in many different countries, most of whom follow one religion or another, and one of them is to mock their beliefs. Fair enough: common courtesy would require that, even if self-interest didn't. But sometimes things come by that you really want to highlight, and there is one in the third paragraph of the next piece.

Tim Bleakley of CBS Outdoor in London says that the sponsors of his advertising campaign couldn't put the flat statement "There is no God" in their ads because it "would have been misleading" for religious people. Does that mean that the believers would have lost their faith if they had seen that written on the side of a bus, Tim? Or what?

February 8, 2009
THE ATHEIST BUSES

If the objective was to undermine people's belief in God, then turning the atheist buses loose in Britain was largely a waste of time, because most British people don't believe in God anyway.

The atheist buses are all over London and some other big British cities by now, with a large ad running down the sides saying: "There is probably no God. Now stop worrying and enjoy your life." But you have to ask: if the sponsors of the ad, the British Humanist Association, felt strongly enough about it to spend £35,000 ($50,000) to put the signs on all those buses, why did they only say "*probably* no God"?

It's not their fault. Tim Bleakley, managing director for sales and marketing at CBS Outdoor in London, which handles advertising for the bus system, explained that advertisements saying flatly that there is no God "would have been misleading" for religious people. "So as not to fall foul of the code, you have to acknowledge that there is a grey area."

When the complaints rolled in anyway, alleging that the ad was offensive to Christians and that the "no God" claim could not be substantiated, the Advertising Standards Authority ruled that the ads were "an expression of the advertiser's opinion and that the claims in it were not capable of objective substantiation." For a non-theological organization, the ASA is pretty sharp.

Never mind all that. The real question is: what did the British Humanist Association think it would achieve with its ad campaign? It's not as though non-believers in Britain were an oppressed minority. In fact, they're not a minority at all. They are the majority, although you have to read the statistics carefully to understand this.

According to the 2001 census, only seven million people in Britain said they had no religion, while thirty-seven million said they were Christian; one and a half million said they were Muslim, half a million were Hindu, 390,000 were Jedi Knights (there was a conspiracy among younger Britons to mock the process by claiming allegiance to the religion of *Star Wars*), 329,000 were Sikhs, and 260,000 were Jewish.

Those numbers suggest that Britain is an overwhelmingly Christian country, with under 20 percent of the population describing themselves as non-believers. Yet three-quarters of the people in Britain do not go to church even once a year. On an average Sunday, only 6 percent of the population is in church, and that figure has been dropping by 2 percent per decade since the 1970s. Something doesn't add up here.

When the International Social Survey Program conducted a more in-depth study of religious belief almost twenty years ago, it asked people if they agreed or disagreed with the statement "I know God exists and I have no doubts about it." In Britain, only 23.8 percent of people said they agreed.

That's a normal number for Europe. In that ISSP poll, most European countries registered between 20 and 30 percent for confident belief in God, although Italy struggled up to 51 percent, Ireland reached 58 percent, and Poland got the prize with 66 percent believers.

What is happening is that people in Britain and many other countries are answering the census question about religion in terms of their cultural heritage (which is, in most cases, Christian), not in terms of their actual beliefs. It all depends on how you phrase the question, but the official figures are misleading. Actual levels of religious belief in Europe are very low.

Moreover, the collapse in belief is continuing, with the youngest least likely to identify with a religion. An Ipsos MORI poll commissioned by the British Library in 2007 found that nearly half of the teenagers in Britain were atheists.

This fits in better with what you actually observe from day to day in most European countries. People are no less moral than they ever were, but religion is simply absent in daily life in Europe, at least compared to the United States, where it seems omnipresent. Yet here's a strange thing: the very first place those bus ads came out was the United States.

The idea started in Britain, but the American Humanist Association moved faster. Their ads appeared on buses in Washington, D.C., in November, saying "Why believe in a god? Just be good for goodness' sake"—and there was little public outcry. Maybe the United States is not that different after all.

The U.S., we are constantly told, has a level of religious belief almost as high as Iran's, and every Gallup poll since 1944 has reported that at least 94 percent of Americans "believe in God or a universal spirit." But look at this wording. If you had any lingering guilt at all about having abandoned your ancestral religion, you'd say yes to that, wouldn't you?

When the ISSP asked its much more rigorous question, only 66 percent of Americans agreed with the statement "I know God exists and I have no doubts about it." That was almost twenty years ago, and it's very likely that the level of belief has fallen since.

The United States is not the same as Europe but it is not invulnerable to the same trends. Which may be why President Obama, while rhyming off the roll call of America's religions in the time-honoured fashion in his election-night acceptance speech, for the first time added "and non-believers."

I was obviously very cross when I wrote this next one, but look at the date. The Israelis were pounding the bejesus (pardon the expression) out of the Gaza Strip once again while the United States, Canada and Britain ran interference for them on the diplomatic front. It seemed just the right time for . . .

December 27, 2008
A CHRISTMAS MESSAGE FROM AHMADINEJAD

There's something about the Middle East that brings out the hypocrisy in people, and never more so than at Christmas. Take, for example, the president of Iran, Mahmoud Ahmadinejad. Britain's Channel Four, in its never-ending quest for cheap controversy, has fallen into the habit of

getting someone to deliver an alternative address to the Queen's traditional Christmas message, and who better than the Iranian lunatic?

That was the intent, obviously, but Ahmadinejad foxed them all with
a low-key talk full of brain-curdling platitudes like the following: "If
Christ were on Earth today, undoubtedly he would stand with the people
in opposition to bullying, ill-tempered and expansionist powers . . . He
would hoist the banner of love and justice for humanity to oppose war-
mongers, occupiers, terrorists and bullies the world over."

Really? Christ lived in the Roman Empire, the very epitome of a
bullying, ill-tempered and expansionist power, and his own native
land, Palestine, was under Roman occupation, but he didn't hoist the
banner to oppose anything. He was certainly in favour of love and
justice, but he said "Render therefore unto Caesar the things which
are Caesar's; and unto God the things that are God's." Don't revolt,
don't even withhold your taxes, because this world does not matter. Only
the next one does.

Muslims are right in grouping Judaism, Christianity and Islam together
as the "Abrahamic religions," the "peoples of the Book," but the differences between them are much wider than the ecumenical fraternity
pretend. Jews and Muslims share a belief in the law and an enthusiasm
for the state that was utterly absent in early Christianity.

Abraham, Christ and Muhammad were all born within a very long
day's drive of one another, and they grew up in slightly different versions
of the same basic culture, but Abraham and Muhammad were both
prominent and powerful men. Christ was not. He was probably illiterate,
and he never showed the slightest interest in politics.

Jesus's followers were initially drawn from the downtrodden and the
excluded, the women and the slaves, and they did not believe that they
could or should engage in earthly politics. They courted martyrdom, and
they eagerly awaited the time when injustice, and indeed the world itself,
would be swept away in the Last Judgment (coming soon to a cemetery
near you). Of course, after a couple of centuries, Christianity became
the state religion of the Roman Empire, and all of that changed.

Mahmoud Ahmadinejad knew none of this, and why should he? He
was just saying the words that somebody slightly better informed (but
only slightly) put into his mouth. It was pious hypocrisy from a man who
has almost no influence on events. The power in Iran lies elsewhere,

with Supreme Leader Ali Khamenei, the Assembly of Experts and the Guardian Council.

The president of Iran has no more power than the vice-president of the United States: he doesn't control the armed forces, he makes no foreign-policy decisions, he is not in the loop as far as the intelligence services are concerned, and he can neither propose nor pass any laws. As Jack Garner, Franklin Roosevelt's first vice-president, said of his own job, being president of Iran is "not worth a tub of warm piss." Ahmadinejad accepted Channel Four's offer because he had nothing better to do that day.

So why pick on this self-promoting but marginal figure? Partly because there is something funny about watching a certifiable religious fanatic struggling to be ecumenical. But also because all politicians who feel pressured to say something positive about the ghastly situation in the Middle East fall into the same empty platitudes. The reality of frozen deadlock, huge hatred and lethal weapons is just too ugly to be addressed in a Christmas message.

25.

LATIN AMERICA

The big event in South America in 2005 was the election in Bolivia of the first-ever indigenous (that is, Indian) president, Evo Morales. Mexico has had some mestizo (mixed-race) presidents and there have been a few elsewhere, but a genuine indio *president who still speaks a native language fluently (Aymara, in Morales's case), in addition to Spanish, is a complete novelty in Latin America. And Morales doesn't just happen to be indigenous; that is his whole political raison d'être.*

December 19, 2005
BOLIVIA: RACE AND REVOLUTION

Bolivia has had more presidents by far than any other South American country mainly because so many of them were overthrown long before their terms ended. They were also all white, even though the majority of Bolivia's population is "indigenous," descended from the Indians whose ancestors already lived there as subjects of the Incan Empire at the time of the Spanish conquest five centuries ago. So, what are the odds that Evo Morales, Bolivia's first indigenous president, will survive a full term of office?

Morales, who won an absolute majority of the votes in last Sunday's presidential election, faces not only the usual hazards of life as the president of South America's poorest country, but also the threat of American intervention to overthrow him. As a socialist whose declared goal is to "end the colonial state" and as a leader of the coca farmers who promises to lift the ban on growing coca leaf, the crop from which cocaine is produced, he is deeply unpopular in Washington.

In the past, South American policies that are unpopular in the United States have frequently proven to be bad for the health of those who propose them. The U.S. found the time to organize the overthrow of the president of Chile in 1973 despite being neck-deep in the Vietnam War, and the election of Morales may finally focus Washington's attention on how countries all over Latin America are rejecting U.S. tutelage.

The main target of Washington's wrath so far has been Venezuela, whose president, Hugo Chavez, has built an unassailable domestic base—he has won eleven elections and referendums in the past seven years—by spending a lot of the country's oil revenues on the health and education of poor Venezuelans. He has built a close relationship with Cuba's Fidel Castro, and he is now providing Venezuelan oil at a discount to other Caribbean and Central American countries (and even to poor Americans).

It is Chavez's incendiary language that gets the headlines—last month he called President George W. Bush a "madman, a killer and a mass murderer"—but his aim is serious: to free all of Latin America from the grip of neo-liberal economic policies, indeed from American influence in general. Last July's launch of TeleSUR, a new television network whose aim is to provide an alternative to U.S.-based news and analysis for all Latin Americans, is a case in point. It is based in Caracas and is 70 percent financed by Venezuela, but it is also backed by the governments of Argentina, Uruguay, Cuba and Brazil.

While the Bush administration has been obsessed by its grandiose plans for reshaping the Middle East, a real transformation has been happening in America's "backyard." Left-wing governments have come to power in

Brazil and Argentina, the two biggest countries of South America, and in a number of smaller countries as well. Furthermore, the continent is seeing more than just a comeback in modern dress by the traditional left.

The Indians and part-Indians who form a downtrodden majority in some of the Andean countries are staging their own comeback. They talk mostly in terms of winning elections and rewriting constitutions, but they basically share the view of Antauro Humala, leader of the Movimiento Etnocaceristas (Nationalist Movement) in Peru: "There are four races, black, white, yellow and copper. We are the copper people and I want us to be recognized as a race."

Hugo Chavez's Indian and black ancestry is written all over his face, and this explains much of his popularity with the majority of mixed-race Venezuelans who felt excluded by the dominant white minority in that oil-rich country. Evo Morales is even more clearly a descendant of the Incas who ruled the central and southern Andes before the white conquerors and settlers arrived, and he wants the two-thirds of Bolivians who share his heritage to at last hold power in their own country.

It will get very fraught in Bolivia when Morales starts rewriting the constitution to include the excluded, as he has already sworn to do, but the ethnic solidarity among Bolivian Indians that has helped him into power will also make it very hard for Washington to overthrow him. So long as he avoids the civil war that some of the more extreme members of the white minority may now try to provoke, he will probably manage to serve a full term in office. What he does with that term may change Bolivia beyond recognition.

Morales is already in his second term as president of the "Plurinational State of Bolivia," having been re-elected with a large majority in late 2009. Whether he will "change Bolivia beyond recognition" is hard to say, but it is unlikely that the indigenous peoples, who represent 55 percent of the country's population, will ever again allow politics to become a game strictly for whites and mestizos.

This is largely a local issue. The only other countries in Latin America to have such a large indigenous population (40–45 percent) are Peru and Guatemala. Elsewhere, the dominant population is either of mixed race or descended entirely from newcomers, like Uruguay (almost all European) or Haiti (overwhelmingly African).

January 2, 2006
HAITI: NO EASY WAY OUT

"We are not going to participate [in the election] without Aristide," said Father Gérard Jean-Juste, whom many Haitians see as the natural successor to Jean-Bertrand Aristide, the priest-president who was overthrown by the United States in 2004. "It's going to be like the election in Iraq. It will be futile."

That was last February, and as part of the process of trying to break Aristide's support among the Haitian poor, the "interim government" installed by the U.S., France and Canada jailed Jean-Juste in July, on the implausible charge that he murdered a journalist. But the elections that might finally give the foreign intervention some legitimacy have just been postponed for the *fourth* time.

They said they were cancelling the vote on January 8 because of problems with the new electronic voting system, but the real problem is that they still don't control a lot of the country. In particular, they still don't control Cité Soleil, the seething shantytown that dominates Port-au-Prince, the ramshackle capital where a third of the 8.5 million Haitians live.

In Cité Soleil, Aristide is still considered the president. When United Nations troops in Haiti conducted a pre-dawn raid there last July, it turned into a five-hour firefight. The UN troops killed the five "gang members" they were allegedly after, but local residents saw the dead men as martyrs for Aristide and placed photos of the exiled president on their bodies. They did the same for the twenty other residents of the slum who they claim were killed by the "blue helmets"—and since then UN troops have rarely dared to enter Cité Soleil.

In fact, all foreigners associated with the military intervention in Haiti are potential targets. In the last ten days of December, three Chilean UN soldiers were wounded in the northern town of Plaisance, a Jordanian soldier was killed in Cité Soleil, and a Canadian soldier was shot dead near a checkpoint just outside the slum. On December 30, two employees of the Organization of American States, one Peruvian and the other Guatemalan, were kidnapped while driving near Cité Soleil.

Haiti is responding badly to foreign intervention because it is a real country with a tragic history. Haitians may have no money, little education and few prospects, but they actually know who they are.

They are a whole country descended from people who were kidnapped from Africa, heirs of the greatest slave rebellion in history two centuries ago. They are the survivors of an attempted genocide by Napoleon, whose strategy for reconquering France's richest colony involved exterminating every black over the age of twelve and restocking Haiti with more docile slaves imported from Africa. They are also the victims of the long, sad aftermath of Haiti's victory and independence.

With all the whites dead or fled, the enslaved former peasants from Africa inevitably ended up being dominated in independent Haiti by the so-called "mulattoes," locally born ex-slaves, many of them mixed-race, who spoke good French and understood how business, government and diplomacy worked. The new mulatto elite created an army, recruited mostly from the black majority, whose main job was to keep other blacks under control and, generation after generation, they cooperated with foreigners to exploit their own fellow-countrymen.

Jean-Bertrand Aristide, a Catholic priest nurtured on liberation theology, became the hero of the poor black masses because he promised to end all that. He was elected president by a landslide in Haiti's first free election in 1990, after the reigning dictator, "Baby Doc" Duvalier, was forced into exile, but the unreformed army overthrew him the next year with the warm approval of the elder Bush administration, which saw him as a dangerous Marxist.

The Clinton administration used 24,000 American troops to put Aristide back in power in 1994, but discovered too late that he was a real revolutionary. Aristide disbanded the army on his return, and when the old elite started using gangs of ex-soldiers to defend their privileges, he used similar gangs recruited from amongst the poor to cow them. His policies were incoherent, his style more that of a demagogue than a democrat, and Haiti remained the poorest country in the Americas—but the poor still loved him. Especially after the U.S. overthrew him again.

The Republican-controlled Congress cut off U.S. aid to Aristide's government in 2000, and the younger Bush administration revived U.S. links with the mulatto elite and their ex-military gangs after 2001. In early 2004, gangs of ex-soldiers launched a revolt that advanced to the outskirts of Port-au-Prince—and a U.S. official arrived at the presidential palace with a group of heavily armed Marines to escort Aristide to the airport.

Washington got diplomatic cover by persuading Canada and France to go along with the operation (they both felt the need to give Bush something after refusing to help him invade Iraq), and it got a 7,400-strong "peacekeeping force" out of the United Nations (which also felt the need to look helpful). But CARICOM, the association of Caribbean countries, still refuses to accept the U.S.-backed coup, and most poorer Haitians see the "interim government" as an American puppet and the UN troops as an occupying army.

Aristide, in exile in South Africa, still sees himself as the legitimate president of Haiti, and so do a lot of Haitians. They will not be allowed to vote for him even if the "interim government" does eventually manage to stage an election, but that means that nothing will be settled and the violence will not abate. Aristide may never return, but the old order cannot be restored.

That article was written in 2006, and not much has changed since, apart from the massive destruction of lives and infrastructure caused by the 2009 earthquake. Haiti is effectively run by the foreign military and foreign non-governmental organizations present in the country, to the extent that it could be said to "run" at all.

Aristide is still in exile, and it is to be doubted that things would improve much even if he did return. His intentions were good, but in power, he proved a very bad manager and a deeply divisive character. But at least he has not got religion.

November 8, 2006
NICARAGUAN TIME WARP

"Ortega is a tiger who has not changed his stripes," warned U.S. ambassador Paul Trivelli before the former revolutionary leader won back the presidency of Nicaragua in the election on November 6. Retired U.S. Marine colonel Oliver North, who took the fall for president Ronald Reagan's administration in the Iran/Contra scandal of the 1980s, showed up to warn that Ortega was as bad as Adolf Hitler. And Daniel Ortega just smiled and said: "Jesus Christ is my hero now."

It's déjà vu all over again as American leaders denounce the Communist threat in Nicaragua and leftist Latin American leaders like Cuba's Fidel Castro and Venezuela's Hugo Chavez celebrate the rise of the "pink tide" in their region. Old images of the Sandinista revolutionaries and their "sandalista" foreign admirers—mostly left-wing youth who came to help the revolution by picking coffee beans and drinking lots of cheap rum—fill the media. Seventeen thousand foreign observers and a thousand journalists came to Nicaragua for the elections. But the whole drama was *Hamlet* without the prince.

Daniel Ortega was once a revolutionary leader, but that was a quarter-century ago. Now he is a populist politician as cynical as any of his opponents, and the likelihood that his election will make any difference to Nicaragua's poor is slim.

The Sandinista revolution that overthrew the Somoza family dictatorship in 1979 might possibly have made some difference to the people at the bottom of society—and the bottom is a long way down in Nicaragua—if the revolution had been left alone to get on with the task. But it was the height of the Cold War and the U.S. didn't want "another Cuba," so the Reagan administration armed and financed an army of right-wing exiles, the "contras," to wage a guerrilla war against the Sandinistas.

President John F. Kennedy's similar attempt to strangle the Cuban revolution in its cradle ended in defeat and ignominy at the Bay of Pigs in 1961, but Ronald Reagan had more luck. He got around a congressional ban on U.S. government aid to the contras by turning a blind eye to White House aide Oliver North's fundraising efforts, which involved selling U.S. arms to Iran with a secret markup that was then passed on to the contras. (When North got caught, Reagan escaped impeachment by claiming that he could not remember having been told about it.)

Ortega was elected president in 1984, but the constant attacks of the contras—between thirty thousand and sixty thousand Nicaraguans were killed in Reagan's war—ensured that the Sandinistas never achieved any real transformation. It's questionable whether they would have done so even without that distraction, for the leading Sandinista leaders were mostly well-intentioned middle-class boys radicalized by the brutality of the Somozas, but with little self-discipline and even less by way of a plan. There were kibbutz-style communal farms for peasants on land confiscated from the rich, and literacy classes for all, but the confiscations were almost random, and too often ended up in the pockets of Sandinista leaders. When Ortega left the presidency in 1990, he bought the confiscated million-dollar mansion of a contra supporter, Jaime Morales, for two thousand dollars—and he still lives there.

Ortega never suspected that he would lose the presidency in 1990, so he invited the whole world to come and observe the election in which he and the Sandinistas were booted out by the disillusioned Nicaraguan voters. In three subsequent runs for the presidency, he never got more than 40 percent of the vote, although Sandinistas continued to control many courts, municipalities and unions. His road back to power, however, was paved by "the pact" of 1999, a flagrantly corrupt deal with then-president Arnoldo Aleman.

At the time, Ortega was facing the charge of having raped his step-daughter and Aleman was embezzling huge amounts of money from the government. So the two men agreed to give themselves lifetime memberships to the National Assembly, which gave them both permanent immunity from prosecution. Ortega also got the threshold for a first-round victory in presidential elections lowered from 50 percent to 40 percent—or even to 35 percent, if the front-runner was five percentage points ahead of the next candidate.

"El pacto" didn't save Arnaldo Aleman in the end. An outraged Congress stripped him of his legal immunity and he was given a twenty-year sentence in 2003 for stealing roughly one hundred million dollars from the Nicaraguan people. But a Sandinista-run court allowed him to serve his sentence at home on his ranch due to "health problems"—and the pact has now given Ortega the presidency with less than 40 percent of the vote. (Under the old rules, there would have been a second ballot, in which the 60 percent of Nicaraguans who didn't want Ortega back would have united behind a single candidate, as they did the last three times.)

Ortega is back, but socialism isn't. He now presents himself as a devout Catholic, and recently voted for an absolute ban on abortion. His vice-president is Jaime Morales, the former contra supporter, whose confiscated mansion he still lives in. And all the excited promises by Venezuela's Chavez to support the new Nicaraguan revolution with cheap oil, and all of Washington's threats to cut aid and trade to a neo-Sandinista Nicaragua, are just time-warp fantasies about what used to be. The revolution was cancelled long ago.

Actually, the whole damn thing is a mirage. I'm certainly not longing for the good old days of dedicated revolutionaries willing to kill and die in pursuit of their dreams of a society utterly transformed, but the current crop just aren't serious. Chavez, for example.

November 28, 2006
NO REVOLUTION IN VENEZUELA

"I'm not a populist, I'm a revolutionary," insisted Hugo Chavez at a press conference (that is, a four-hour monologue) in early November. But the Venezuelan president is in fact a populist, not a revolutionary—a populist with a great deal of money to hand out, thanks to the record oil prices of the past two years, so a Chavez victory in the presidential election on December 3 was never in doubt. The real question is what he is really doing with all that money and power.

Chavez rejoices in annoying the U.S. government with revolutionary rhetoric, regularly denouncing President Bush as "the Devil," and when Washington responds with bluster and veiled threats it just fortifies his popularity at home. But so far, after eight years in power, he has attempted nothing that could be called a revolutionary transformation of Venezuelan society. In fact, the rich are just as rich as they ever were.

The lives of many of the poor have certainly gotten better under Chavez—much improved medical care, free literacy classes, subsidized grocery shops selling basic foods at cut prices, cheap start-up loans for businesses—but that is just oil income diverted straight into services for the poor. Even the seventeen thousand Cuban doctors provided by Fidel Castro to run the free clinics that have appeared all over the country fit the pattern, for Chavez pays Cuba for them with ninety thousand barrels per day of free oil.

There is nothing wrong with spending some of your oil income like this, especially if you think the price of oil will remain high for a long time, but it is not revolutionary. Rather, this is exactly how many oil-rich kingdoms with deeply conservative rulers ensure decent lives for their poorer citizens and political stability for themselves.

In Venezuela, it is now the political norm. The main challenger in this election, Zulia state governor Manuel Rosales, tried to outbid Chavez by promising to issue special black debit cards ("Mi Negra") with between $270 and $450 of credit on them to 2.5 million poor families. You can't get much more populist than that.

So what, other than calling the United States bad names, qualifies Chavez as a "revolutionary"? He has gained power by perfectly legitimate democratic elections. He has taken almost nothing new into state ownership except for some—but very few—privately owned sugar plantations. The country still has a free press (95 percent of which opposes Chavez), and the middle class is doing so well that new car sales have tripled in Venezuela since 2004.

On a recent visit to Belarus, the last Communist country in Europe, Chavez expressed his deep admiration for Vladimir Ilyich Lenin, but one suspects that Lenin would not have reciprocated. One even wonders what Chavez's great pal Fidel Castro privately thinks of him. (Actually, I think I can guess: "A well-intentioned man, but an ideologically immature populist with a short attention span.")

Chavez, together with Evo Morales of Bolivia, is the only evidence for the wave of radical leftist regimes that are allegedly sweeping to power in Latin America, and he is not a very convincing piece of evidence. Elsewhere, the alleged standard-bearers of leftist radicalism are mostly burnt-out cases like Daniel Ortega in Nicaragua, once the leader of the Sandinistas but now a Catholic social conservative, or Alan Garcia, the once radical Peruvian politician who was recently re-elected to the presidency on a platform of fiscal responsibility.

The real promoters of change in Latin America are centre-left politicians like Brazil's President Luiz Inácio "Lula" da Silva, Argentina's Nestor Kirchner and Chile's President Michelle Bachelet, but they are social democrats in the classic Western European mould and they mostly avoid anti-American rhetoric. In the end, they will do far more to undermine Washington's stranglehold on Latin America than Chavez, Castro and Company, and far more good for their people, too.

Chavez, like Castro, is good at revolutionary theatre, but he has little of Castro's underlying seriousness. Often he offers nothing but froth and bombast, as when he celebrated the two hundredth anniversary of the Venezuelan flag last March by introducing a new version in which the white horse, rather than going from left to right, goes from right to left. "The white horse is now liberated, free, vigorous, trotting towards the left, representing the return of Bolivar and his dream!" he told the crowd. "Long live the Fatherland!"

Chavez promises to get serious about the revolution after this election, starting with redistributing most of the land to the peasants (currently, 5 percent of landowners hold 80 percent of the country's land), but there is no particular reason to think that he really means it this time. He is a narcissist and an accomplished populist, with oil money to burn. He may even turn out to be Venezuela's Peron, hanging around to blight the country's politics for decades after his own time is up, thanks to a dedicated following among the poor.

But he is not a revolutionary, and the proof lies in his own definition of the word: "It's like love. You have to make love every day in many ways. Sometimes carnally, sometimes with your eyes, sometimes with your voice. A revolution is love."

Right on, Hugo.

Fidel Castro, on the other hand, is certainly a serious man. Not a particularly successful man, unless you count almost fifty years in power as success in itself, and he couldn't even have achieved that without constant (though inadvertent) support from the U.S. government. But nobody ever accused him of being shallow.

March 23, 2007
CUBA: WHAT IF HE COMES BACK?

For anyone who knew the old Soviet Union, a visit to Cuba is always a trip down memory lane. From the ubiquitous revolutionary slogans and the absence of advertising to the cautious shorthand in conversation (stroking the chin means Fidel Castro) and the sour, fatalistic jokes, it is a Communist country of the classic era. But, this time, I kept thinking about an old Soviet joke that had not made it to Cuba (though I have now done my best to get it started there).

A rising young apparatchik in the Soviet Communist Party, starting to enjoy the privileges that come to high officials of the regime, brings his peasant mother to Moscow from her distant, impoverished village and installs her in a grand apartment in the Arbat. His mother, instead of being delighted, just falls silent and looks worried. So he takes her to one of the special Party shops, a wonderland of Western consumer goods unavailable to ordinary Russians, and tells her to buy anything she wants. She buys only a kilo of oranges, and looks even more troubled.

Desperate to please her, he takes her to dinner at the Praha, the grandest and most expensive restaurant in the capital, but by now, there's no denying it. This display of privilege is not impressing her; it's frightening her half to death. So her son finally asks her straight out: Isn't she pleased with what he has accomplished? Isn't she proud of him?

"It's wonderful, darling," she replies. "But what will happen to us if the Communists come back?"

The question in Cuba is: what will happen if Fidel comes back? It has been eight months since he fell gravely ill and handed the president's powers over to his brother Raul, and the "transition" is complete. Fidel's lengthy illness created the ideal circumstances for an orderly handover of power, and by the end of last year the new collective leadership was firmly in charge. Most people were quietly relieved that it was all over.

It felt a bit strange no longer having Fidel on television all the time nagging and exhorting the population, a larger-than-life father figure, but, after forty-seven years of it most people were very tired of being treated like backward children. There was enormous respect for Fidel in Cuba, but there was also enormous weariness of him, combined with a great secret fear of what would happen when he finally went.

Partly it was just fear of the unknown—80 percent of Cuba's population have known no other leader—but it was also fear of chaos, because everybody knew that the United States would use Castro's death to try to change the regime. As Wayne Smith, former head of the U.S. diplomatic mission in Havana, said recently, Cuba has the same effect on the U.S. that the full moon has on a werewolf. Washington doubtless had all sorts of regime-change projects ready to launch as soon as the Old Man died.

Even Cubans who don't like Castro don't want abrupt political collapse and perhaps great violence. Neither do they believe that life would necessarily be better for the people who live in Cuba now if all those Cuban refugees in Miami and all of their money suddenly flooded back. They'd just buy up the island and take over again. So a smooth transition to the next generation of the Communist leadership is better than the chaos that would have followed if Fidel had just died suddenly one day.

The new leadership is collective, with brother Raul out front as chairman of the board. Its members are well known and respected by the Cuban public—people like Felipe Perez Roque, the foreign minister; Ricardo Alarcon, head of the National Assembly; Ricardo Lage, now in charge of energy; and Francisco Soberon, governor of the Central Bank—and they can expect a couple of years' grace to show that they can grow the economy faster and give Cubans more freedom without destroying the welfare state that gives people free education and health care.

Or rather, they did expect a couple of years' grace—but then Fidel started to get better. He is still far from fit, but he is out of bed and on the phone, and the spectre looms that he might decide he is well enough to take over again.

"[Fidel cannot participate in decision-making] the same way he did before because he has to dedicate a good part of his time to recuperating physically," said Ricardo Alarcon last week. "To what extent he will go back to doing things the way he did, the way he is accustomed to, it's up to him." And it really is up to him. Fidel Castro so dominates modern Cuban history, and the reflex respect that all his colleagues feel towards him is so deep, that nobody would dare tell him he can't take back supreme power.

But it would be a disaster for the regime. Many Cubans revere Fidel, but few want him back in power, jerking them around again with his constant, arbitrary changes of policy. Moreover, the odds are very much against another smooth transition of power sometime in the future, when death finally does take Fidel. Miracles happen, but not with any regularity.

26.

MISCELLANY II

It's not having a billion speakers that decides which of the planet's many tongues becomes the "world language." What decides the issue is which language people choose when they are trying to communicate and neither speaks the other's language.

October 25, 2004
A (MUCH RESENTED) WORLD LANGUAGE

Predictably, the French were furious. A commission looking into the future of the French education system recommended last week that English, which it called "the language of international communication," be made compulsory in French schools, and the usual suspects erupted in outrage. It would be the final surrender, an acceptance that English had replaced French as the international language, and they were damned if they would let it happen.

Most of the world thought that this battle ended about fifty years ago, shortly after the Second World War, when America emerged as the new superpower and its language became the normal medium of communication in international business and diplomacy. English had been gaining ground on French since Britain replaced France as the reigning superpower over a century before, and the rise of the United States settled the issue. Except in France.

It's hard losing an advantage that your country has enjoyed for a long time, but the French went into denial about it. Some 97 percent of students in France study English at some point, but there is no official pressure to learn it well, and the French lag far behind their German, Italian and Spanish neighbours in their command of English. This impairs France's international competitiveness and the commission was merely suggesting a remedy.

Foolish commission. They should have known. Politicians and intellectuals queued up in the French media to denounce them as defeatist. The dominance of English is merely a transitory thing, they argued, and should not be pandered to. Typical was Jacques Myard, a member of parliament for the ruling Union pour un Mouvement Populaire (Union for a Popular Movement Party) who announced: "English is the most spoken language today, but that won't last." Arabic, Chinese, Japanese and Spanish would become increasingly important, he predicted, and the position of English would erode.

It's obvious why they like this prophecy so much. They all hope that the rise of these other languages and the relative decline in the importance of English will lead to a polyglot world where French would at least regain a position as one of the equal leading languages. (French has only seventy-five million native speakers in the developed world, but there is a huge additional reservoir of potential French-speakers in the former French colonies in Africa.)

Is this just wishful thinking, or is it really the shape of the future? Size matters: no language has ever risen to become the regional or global lingua franca without having a lot of speakers and a powerful state behind it. But once a language has achieved that dominant position, it is such a useful device for international intercourse that it doesn't necessarily fall into disuse when the power of its original speakers declines. A thousand years after the Roman Empire in the West was overrun by barbàrians, educated Europeans still used Latin to communicate with one another.

The United States does not face the fate of Rome, but it will bulk much less large in the world in fifty years' time than it does at the moment: other economies are growing much faster, especially in Asia. If there is more business to be done, many more foreigners will take the trouble to learn Chinese, Arabic, and Spanish—and Portuguese, Russian and Indonesian—than do so at the moment. But nobody is going to learn them *all*: everybody will still need a common language, and it will still be English.

It helps that India, which is destined to be the most populous nation of all, already uses English as a lingua franca within its own borders to cope with the multiplicity of other official languages in the country. By 2050, when China will be the largest economy, the U.S. second and India third, two of the three most powerful countries in the world will be effectively English-speaking for international purposes. But this merely reinforces a phenomenon that has already gained huge momentum.

Over the past twenty years, the switch to English as the first foreign language taught in schools has accelerated worldwide. In the formerly Communist countries of Eastern Europe it has replaced Russian and, in Russia itself, English is now obligatory in the schools. More recently it has been made compulsory in Chinese schools: it is now practically impossible to gain admission to a Chinese university without a decent command of English.

To the intense irritation of the French, English has even become the de facto working language of the European Union, although only two out of twenty-five member states (Britain and Ireland) are mainly English-speaking. An avalanche has occurred, and avalanches are irreversible.

A globalized world needs a common second language so that Peruvians can talk to Chinese and Hungarians can communicate with Ethiopians. It is an accident of history that the dominant global power was English-speaking at the time when this need became apparent, but the investment that hundreds of millions of people have already made in learning the language guarantees that this accident will have permanent results.

But it does make the French very cross.

The world capital of conspiracy theories used to be the Middle East, and the region was certainly awash in such theories after 9/11. Half a decade later, however, the United States itself was seething with equally bizarre theories, thanks to dedicated amateurs distributing their work on the Internet.

Dealing with questions from sincere people who were taken in by these theories took up a lot of my time, mostly because such theories were only obviously nutty if you knew how the intelligence world actually worked. Eventually I wrote this column in response.

March 8, 2007
LOOSE SCREWS

The 9/11 conspiracy theory is back, in a much more virulent form, and normally sane people are being taken in by it: I am getting half a dozen earnest emails every day telling me I must see a film called *Loose Change*. It has been around in various versions for almost two years, but it now seems to be gathering converts faster than ever.

Well, I have seen it, and I concede that it is a much slicker, more professional product than other 9/11 conspiracy films, and therefore more seductive. But the argument is pure paranoid fantasy, and it is rotting people's brains.

There have always been two kinds of 9/11 conspiracy theories. The lesser version held that the Bush administration had advance intelligence of al-Qaeda's plans but chose to ignore the warning because the attacks suited its purposes. The greater version insisted that there was no al-Qaeda involvement at all and that the attacks were carried out by the U.S. government itself, perhaps with Israeli help.

Until recently, the greater conspiracy theory was largely confined to the Arab world, where many people are in complete denial about any Arab involvement in the atrocity. Few Americans took that version seriously, but many wondered whether the intelligence lapses had really been accidental. If you believe that they weren't, then you have bought into the lesser conspiracy theory.

Even this more modest conspiracy theory, in which the U.S. government learned of Osama bin Laden's intentions but decided not to stop him, requires the complicity of some very senior people. If the information got into the system, then the people who would have known about it included the heads of the Central Intelligence Agency and the Federal Bureau of Investigation (George Tenet and Louis Freeh), the national security adviser (Condoleezza Rice), the secretaries of defence and state (Don Rumsfeld and Colin Powell), plus Vice-President Cheney and perhaps President Bush.

Getting away with it also would have required the permanent silence (or silencing) of at least a dozen lower- and mid-level intelligence analysts in Washington. Intelligence like this only gains credibility within the system when there are multiple sources confirming it, so the people who saw the raw intelligence, collated it and passed it up the line would know that the senior people had received it. And the senior people would know that they knew.

I don't believe in the lesser conspiracy theory because I don't think that Tenet, Rice, Powell and others would have deliberately allowed thousands of Americans to be killed like that. I don't believe even Dick Cheney would have done that. And I note that there has been no inexplicable wave of sudden deaths among junior intelligence analysts in Washington.

I do believe, however, that 9/11 served the purposes of the neo-conservatives. They were already pressing to attack Iraq as part of a larger plan, dating back to the late 1990s, to relaunch *Pax Americana* and re-establish American hegemony in the twenty-first century world. I agree that they were adroit in seizing on 9/11 as a way of enlisting popular support for their project. But that's all.

As for the greater conspiracy theory, of which the movie *Loose Change* is the most prominent manifestation, it is just plain loony. Yet more and more people are falling for it in the West, where it was once the exclusive domain of people with counter-rotating eyeballs and poor personal hygiene. You cannot overstate the impact of a well-made film.

Loose Change confidently asserts that the twin towers were brought down by carefully placed demolition charges, not by the fires ignited by the planes that hit them; that the Pentagon was struck by a cruise missile and not by a plane at all; and that the fourth "hijacked" plane, Flight 93, did not crash in a field in Pennsylvania but landed at Cleveland airport, where the passengers were taken into a National Aeronatics and Space Administration building and never seen again.

What about all the calls that the passengers on Flight 93 made on their phones? Their voices were cloned by the Los Alamos laboratories and the calls to their relatives were faked. The FBI was in on it, the CIA was in on it, the U.S. Air Force was in on it (except, of course, those personnel who were killed at the Pentagon), and the North American Aerospace Defense Command was in on it (but they kept the Canadians in the organization out of the loop).

The security companies guarding the World Trade Center were in on it, New York Mayor Rudy Giuliani was in on it, the Federal Aviation Administration was in on it, NASA was in on it, and the Pentagon was in on it. At least ten thousand people were in on it. They had to be, or it couldn't have worked. And, more than five years later, not one of them has talked.

Nobody has got drunk and spilled their guts. Nobody has told their spouse, who then blabbed. Not one of these ten thousand guilty people has yielded to the temptation for instant fame and great wealth if only they blow the whistle on the greatest conspiracy in history. Even the Mafia code of silence is nothing compared to this.

In normal times you wouldn't waste breath arguing with people who fall for this kind of rubbish, but the makers of *Loose Change* claim that their film has already been seen by more than one hundred million people, and looking at my incoming email I believe them. This is a real problem, because by linking their fantasies about 9/11 to the Bush administration's deliberate deception of the American people in order to gain support for the invasion of Iraq, the filmmakers bring discredit on the truth and the nonsense alike.

You almost wonder if they are secretly working for the Bush administration.

I didn't put the next piece in the China section of this book because it's not really about China, and I didn't put it in the "colonies" section because there isn't one: almost all the world's other colonies already have their independence. So it ends up in "Miscellany," but that doesn't mean that it's a minor issue.

All the world's other colonial empires have had to let their colonies go, including the Soviet empire. Can the Chinese empire hold on to its colonies? That remains to be seen.

July 14, 2009
CHINA: TROUBLE IN THE COLONIES

"The incidents in China are, simply put, a genocide. There's no point in interpreting this otherwise," said Turkey's Prime Minister Recep Tayyib Erdoğan last Friday. He was talking about the deaths of at least 184 people in the recent street violence in Xinjiang (also spelled Sinkiang), the huge province that occupies the northwestern corner of China.

A majority of Xinjiang's people are Uighurs. They are Muslims who speak a language closely related to Turkish, so Erdoğan's comments were bound to appeal to his audience in Turkey. The Chinese government, predictably, condemned his charges as "irresponsible and groundless." The Chinese government was right—but also terribly wrong.

It wasn't a genocide. The deaths of 184 people, for whatever reason, do not constitute a genocide. Moreover, as Erdoğan was claiming that there had been a genocide against the Uighurs, but three-quarters of the people killed in the riots were Han Chinese. "Genocide" is a word that should only be used very precisely, and Erdoğan owes Beijing an apology.

There is no doubt that this violence started as an Uighur attack on Chinese immigrants. However, Beijing owes the Uighurs more than just an apology, for it is Chinese policy that drove them to such desperate measures.

The Chinese authorities genuinely believe that the development they have brought to Xinjiang has been for the Uighurs' own good, even if it has also brought huge numbers of Han Chinese immigrants to the province. But they are certainly not unhappy to see this frontier province, which was 90 percent Uighur and Muslim sixty years ago, become a place where most of the people are instinctively loyal Han Chinese.

More importantly, they lack the cultural imagination to see that this process will be profoundly alienating for the Uighurs. It may sound preposterous, but most of the men who rule China simply could not come up with an answer to the question "Why don't they want to be Chinese?" So if there are anti-Chinese riots in Xinjiang, it must be "outside agitators stirring up our Uighurs."

That is how Beijing explained the riots to itself and to the nation. As Xinjiang's Communist governor, Nur Bekri, said in a televised address: exiled Uighur leader Rebiya Kadeer "had phone conversations with people in China on July 5 in order to incite [the violence]." Beijing explained the even bloodier anti-Chinese riots in Tibet in March of last year in exactly the same way, except that that time the outside agitator was the Dalai Lama.

What's more, most Chinese believe it. They have been taught that Xinjiang and Tibet have been an integral part of their country since time immemorial. They also believe the Uighurs and Tibetans who live in those places are (or should be) profoundly grateful for the development and prosperity that have come to their provinces as a result of their membership in the Chinese nation.

The gulf of incomprehension is reminiscent of the gap between the Russian and non-Russian inhabitants of the former Soviet Union before it collapsed in 1991. Almost all Russians believed that the non-Russians were (or should be) grateful for all that had been done for them, and even resented the fact that they got more investment per capita than the Russians themselves. As for the non-Russians, they took their independence as soon as they could.

The truth is that the Chinese empire first took effective control of Tibet and Xinjiang in the same period when the Russian empire was conquering the other Central Asian countries. Whatever vague claims to "suzerainty" Beijing can dredge up from the more distant past, they do not convince the Uighurs and the Tibetans themselves, who would cut loose from China instantly if they got the chance.

It's called decolonization, and China is the last holdout. The only way it can ensure a different final outcome to that of the other empires is to swamp the local people with Han Chinese immigrants—and that, oddly enough, is the principal result of its "development" policies. The development creates an economy that the local people are not qualified to work in, and Chinese immigrants come in to fill those jobs instead.

The Tibetan Autonomous Region still has a large Tibetan majority, but in Xinjiang the Uighurs are already down to 45 percent of the population, while the Han Chinese are up to 40 percent. The Uighurs feel that their country is disappearing in front of their eyes, and they are right. So they attack innocent Chinese immigrants, which is shameful but all too understandable. Chinese mobs attack them back, which is equally shameful and equally understandable.

It is already ugly, and it's probably going to get a good deal uglier. The repression needed to hold down Xinjiang and Tibet may lead to increased repression in China in general, and it will almost certainly lead to more violence in the colonies.

And finally . . . a piece about the left-right conflict.

August 28, 2009
LEFTIST TRIUMPH IN SAMOA

At last the tide has turned. After centuries of huge advances by the rightists, those who drive on the left finally have a victory to celebrate. On September 7, Samoa will stop driving on the right and start driving on the left. Naturally, those who oppose the change are predicting disaster.

"So we just wake up one morning and pull out of our driveways onto the other side of the road, do we?" says Tole'afoa Solomona Toa'iloa, who heads People Against Switching Sides. "Cars are going to crash, people are going to die, not to mention the huge expense to our small country."

But Prime Minister Tuila'epa Aiono Sailele Malielegaoi is not impressed: "All this talk about accidents is just stupid. The 7th and the 8th are holidays to help people get used to it, and after that they'll be driving more carefully than ever because it will be so different." All the nearby islands, except American Samoa, drive left, he points out, and it's cheaper to import cars from Australia, New Zealand and Japan (which drive on the left) than from the United States.

It's much ado about nothing; I switch back and forth several dozen times a year. My work takes me to both sides of the road, and my family connections divide right down the middle: Canada right, Britain left, France right, South Africa left, and Argentina both (left until 1946, right since then). If the steering wheel is on the left side of the car, you drive on the right side of the road, and vice versa. A monkey could do it.

Nevertheless, this is a big deal: the first time any country has switched sides since Burma swung right in 1970 (which made very little sense, since most of the countries around it drive on the left, but General Ne Win's soothsayer told him to do it). And *nobody* has switched from right to left in living memory.

The rightists won because the United States drives on the right, and the year of victory was 1946. That was when the U.S. embassy in Beijing threw a party to celebrate the Nationalist Chinese government's decision that China would drive on the right. (Previously most of northern China had driven right, while southern China drove left.) In the same year, the project for a Pan-American Highway persuaded the last left-driving holdouts among the Latin American countries to switch.

Only one-third of the world's 6.7 billion people live in countries that still drive left. That is not likely to change much now, for once you start building high-speed, controlled-access highways, all the concrete you have poured locks you into your existing choice.

How did we end up split like this? There is plenty of historical evidence for both sides. Deeply rutted tracks on one side of an old road from a quarry used in Roman times in England, and shallower ruts on the other side, support the hypothesis that the Romans drove on the left, for example—but the evidence from other Roman roads in Turkey suggests the opposite.

The real answer, probably, is that there was so little long-distance road traffic that you didn't need uniformity. Some bits of the empire drove left and other parts right, and nobody cared.

Indeed, the same situation still pertained in nineteenth-century Europe. Both Spain and Italy, for example, had a patchwork quilt of local rules. However, most places that had been conquered by Napoleon drove right, while those that had escaped French occupation mostly drove left (Britain, Russia, Portugal, Sweden, the Austro-Hungarian Empire).

It's all over in Europe now. The Bolsheviks took Russia to the right after the First World War (on the roads, at least). Mussolini made all the Italians drive right, and the Spaniards and Portuguese changed over in the 1920s. Hitler forced the remnants of the Austro-Hungarian Empire (Austria, Hungary, Yugoslavia, Czechoslovakia) to drive right in the late 1930s, and Sweden and Iceland finally switched in the late 1960s.

And then there's Canada. Part of it (Quebec west to the Rockies) used to belong to the French Empire, while the rest (the Maritimes in the east and British Columbia in the west) was British more or less from the start. So the central provinces drove on the right, while the extremities drove on the left.

The latter switched to the right in 1922–23—but my own native country, Newfoundland, only joined Canada in 1949, so it didn't switch from left to right until 1947. There is a story about how they eased the transition there, however, that may be of assistance to those anxious Samoans.

Newfoundlanders, in the Child's Garden of Canadian Stereotypes, fill the same role as the Laz in Turkey, Karelians in Finland, or Tasmanians in Australia. There are hundreds of "Newfie" jokes about how stunned we are. We laugh and go along with the joke, and then later, at night, we sneak into their homes and strangle their offspring.

The story is that the Newfoundland government was worried about how its people would handle the switch from left to right, until one minister solved the problem. "Let them get used to it a bit at a time," he said. "The people whose names start with A to D can switch on Monday, E to K will switch on Tuesday . . ."

27.

SOUTHEAST ASIA

Beginning with "People Power" in the Philippines in 1986, Southeast Asia is where the modern wave of non-violent democratic revolutions started. It's also (with the possible exception of South Africa) the part of the newly democratic world where the gulf between the rich and poor is greatest. As such, it has become a huge, uncontrolled experiment in whether democracy can enable the poor to change their fate.

September 22, 2004
NEW DEMOCRACIES

Vote for "the prettiest candidate," said Indonesia's President Megawati Sukarnoputri as the presidential election campaign got underway, and the voters took her at her word. On September 20, they voted overwhelmingly for her former chief security minister, Susilo Bambang Yudhoyono.

He's no beauty, but neither is she—and at least he does sing very nicely. None of his campaign rallies was complete without a rendition of "Rainbow in Your Eyes" by the former four-star general and his wife, Kristiani Herrawati. The voters loved it.

Mr. Yudhoyono is actually quite a serious man who was seen by his army colleagues as efficient and incorruptible, but even his closest adviser, Muhammad Lutfi, admitted: "This election is not about policy. This is a popularity contest so we sell [him] like a brand image." It's enough to give you doubts about the future of Indonesia's new democracy.

It's not just Indonesia. There has been an avalanche of new democracies in the past twenty years, and there are doubts about the quality of democracy in a lot of them. At the same time, many people in these countries have become nostalgic for the sheer stability of the old regimes: in a poll conducted by the Asia Foundation last December, 53 percent of Indonesians agreed with the statement "We need a strong leader like Suharto [the former dictator, overthrown in 1998] . . . even if it reduces rights and freedoms."

The new democracies of the world are full of people who are not too sure that it was all such a good idea: East Germans who miss the threadbare economic security they had in their part of the old divided Germany; Filipinos who elected an ignorant and corrupt former movie star as president because he played heroic roles in movies; South Africans who blame the huge crime rate on their post-apartheid freedoms.

The United Nations Development Programme has calculated that eighty-one countries moved towards democracy in the 1980s and 1990s. By 2002, 140 of the world's almost 200 independent nations had held multi-party elections. The only really big countries where elections either don't happen at all or have no discernible impact on who runs the place are China and Pakistan.

It has been an astonishingly rapid transformation—which may explain why people seem so ungrateful for their liberation. The voters are inexperienced, so demagoguery works better than in the older democracies (not that it doesn't often work in those countries, too). There is also the disillusionment that comes when people realize that changing the political system does not solve all the country's problems. It just changes our way of dealing with them, hopefully for the better, but it's bound to take some time for the benefits to become apparent.

When a society opts for democracy it is betting that the collective

wisdom of the majority is superior to the judgment of any single powerful individual or group. This is almost certainly true in the long run but
can be quite wrong in the short run. On the other hand, the kind of
individuals who rise to power in tyrannies are even more prone to catastrophic errors of judgment.

Take Indonesia. The thirty-year Suharto dictatorship, which covered
most of the country's independent history, delivered economic growth
but siphoned off most of the profits for the benefit of a narrow elite of
the dictator's cronies and collaborators. The three presidents who have
governed the country in the six years since Suharto's overthrow—chosen
by a parliament where interest groups that were powerful under the old
regime still had much influence—were disastrous in different ways, but
all were incapable of addressing Indonesia's problems effectively.

By contrast, in the first election where Indonesians were allowed to vote
for a president directly, they have rejected the do-nothing incumbent,
Megawati Sukarnoputri, the not-very-bright daughter of independence
hero Sukarno, and the man who was tipped as her successor, indicted war
criminal General Wiranto, in favour of the plodding sincerity, dogged honesty and fine singing voice of Susilo Bambang Yudhoyono. The popular
wisdom may not be all that sophisticated, but it probably isn't wrong, either.

*The Indonesian voters got it more or less right. The human-rights situa-
tion in the country improved, the long separatist war in Aceh ended,
corruption dropped, and the economy grew at 5 percent or better in each
year of Yudhoyono's first term. He was re-elected with almost two-thirds
of the votes in 2009.*

*Whereas in Burma, voting can be a life-threatening activity. Any kind
of dissent is.*

October 2, 2007
BURMESE TRAGEDY

Empty monasteries, severed telecommunications, and a sullen, beaten
silence that seems to envelop the whole country. It doesn't just feel like
a defeat for the Burmese people; it feels like the end of an era. It was an
era that began at the other end of Southeast Asia two decades ago, with

the non-violent overthrow of the Marcos regime in the Philippines by "people power" in 1986.

For a while, non-violent revolutions seemed almost unstoppable: Bangladesh, South Korea, Thailand and Indonesia all followed the Filipino example, overthrowing military rule and moving to open democratic systems after decades of oppression. China itself almost managed to follow their example in the Tiananmen episode of 1989, and then the "contagion" spread to Europe.

The Berlin Wall came down in late 1989, the Communist regimes of Eastern Europe melted away with scarcely a shot fired, and by 1991, the Soviet Union itself had gone into liquidation. It was the threat of similar non-violent action that finally brought the apartheid regime in South Africa to the negotiating table in the early 1990s. Right into the twenty-first century the trend continued, with undemocratic regimes being forced to yield power by unarmed protestors from Serbia to Georgia to Nepal. But there were always the exceptions, and exceptions are always instructive.

The greatest exception, in the early days, was Burma itself. Entranced by the seeming ease with which their Southeast Asian neighbours were dumping their dictators and emboldened by the transfer of power from General Ne Win (who had been in power for a quarter-century) to a junta of lesser generals, Burmese civilians ventured out on the streets in 1988 to demand democracy. In Rangoon the army slaughtered three thousand of them, whisking the bodies away to be burned, and the protestors went very quiet.

Non-violent protest is a powerful tactic, but no tactic works in every contingency. To be specific, non-violent protest does not work against a regime that is willing to commit a massacre, and can persuade its troops to carry out its orders.

The emotion that non-violence works on is shame. Most people feel that murdering large numbers of their fellow citizens on the streets in broad daylight is a shameful action, and even if the privileged people at the top of a regime can smother that emotion, their soldiers, who have to do the actual killing, may not be able to.

If you cannot be sure your soldiers will obey that order, then it is wise not to give it, since you present them with a dilemma that can only be resolved by turning their weapons against the regime. Better to negotiate a peaceful withdrawal from power. Non-violent revolution often succeeds, but not if the army is isolated from the public.

The Burmese army is profoundly isolated from the civilian public. Its officers, over the decades of military rule, have become a separate, self-recruiting caste that enjoys great privileges, and its soldiers are country boys—not one in a hundred is from Rangoon or Mandalay. The regime has even moved the capital from Rangoon to the preposterous jungle "city" of Naypyidaw, a newly built place whose only business is government, in order to increase the social isolation of its soldiers and servants.

So, after nineteen years, when the protestors came out on the streets again in the bigger Burmese cities, led this time by monks whose prestige made many believe the army would not dare touch them, the regime simply started killing again. The death toll this time was probably no more than a tenth of that in 1988, for people got the message very quickly: nobody who defies the regime is safe. Not even monks.

The Burmese are now pinning their hopes on foreign intervention, but that is never going to happen. It never played a decisive role in the non-violent revolutions that succeeded, either. Sooner or later, the extreme corruption of the army's senior officers will destroy its discipline, but meanwhile it is probably more years of tyranny for Burma, with only Aung San Suu Kyi, the heroic symbol of Burmese democracy, who lives under semi-permanent house arrest, to bear witness against it.

It is not the end of an era, however. In other places, against other repressive regimes, non-violence still has a reasonable chance of succeeding. It has just never worked in Burma.

The litmus test for Southeast Asian democracy is Thailand because matters have gone much further there. The poor have actually mobilized politically, and the old and new elites are fighting hard to safeguard their privileges. The army has been back on the streets, and, as this book goes to press, the final outcome of the battle between the "red shirts" and the "yellow shirts" is still unclear. It may remain so for years.

April 15, 2009
CLASS WAR IN THAILAND

Thailand's Prime Minister Abhisit Vejjajiva was humiliated last week when red-shirted protesters overran the summit of Asian leaders that he was hosting and forced him to evacuate them by helicopter, but now he is back in control. The "reds" have been driven off the streets of Bangkok by the army, and the "yellows," who fought them last year, have not come out in force either. For the moment, peace has been restored.

The whole situation seems as arcane as the street battles of the blues and greens in Byzantium fifteen centuries ago. It certainly doesn't sound like modern politics, and indeed, it is not like politics in mature democratic countries like France or India. But it is (apart from the coloured T-shirts) a great deal like nineteenth-century European politics.

Thailand's democracy is less than twenty years old, and it was the growing Thai middle class that made it happen—just as it was the middle class in European countries that made the revolutions happen there in the 1800s. In both cases, they were doing it for themselves, not for the poor.

As the history of a hundred ancient empires demonstrates, the poor and the downtrodden never launched a democratic revolution. It didn't occur to them to demand their democratic rights, because they lacked the education and the perspective even to think in those terms. Democracy only got onto the political agenda when a large and literate middle class appeared.

The European middle class mainly wanted political equality, as they were already doing quite nicely economically. But, no sooner had they won it than they discovered to their horror that the poor were also infected by this idea of equality. At that point, the newly empowered middle class faced a stark choice: either make a political deal that brought the poor into the system economically, or live forever in fear of the day when angry mobs broke into their homes. In Europe, it took most of the nineteenth century and a good deal of the twentieth to come up with a deal that worked, but in the end, various versions of the welfare state did the trick.

Most of the former colonial countries inherited the democratic system. They didn't all make it work but at least they knew the rules, including how to get the poor to accept the system. Whereas Thailand, almost uniquely in southern Asia, was never colonized.

In 1992, middle-class Thais, overwhelmingly Bangkok-based, drove the army from power in a non-violent revolution that brought genuine democracy to the country for the first time. It was an exhilarating and long overdue event, but the Thai middle class really didn't anticipate what was going to come next.

Give a country a democratic system, and pretty soon the poor will figure out how to use it for their own purposes. Their leader and voice in Thailand was Thaksin Shinawatra, an ex-cop from humble origins who became a telecommunications billionaire. He was a demagogue who cut as many corners in politics as he did in business, but he genuinely represented the poor, both urban and rural, and they voted for him in the millions.

Thaksin won power in 2001, and began pushing through measures to give the poor access to cheap loans, medical care and other things that the middle class took for granted. The poor loved him for it, but the urban middle class was appalled: they had lost control of politics, and their money was being spent on ignorant peasants.

Thaksin was overthrown by the army in 2006 and his party was banned. Then, as soon as democracy was restored, the poor voted for his allies and the new party they had formed. So the new government also had to be overthrown, a task that was accomplished last year by the yellow-shirted supporters of the People's Alliance for Democracy.

In many ways, the PAD is typical of conservative parties seeking to rein in the demands of the poor. It is backed by the army, the senior bureaucracy and the upper middle class, but its street fighters are drawn mostly from the aspiring lower middle class. However, this being Thailand, there is one big difference: the PAD actually wants to take the vote away from the poor.

In the parts of the world that know democracy better, the notion that the demands of the poor can be dealt with simply by disenfranchising them seems crazy—and we have the history to prove it. At the moment, however, it clearly doesn't sound like a crazy idea to many middle-class Thais.

Really bad outcomes to this impasse are possible, including a return to permanent military rule, although that would now require repression on an almost Burmese-like scale. But the likelier outcome is that the Thais will find some way out of their current blind alley and back to democratic normality.

The whole history of the past two centuries proves that you have to compromise with the poor. You don't have to give them *all* your wealth, but if you want to live in a stable and prosperous country, then you do have to share it.

28.

ISRAEL-PALESTINE II

"Turning point" is generally the wrong phrase to apply to events in the Israeli-Palestinian relationship, because it implies a change of direction. When things go from bad to worse, along an entirely predictable trajectory, it is not a turning point. Perhaps it would be more accurate to describe what happened in June 2007 as a milestone.

A milestone on the road to where? Don't ask. You know.

June 14, 2007
THE ISLAMIC REPUBLIC OF GAZA

"I like this violence . . . It means other Palestinians are resisting Hamas," said a U.S. official some months ago to Alvaro de Soto, the United Nations envoy to the Middle East, according to de Soto's confidential "End of Mission Report," leaked to the *Guardian* last week.

This certainly fits with what we know about U.S. policy at the time.

The policy was to block international cooperation with the shaky Palestinian coalition government, including both Hamas and Fatah elements, that had been cobbled together after a year's delay, and to build up Fatah's militia for a showdown with Hamas. That showdown came last week in the Gaza Strip, and Hamas won it.

In less than a week, at the cost of about a hundred lives, Hamas eliminated almost all of Fatah's strongholds in the Strip, and now the question is: were the United States and Israel being naïve boycotting Hamas and backing Fatah, or was their real goal all along to split the Palestinians?

In a sense this confrontation has been coming for years. The Gaza Strip is an overcrowded open-air prison where living conditions are vastly worse than in the West Bank, so it has always been a breeding ground for extremism. Nevertheless, the change is dramatic: where yesterday there was one "Palestinian Authority" seeking to build an independent state in the West Bank and the Gaza Strip—the bits of former Palestine that were not incorporated into Israel after the war of 1948—there are now two rival authorities with very different aims.

The West Bank is still run by the familiar institutions built up over forty years by the late Yasser Arafat: Fatah, the Palestine Liberation Organization, and the Palestinian Authority, the proto-government of what the Oslo Accords of 1993 envisaged as an independent Palestinian state. The PA, currently led by President Mahmoud Abbas, remains committed to a "two-state" solution in which Israel and a Palestinian state share former Palestine.

The Gaza Strip, however, is now controlled by Hamas, an Islamist organization that rejects peace with Israel. Its vision is a single Palestine reunited under Islamic law, a country in which Palestinian Arabs would be the clear majority. (There are currently 5.5 million Jews and 4.5 million Arabs in the lands under Israeli control, but millions more Palestinian refugees live in the surrounding countries.) Hamas says that native-born Jews would be welcome to stay, but the state of Israel would have to vanish.

The state of Israel is not going to vanish, of course—it has by far the strongest army in the region, the unquestioning support of the United States and lots of nuclear weapons—but this marks the definitive end of the peace process that began fourteen years ago. The Israelis blame the Palestinians, and the Palestinians blame the Israelis (and they are both right), but there will be many more years of violence before there is any return to serious peace talks.

The last exit before this disaster was probably passed seventeen months ago, when the Palestinians elected a Hamas government in a fair and free election, and Israel and the West refused to have anything to do with it: the Palestinians had made the wrong choice and they would just have to be bludgeoned into changing their minds. What followed was a political boycott, a financial blockade and, in the case of the Gaza Strip, an almost complete physical blockade as well.

The aim was to push Fatah and the Palestinian Authority into defying the election results and taking Hamas on in an open civil war. What the boycott and blockades actually did, of course, was to further impoverish and radicalize the population, especially in the Gaza Strip. The civil war duly arrived, in the end, but in the Gaza Strip, Hamas won it. It never had any chance of winning in the West Bank, where there was little fighting and Fatah remains in control, and now there are two Palestinian proto-states where there used to be one.

Back to the original question: were the U.S. and Israel being naïve and clumsy in trying to push the Palestinians into a civil war that was bound to end with Fatah controlling the West Bank and Hamas ruling the Gaza Strip—or were they being devious and very clever? If the goal was to take the spotlight off the continuing expansion of Jewish settlements in the West Bank, to free Israel from pressure to negotiate with the Palestinians, and to destroy the prospect of a viable Palestinian state for at least a generation, this much has certainly been achieved.

The only losers are the ten million people, Jewish, Muslim and Christian, who live between the Jordan River and the Mediterranean sea. They have been condemned to another generation of war.

What always puzzled me was the inability of most people in the English-language media to call a spade a spade. It was like the Monty Python pet-shop sketch, with the customer pointing out that the parrot was dead and the pet-shop owner insisting that it was just "pining for the fjords" or "shagged out after a long squawk."

The peace process was utterly, unarguably, irreversibly dead, and yet the Western media went along with the pretense that it was still alive. The U.S. media were the worst, slavishly printing every State Department press release as if it were actual news or independent analysis. (The Canadian media weren't much better.)

October 16, 2007
THE CORPSE TWITCHES: THE MIDDLE EAST "PEACE PROCESS"

"We are at the beginning of a process," said U.S. Secretary of State Condoleezza Rice after her four-day tour of the countries closely involved in the Arab-Israeli confrontation. But the peace process really began with the Oslo Accords in 1993, and it died when Ariel Sharon became prime minister of Israel in 2001. The last nail was hammered into its coffin with the takeover of the Gaza Strip this year by Hamas, which flatly rejects the idea of Palestinian and Israeli states living side by side. Dr. Rice can make the corpse twitch, but she cannot make it walk.

Faced with almost universal cynicism about her proposed Middle East peace conference in the state of Maryland next month, she protested: "I have better things to do than invite people to Annapolis for a photo-op." Nevertheless, the suspicion lingers that this conference is just part of a last-minute legacy project to salvage President George W. Bush's reputation.

Secretary Rice insisted that this is "the most serious effort to end the conflict in many, many years"—but the wasted years are those of Bush's presidency. The last serious American attempt of this sort was at Camp David seven years ago, in the last year of Bill Clinton's presidency. That was another rushed legacy project, but it came a lot closer to success than this one will.

The "two-state solution," the basis of the Oslo deal, assumed that Israelis would settle for the four-fifths of former Palestine that was already within their legal borders, and that Palestinians would settle for the remaining fifth. It was not unrealistic at the time, for Palestinians were very tired after a quarter-century of military occupation and most Israelis had concluded that they could not afford to hold down the occupied territories forever. But it never quite happened.

The Israelis could not agree among themselves on how much of the territories to give back. The Palestinians felt that they had made their final concession by recognizing Israel within its pre-1967 borders, and

wanted all the conquered land back. On both sides there were also rejec-
tionists: Israelis who insisted on Israel's inalienable right to all of the
occupied territories, and Palestinians who refused to accept the legitimacy of Israel. Time passed, patience eroded and hope died.

There is another reason, beyond sheer fatigue and disillusionment,
for the collapse of the peace process. The Islamist parties and groups
that are the main opposition to the existing regimes in most Arab countries have always condemned the idea of making peace with Israel. Their
organizations are illegal in many countries, but their views on Israel are
very popular.

In some thirty years of trying, the Islamists have not managed to win
power in any Arab country, either through elections (where that is theoretically possible) or by revolution, but now they have the wind in their
sails. The exploits of the Islamists who have come to dominate the anti-
American insurgency in Iraq, and more recently Hezbollah's success in
withstanding the Israeli assault in southern Lebanon last year, have made
them the heroes of the Arab street, and given Islamist parties everywhere
a better chance of gaining power.

And now, even those Israelis who genuinely want a deal are increasingly reluctant to hand over territory in return for peace since they cannot
be sure that the regimes they are dealing with will stay in power. What if
Israel finally gave the Golan Heights back to Syria in return for a peace
treaty, and then, a few years later, President Assad was overthrown by
Islamists who repudiated the treaty and re-militarized the Golan?

Even existing peace treaties are at risk. What if the Islamists were to
come to power in Egypt one day? In the 2005 election, the semi-legal
Muslim Brotherhood (it can run candidates in elections, but only as
"independents") increased its seats in parliament fivefold, from 17 to 88,
despite the usual vote-rigging, media manipulation and intimidation.

It really is over. There will be no comprehensive Arab-Israeli peace
deal this decade. In the next decade there could even be a war.

*It is remarkable how some people grow into their responsibilities. Ehud
Olmert was almost a caricature of the right-wing Israeli politician for most
of his career, trotting out the easy clichés whenever his ultra-nationalist
policies were challenged. As mayor of Jerusalem, he was ruthless in moving
Arabs out and moving Jews in. But then he became prime minister, with*

ultimate responsibility for the fate of the whole Zionist enterprise, and he started to think strategically.

It happens like that a lot, actually.

November 29, 2007
ISRAEL SIXTY YEARS ON: PARTITION OR APARTHEID

Israeli Prime Minister Ehud Olmert was just back from the Annapolis summit where President George W. Bush tried to reboot the moribund Israeli-Palestinian peace talks. More importantly, last week was also the sixtieth anniversary of the United Nations vote that divided British-ruled Palestine into a Jewish and an Arab state. That promised Arab state still doesn't exist, of course, but if the peace talks fail to produce it in the end, Olmert told the newspaper *Haaretz*, then Israel is "finished."

"If the day comes when the two-state solution collapses," Olmert said, "and we face a South African-style struggle for equal voting rights for the Palestinians in the [occupied] territories, then, as soon as that happens, the State of Israel is finished. The Jewish organizations which were our power base in America will be the first to come out against us, because they will say they cannot support a state that does not support democracy and equal voting rights for all its residents."

It was an extraordinary thing for a right-wing Israeli politician to say: Israelis usually erupt in fury if anybody suggests a comparison between their country and apartheid-era South Africa. However, Olmert wasn't talking about the country as it is now—seven million people, of whom about five and a half million are Jews—but about the country that would exist if the peace talks fail definitively and the four million Palestinians in the occupied territories remain under Israeli control indefinitely.

They have already been under Israeli military rule for forty years, and fifteen years of on-and-off peace negotiations have made little progress towards a Palestinian state. The Arab population both within Israel and in the occupied territories is growing much faster than the Jewish population, even allowing for Jewish immigration. Sometime soon, there will be more Palestinians than Jews within the borders of the former British mandate of Palestine for the first time since the war of 1948–49.

Most of the Palestinians who lived within what is now Israel fled or were driven out during the 1948–49 war. Subsequent Jewish immigration, combined with the fact that many of the Palestinians fled beyond the borders of the old British mandate, meant that Jews were still a large majority overall even when Israel conquered all the remaining lands of former Palestine in the 1967 war. And so, for a long time, the "demographic question" did not trouble Israelis much.

There were still far fewer Palestinians in the late 1980s, when Yasser Arafat persuaded the Palestine Liberation Organization to adopt the goal of a Palestinian state within the West Bank, the Gaza Strip and East Jerusalem (which is considerably less territory than it was given under the United Nations partition plan of 1947). That led to the era of the peace process, but for various reasons, and with much blame on both sides, the negotiations never succeeded.

Now the Palestinians are within sight of becoming a majority in the whole of the territory between the Jordan River and the Mediterranean sea, and some of them are starting to abandon that compromise goal. Let us have a single democratic state in all of these lands, they say, and we don't mind if Israel never returns to its 1967 borders. We will just demand our equal democratic rights within this larger country that includes all the land now controlled by Israel, and our votes will change Israel from a "Jewish democracy" to a multi-ethnic, post-Zionist democratic state. (Hamas, which controls the Gaza Strip, has already adopted this strategy.)

This is the spectre that haunts Ehud Olmert and every other thinking Israeli. If you cannot make the two-state solution work, then you get the one-state solution, and Palestinians will soon be a majority within the borders of that single state.

Israel has the military power to deny the vote to Palestinians in the occupied territories indefinitely, but, in that case, it will look more and more like apartheid-era South Africa, with the West Bank and the Gaza Strip as its Bantustans. Even its American supporters will turn away in the end, and Israel will be, as Olmert put it, "finished."

That would not happen next year, or even in five or ten years, but the possibility is now permanently on the table. Even on the right, many Israelis have concluded that a Palestinian state is essential to the long-term survival of a Jewish state—but many others still think that a two-state deal is either undesirable or impossible, and hope that the current round of peace talks fails.

They will probably not be disappointed, for Olmert's cabinet would collapse if he made any major concessions on Jerusalem or Palestinian refugees in the talks. His negotiating partner, Mahmoud Abbas, only controls half of the Palestinian population in the occupied territories. Eighty-three percent of Israelis think that there will be no peace deal in the next year, and expectations among Palestinians are even lower. Still the question is as valid as ever: "if not now, when?"

What kept Ehud Olmert in office right down to the middle of 2008, despite the disastrous miscalculation of his 2006 war against Lebanon, was the fear on the centre and left of Israeli politics that the only alternative was a return to power by Binyamin Netanyahu, who had recaptured the leadership of the right-wing Likud Party. However, Olmert was dogged by corruption charges for his whole time in office, and eventually he was forced to resign and face them.

By the time he left office, he finally understood the strategic realities of Israel's situation fully, but there was nothing he could have done about them. Israeli politics is still paralyzed by the great division between those who think the "demographic danger" requires major compromises on territory, and those who do not.

October 2, 2008
EHUD OLMERT: THE TRUTH, TOO LATE

Israeli Prime Minister Ehud Olmert was well aware that he resembled the generals who join a peace movement as soon as they retire. "I have not come here to justify my actions over the past 35 years," he said. "For a large portion of that period, I was unwilling to look reality in the eye."

Olmert, who has resigned but will stay in office until a new government is formed or an election is called, gave a valedictory interview to the newspaper *Yedioth Ahronoth* on September 29, and said something that no previous Israeli prime minister has ever said. He declared that if Israel wants peace, it must withdraw from almost all the lands it occupied in 1967. Unfortunately, it's probably too late.

Not only is it a bit late for Olmert to tell the Israeli public this harsh truth, since he is leaving power now. It's also too late for Israelis to act on his advice even if they accepted it, because the situation has changed.

That isn't Olmert's own view. What he says is: "We have an opportunity that is limited in time, in which we can perhaps reach a historic deal in our relations with the Palestinians and another historic step in our relations with Syria. In both cases, the decision we must reach is a decision that we have been refusing to accept for the past four decades."

If Israel wants peace with Syria, he says, it must give back all of the Golan Heights. If it wants peace with the Palestinians, "we must . . . withdraw from almost all of the [occupied] territories, if not all of them. We will maintain control of a certain percentage of the territories [where the big Jewish settlements are], but we will have to give the Palestinians a commensurate percentage of our land, because without this, there will be no peace."

Not only that, but Olmert now says that Israel must let go of predominantly Arab East Jerusalem, which the Palestinian Authority wants as the capital of its future state. A "special creative solution" would get around the question of sovereignty over the disputed sacred sites in the Old City.

If Israel had been willing to make such a peace deal in the 1990s, it could have worked, but the only Israeli leader of that era who might eventually have offered such terms to the Arabs was Yitzhak Rabin. Since Rabin was murdered by a right-wing Jewish extremist in 1995, no other Israeli prime minister has been willing to go so far—including Olmert during his two and a half years in power.

But the new reality, which Olmert does not acknowledge, is that no Israeli leader will be free to make that deal in the next five or ten years. It is the right deal to make in Israel's own long-term interests, but only if the Arab partners can guarantee that Israel will get permanent peace in return for giving back the land, and the Arab leaders with whom Israel might make this deal cannot really guarantee that anymore because they don't even know if they will survive.

Consider Syria. The old dictator died in 2000 after a mere thirty years in power and his son still rules there eight years later, but the country is much less stable than it used to be. Many elements in Syrian society have been sharply radicalized by the American invasion of Iraq and the flood of refugees from that country. Nobody knows if Syria is heading for a revolution, but the possibility certainly exists.

If there were a revolution in Syria the winners would almost certainly be Islamists who reject any peace with Israel. So what Israeli leader in the next five or ten years could sell the public on a peace that returned the Golan Heights to Syrian control? A few days of violence in Damascus could turn that peace into a nightmare that sees a hostile Syrian army back on the heights that overlook northern Israel.

In the case of the Palestinians, the Islamists of Hamas are already in control of the Gaza Strip, and there is no single Palestinian authority for Israel to make a peace deal with. The notion of an Israeli-Palestinian peace settlement in the current circumstances is purely a fantasy that is maintained to indulge the Bush administration.

Even Egypt, whose peace treaty with Israel is almost thirty years old, is not a reliable partner anymore. If there were to be a truly free Egyptian election in the next five years, the Muslim Brotherhood would probably form the next government—and they have already said that their first act would be to hold a referendum on the Egyptian-Israeli peace treaty. It would probably be rejected by the voters.

So, even if Israeli voters were willing to listen to Ehud Olmert in principle, they would not dare to act on his advice now. Perhaps, in time, the likelihood of Islamist regimes coming to power in Israel's neighbours will shrink. Perhaps there will then be a majority of Israeli voters willing to back the kind of deal that Ehud Olmert has just outlined. But not this year, not this decade, and probably not this generation.

Three months after his "valedictory" interview, Ehud Olmert was still in office, hanging on in order to hold his coalition together until the next election, scheduled for February 2009. And in order to improve the chances of his own Kadima Party in that election, he was fighting another war: an extremely one-sided one, in which Israel was hammering the Gaza Strip with heavy weapons in retaliation for homemade rockets being fired from there at southern Israeli cities.

Everybody knew that it was completely pointless, but it was neverthe-less an emotional and political necessity in Israel.

December 31, 2008
BATTLEFIELD GAZA

Yosef Sheinin, the chief rabbi of Ashdod, was understandably distraught at the funeral of Irit Shetreet, one of four Israelis to be killed by Palestinian rockets since Israel launched its bombing campaign against the Hamas-ruled Gaza Strip on Sunday. However, he was wrong to say that her death was "the latest manifestation of 3,000 years of anti-Jewish hatred." The hatred is real but its sources are a good deal closer both in time and in space.

Western media coverage of current affairs rarely goes into the origins of those events: even what happened last year or ten years ago is treated as ancient history. So the fury and despair of the million and a half residents of the Gaza Strip can easily seem incomprehensible—the "bottomless hatred of wild beasts," as Sheinin so delicately put it. Why do these Palestinians fire murderous rockets at innocent civilians in Sderot, Ashkelon, Ashdod, even Beersheva?

Because that's where they come from. Only about one-fifth of the Gaza Strip's population is descended from people who lived in that barren stretch of land before 1948. The rest are people, or the children or grandchildren or great-grandchildren of people, who were driven out of what is now Israel during the 1948 war, or simply fled in fear and were not allowed to go home again afterwards. Their former homes were mostly in the south of former Palestine, in places like Sderot, Ashkelon, Ashdod and Beersheva.

This does not give them the right to launch rockets at the people who now live in those towns, of course, any more than Israel has the right to use its massive air power to pound the crowded Gaza Strip. But it does provide some context for what is happening now—and indeed, happens every year or so. This struggle is still about what it has always been about: the land. And the fact that Israel is killing a hundred Palestinians for every dead Israeli does not mean that the Israelis are winning.

Israel cannot actually lose this fight since Hamas, the Islamist organization that now controls the Gaza Strip, is distinctly short of F-16s, tanks and unmanned aerial vehicles carrying Hellfire missiles. And Israel will not lose a lot of soldiers—more than a couple of dozen—even if it invades the Gaza Strip on the ground for a while, because Hamas is not like Hezbollah, the Shia militia in southern Lebanon that fought the Israelis to a standstill in the 2006 war.

Hamas does not have the discipline or the weapons that Hezbollah had. It cannot even prevent Israeli infiltration of its own ranks, which is why its leaders die like flies in Israeli air strikes and "targeted killings," whereas Hezbollah successfully purged its ranks of informers and has not lost a single senior leader to Israeli assassination for more than a decade. The Israelis can do pretty much what they want to the Gaza Strip—but they cannot win.

Ehud Olmert, Israel's interim prime minister, and Tzipi Livni, his successor as head of the Kadima Party, and Binyamin Netanyahu, head of the Likud Party and Livni's principal rival for the prime ministership in next month's Israeli election, all know that. They are all old enough to have watched Israel try to bash the Palestinians into submission half a dozen times before, and they know it does not work. But that is strategy, and this is politics.

For Israel's political leaders, this is mainly about looking tough in front of an electorate that just wants someone to "do something" about the Palestinians and their rockets. Nothing much can be done, short of a peace settlement generous enough to reconcile them to the loss of their land, but Israeli politicians have to look like they are trying. Hundreds of people are dying in the Gaza Strip to provide that show.

The Hamas leaders are equally cynical, since they know that every civilian death, and even every militant's death, helps to build popular support for their organization. The dead are pawns, and the game is politics. No wonder there is such a lack of enthusiasm elsewhere for spending much effort on trying to persuade the two sides to agree to a ceasefire. They will stop only when they have achieved their (purely tactical and short-term) political goals.

There is a more profound issue behind all this, which is Israel's right to exist versus the right of the Palestinians to their homeland, but we shouldn't get carried away with the unique moral dimension of all that. It's just one more conquerors-versus-previous-inhabitants conflict, like the European settlers versus the Indians in the Americas in the eighteenth century—or, for that matter, the Israelites versus the Canaanites three thousand years ago.

Those earlier conflicts were all settled by force, but the world has changed and force doesn't work so well anymore. Israel has the power to hammer the Palestinians endlessly, but they don't give up and go away. They cannot, and neither can the Israelis. Neither side can eliminate the other, as has been amply and repeatedly demonstrated.

That doesn't necessarily mean that this conflict will ultimately be settled by peaceful negotiation and compromise. It may mean that there will be no solution of any sort for the foreseeable future, just an endless series of bloody, indecisive clashes like the present one. Happy New Year.

Israel's three-week war against Hamas in Gaza in 2008–09 ended up looking a lot like its war against Hezbollah in Lebanon in 2006, which could hardly be called a success. It lasted about as long, killed about as many Arabs, and ended with Hamas, like Hezbollah, still able to fire rockets at Israel.

That pretty well guaranteed that Binyamin Netanyahu, the Likud Party leader and the ultimate rejectionist, the man who successfully sabotaged the Oslo Accords and effectively killed the "peace process" during his last term as prime minister in 1996–99, would form the next Israeli government. But Ehud Olmert had one more service to do us before he left the scene.

January 15, 2009
ISRAELI TAIL, AMERICAN DOG

Ehud Olmert really doesn't care anymore. He is serving out his time as Israel's prime minister until next month's election, but then will spend a long time fighting the corruption charges that forced him to resign, and he won't be going back into politics afterwards even if he wins. Not after two bloody, futile wars in three years, he won't. So he's very angry, and he tells it like it is.

On Thursday, January 8, he had a problem. The U.S. secretary of state, Condoleezza Rice, was going to vote for a United Nations Security Council resolution that called on both Israel and its Palestinian enemy, Hamas, to accept a ceasefire in the Gaza Strip. Indeed, she had been largely responsible for writing it, and Olmert was furious. He wanted more time to hammer Hamas, so he phoned up George W. Bush and yanked on his choke chain.

According to Olmert's account of what happened, given in a speech on January 13 in the southern Israeli city of Ashkelon, "I said, 'Get me President Bush on the phone.' They said he was in the middle of giving a speech in Philadelphia. I said, 'I don't care: I have to talk to him now.' They got him off the podium, brought him to another room and I spoke to him."

"I told him, 'You can't vote in favour of this resolution.' He said, 'Listen, I don't know about it. I didn't see it. I'm not familiar with the phrasing.'" So Prime Minister Olmert told President Bush: "I'm familiar with it. You can't vote in favour."

Bush did as he was told: "Mr. Bush gave an order to Secretary of State Rice and she did not vote in favour of it—a resolution she cooked up, phrased, organized and manoeuvred for," said Olmert triumphantly. "She was left pretty shamed, and abstained on a resolution she arranged." The Security Council passed the resolution 14–0, but the United States, its principal author, abstained.

Senior Israeli politicians are usually much more circumspect about the nature of their relationship with the occupants of the White House, and Olmert's colleagues were appalled that his anger had led him to speak so plainly. It is one thing to talk to the president of the United States that way. It is quite another thing to reveal to the American public that Israeli leaders talk to U.S. presidents in that tone of voice.

The Bush administration, deeply embarrassed, tried to deny Olmert's account of the conversation. The State Department spokesperson, Sean McCormack, said that the story was "just 100 percent, totally, completely not true," and the White House deputy press secretary, Tony Fratto, said more cautiously that "there are inaccuracies" in Olmert's account of events. Olmert's office replied curtly that "the prime minister's comments on Monday were a correct account of what took place." He really doesn't give a damn anymore.

There is little reason to doubt Olmert's story: he may be extremely cross, but why would he make it up? After all, he did get his way. And there is every reason to doubt the Bush administration's denials. Not only does the story humiliate Bush personally, but it gives wings to the suspicion, already widespread in the United States, that under Bush the Israeli tail has consistently wagged the American dog.

Merely to mention this issue is still to court accusations of anti-Semitism, but the fear of such accusations, which once silenced any serious examination of Israeli influence on American foreign policy, has dwindled in the past few years. Indeed, Olmert's little indiscretion has opened up a wider question: is it normal for Israeli leaders to speak to American presidents like this?

There can be little doubt that Ariel Sharon, Olmert's predecessor, also spoke to Bush in a bullying way, because he bullied everybody. Did Binyamin Netanyahu give orders to Bill Clinton? Probably not, because silken menace is more his style, but he certainly got his way almost all of the time. Did Yitzhak Shamir talk to George H. W. Bush that way? He wouldn't have dreamt of it, and the senior Bush would never have stood for it.

These discussions usually end up being about the alleged power of the "Jewish lobby" over U.S. foreign policy, and in Congress it is obviously huge. The vast majority of the members of Congress will always vote for bills that involve aid or support for Israel, in many cases because they know what will happen at the next election to those who don't. But the key foreign policy decisions are made in the White House, not in Congress, and the presidency is different.

At the top, it really depends on who the president is. Ronald Reagan always gave Israel everything it wanted, whereas Bush senior forced Shamir to start talking to the Palestinians after the first Gulf War and paved the way for the Oslo Accords and the peace process. The United States is still a sovereign country and it can choose its own Middle East policy, if it wishes.

Which way will it go under the new administration? Well, can you imagine Barack Obama letting an Israeli prime minister talk to him like that?

29.

DISASTER POLITICS

Over the last forty or fifty years there has been a rapid accumulation of threats to life on Earth as we know it—or rather, there has been a rapid growth in our knowledge of such threats. They were always there; we just didn't know about them.

For most of human history, the world seemed to be a safe stage upon which to play out our human dramas, but it turns out that we can be ambushed at any time by many different natural disasters that would affect much or all of the world: asteroid strikes, mega-tsunamis, global plagues and massive bursts of gamma radiation from collapsing stars, to mention only the leading candidates.

April 15, 2005
THINGS WE KNOW NOW

Things we know now that we didn't know twenty years ago:

We know that most stars have planets: in the past decade astronomers have identified around two hundred planets circling nearby stars. They are all gas giants like our own Jupiter and Saturn—only massive planets like these can be detected by our present techniques—but most stars are probably also surrounded by smaller, rocky planets like Earth that we cannot yet detect. How likely is it that our own solar system, which contains four gas giants and five smaller, rocky planets, is unique in a universe of gas giants?

We know that there are abundant quantities of organic molecules, the chemical building blocks of life, in interstellar space, and the hypothesis that life on Earth was seeded from space, first advanced by astronomer Sir Fred Hoyle, gains ground by the day. But if that is how life emerged on Earth, then why not on many of those trillions of other planets in this enormous universe?

We also know that relatively local events like asteroids or comets crashing into planets can devastate the entire biosphere: there have already been five known "extinction events" in the history of life on Earth. And now we know that distant cosmic phenomena like collapsing stars can have just as great an impact. Dr. Adrian Melott of Kansas University and his colleagues have just made a convincing case that the first of those events on Earth, the Ordovician extinction of 440 million years ago, was caused by a ten-second burst of gamma rays emitted by a dying star several thousand light years from here.

Unlike the two mass extinctions known to have been caused by asteroid strikes, 251 million years ago at the end of the Permian period and 62 million years ago when the dinosaurs disappeared, the Ordovician one happened at a time when most life on this planet was still in the seas and nothing had even developed a backbone yet. About 60 percent of the marine species then in existence suddenly vanished from the geological record, but there is no asteroid collision associated with this upheaval.

Until recently, the only explanation we had for the Ordovician extinction was the sudden onset of an ice age, but that didn't really make a lot of sense. Even severe environmental stress and loss of habitat caused by falling sea levels shouldn't have killed off 60 percent of existing species—and besides, why did the planet suddenly tumble into an ice age after a long period of stable, warm climate? So along come astronomer Adrian Melott, his colleague, palaeontologist Bruce Lieberman, and other colleagues at Kansas University with a much more plausible—and worrisome—explanation.

Stars above a certain size have a life cycle that ends with collapse into a black hole—and, as they collapse, they emit a pulse of energy, mostly made up of gamma rays, that is so intense that it carries all the way across the universe. It is a highly directional pulse, however, and it can only be detected if your home planet happens to lie within the cone of radiation from the particular star in question.

Down here on the Earth's surface, astronomers only detect about one gamma-ray pulse a month: the thick blanket of atmosphere muffles most of the weaker, more distant ones. But these stellar collapses are happening all the time here and there in the universe, and satellites simultaneously scanning all parts of the sky for these brief bursts of radiation would see about a dozen a week.

We are caught in the cone of gamma radiation from one dying star or another about a dozen times a week. Most of them are safely millions of light years distant—but it has been calculated that if such an implosion occurs within six thousand light years of us, and happens to emit its beam of gamma radiation in our direction, it would strip the protective ozone layer off our planet and leave all life on the surface exposed to deadly ultraviolet radiation for up to five years. It would also fill the upper atmosphere with nitrogen oxides that absorb the sun's heat and could easily push the Earth into an ice age.

Dr. Melott and his friends believe that this double-whammy is what caused the Ordovician extinction 440 million years ago. What actually happened—first a rapid die-off of many species that were presumably killed by UVB radiation, then an ice age to finish the job—fits the profile of a gamma-ray event very closely. They also calculate that such an event is only likely to hit the Earth two or three times per billion years, so it won't have an immediate impact on real-estate prices. But the larger pattern that emerges from all this is not pretty.

We inhabit a universe in which there are probably trillions of planets that broadly resemble the Earth and many, if not most of them, may be home to life of one sort or another. Nobody has a clue how many might harbour consciousness or intelligence, now or in the future, or how many have done so in the past, but even that number could easily be in the billions. And we have reason to suspect that each year hundreds or thousands of these planets are hit by close-range bursts of gamma rays from collapsing giant stars.

We know a lot more about the universe than we used to, and the knowledge is not very comforting.

Of course, as the science improves some of the conclusions have to be changed. The asteroid strike at the end of the Cretaceous era that killed off the dinosaurs sixty-two million years ago has been confirmed by a dozen different kinds of evidence—they have even found the crater it left, on the coast of Mexico's Yucatan Peninsula—but it turns out that the even bigger end-Permian extinction ("the Great Dying") probably was not due to an asteroid. In the article above, I said that it was, but my information was a year or so out of date.

Scientists have been looking for the same telltale signature of a big asteroid strike in the geological record at the times of the other mass extinctions, and they have not found them. Now the leading suspect for the end-Permian event, and for the three other biggest mass extinctions in the geological record, is runaway global warming caused by massive volcanic eruptions that lasted thousands of years. The hypothesis is that the warming produced stratified, largely oxygen-free oceans that were taken over by sulphur bacteria that emitted vast amounts of hydrogen sulphide gas, destroying the ozone layer and poisoning most land-dwelling life directly. Does that make you feel better?

Asteroids, at least, are relatively straightforward. You might be able to deflect an asteroid on a collision course with the Earth if you had spent the money and acquired the relevant technological capabilities in space beforehand. Otherwise, you just tuck your head between your knees and kiss your ass goodbye. There's not much you can do about massive volcanic eruptions, either. But many of the potential disasters we face pose acute political dilemmas. Like Cumbre Vieja, for example.

November 3, 2004
UNSTOPPABLE GEE-GEES

The western flank of the Cumbre Vieja volcano on the island of La Palma in the Canary Islands is going to slide into the Atlantic one of these days: a diagonal fracture has already separated it from the main body of the volcano, and only friction still keeps it attached. "When it goes, it will likely collapse in about 90 seconds," said Professor Bill McGuire, director of the Benfield Grieg Hazard Research Centre at University College London. And when it goes, probably during an eruption, the splash will create a mega-tsunami that races across the Atlantic and drowns the facing coastlines.

Fortunately, the nearest coast to the Canary Islands, where the waves will be around one hundred metres high when they hit, is lightly settled Western Sahara. Few people living in the densely populated coastal plains of Morocco, southwestern Spain and Portugal will survive either, but the waves will drop in height as they travel. The coasts of southern Ireland and southwestern England will also take a beating, but by then the wave height will be down to about ten metres.

The real carnage will be on the western side of the Atlantic, from Newfoundland all the way down the east coast of Canada and the United States to Cuba, Hispaniola, the Lesser Antilles and northeastern Brazil. With a clear run across the Atlantic the wall of water will still be between twenty and fifty metres high when it hits the eastern seaboard of North America, and it will keep coming for ten to fifteen minutes.

Worst hit will be harbours and estuaries that funnel the waves inland: goodbye Halifax, Boston, New York, Philadelphia, Baltimore and Washington, D.C.; Miami and Havana go under almost entirely, as will low-lying islands like the Bahamas and Barbados. Likely death toll, if there is no mass evacuation beforehand? A hundred million people, give or take fifty million.

The last time the volcano erupted, in 1949, its whole western side slid four metres down towards the sea, and even now it is still slipping very slowly downwards. Given the scale of the catastrophe if the next eruption sends this mountain crashing into the water, Dr. McGuire is angry that there is so little monitoring equipment on La Palma to give advance warning: "The U.S. government must be aware of the La Palma threat.

They should certainly be worried, and so should the island states in the Caribbean that will really bear the brunt of a collapse."

"They're not taking it seriously," McGuire concluded. "Governments change every four or five years and generally they're not interested in these things." It was a classic scene, revisited in every natural disaster movie: crusading scientist calls feckless governments to account, squalid politicos ignore the call. The science journalists couldn't wait to get their pieces into print.

But hold on a minute. Haven't we heard about this threat before? What's new this time? Nothing, except that there hasn't been a stampede to cover La Palma with seismometers. Now, why do you think that is?

Suppose that the governments whose coastlines are at risk, from Morocco to the U.S., did get a warning that Cumbre Vieja was waking up again. What would they do with the warning? Evacuate one or two hundred million people from the low-lying lands indefinitely?

They don't know if there is really going to be an eruption (seismology is not that precise), or how big it might be, or whether this will be the one that finally shakes the side of the mountain loose. It could happen in the next eruption, but it might not happen for a thousand years.

No national leader wants to evacuate the entire coast for an indefinite period of time, causing an economic and refugee crisis on the scale of a world war, for what might be a false alarm. But nobody wants to ignore a warning, and perhaps be responsible for tens of millions of deaths. From a political standpoint, it's better not to have the warning at all.

Natural disasters that can affect the whole planet are known to scientists as "global geophysical events"—gee-gees, for short—and they come in two kinds: ones you might be able to do something useful about, and ones you can't. When governments are faced with the first kind they can respond quite sensibly.

Since we first realized two decades ago that asteroids and comets smashing into the Earth have caused mass extinctions, a U.S. government project has identified and started to track three thousand "near-Earth objects" whose orbits make them potentially dangerous. In another generation, we may even be able to divert ones that are on a collision course—and if there's one gee-gee that you would want to prevent above all others, that's the one. But there's no similar remedy on the horizon for volcanoes or earthquakes, or the tsunamis they might cause. About these, we just have to keep our fingers crossed.

We had a very close call with an asteroid strike less than a million years ago: not a near miss, but an actual collision with a monster the size of the end-Cretaceous asteroid that miraculously did not cause a mass extinction. At the International Geophysical Congress in Glasgow on August 18, 2004, Dr. Frans van der Hoeven of Delft University of Technology in the Netherlands revealed that a similar asteroid hit Antarctica only 780,000 years ago, a mere blink of an eye in geological time. We are still here for three reasons, all of them flukes.

First, the asteroid broke up just before hitting the Earth, creating five smaller impact craters over an area measuring 2,100 by 3,800 kilometres rather than a single huge impact crater. Second, most of the pieces melted in the deep eastern Antarctic ice cap before cratering the underlying bedrock, which limited the amount of dust released into the atmosphere. And finally, there was already permanent winter over most of the planet, so it was much less of a shock to the biosphere than it would be if it happened today.

"The extraordinary thing about this meteor strike is that it appeared to do so little damage," said Professor van der Hoeven. "Unlike the dinosaur strike there is no telltale layer of dust [in the geological record] that dem-onstrates the history of the event. It may have damaged things and wiped out species but there is no sign of it." Apart from the craters, the only indi-cation that something big happened 780,000 years ago is that the Earth's magnetic field reversed at just that time. I could build a whole religion around a piece of luck that big, but I shall refrain.

30.

JAPAN

Something very important happened in Japan over the past five years: it stopped being a one-party state. It always had genuinely free elections, of course, but for fifty years (with the exception of a single year) the Liberal Democratic Party always stayed in power. Then it lost the plot, and soon afterwards it lost power.

The right wing of the LDP was always home for most Japanese nationalists (except the really crazy ones), but they were always kept on a short leash. Then, in 2006, one of their own, Shinzō Abe, became prime minister.

September 23, 2006
SHINZŌ ABE AND A "NORMAL" JAPAN

"We just ignore them!" said the man at the think tank in Beijing, a senior adviser to the Chinese foreign ministry, and burst out laughing.

He laughed because it is a long and daunting list of people to ignore: the American journalists and academics who predict an eventual war with China; the U.S. armed forces, which are transferring more and more hardware to the western Pacific; and the Bush administration officials whose search for allies in Asia to help them "contain China" culminated in a quasi-alliance with India last year. He also has to ignore the counterparts of those people in the Chinese military-industrial complex, who try to use all that foreign activity as evidence that China must pour many more resources into defence. He is a busy man.

The reason he (and most of the Chinese foreign-policy establishment) deliberately ignore them all is because taking the "American threat" seriously and trying to match it would just play into the hands of the hawks on both sides. There is no objective reason that makes a U.S.-Chinese clash inevitable but preparing for it, or even talking too much about it, actually makes it more possible.

It's an admirably sane attitude, founded on the obvious fact that China would be far worse off in any confrontation with the United States today than it would be in ten or twenty years' time, when rapid Chinese economic growth will have narrowed the gap between them. So, even if you believe a clash is inevitable sooner or later (which most Chinese analysts don't), then it's a good idea to have it much later, not today.

I heard the same argument from half a dozen other influential foreign-policy analysts in Beijing two weeks ago, and this should have been reassuring, if not for the fact that every one of these experts, having patiently explained that there were no threats on the horizon that could deflect China's "peaceful rise" to great-power status, then added: "except Japan." That is quite an exception, as Japan has the world's second-biggest economy and is right on China's doorstep.

Which brings us to Shinzō Abe, the new prime minister of Japan. Elected as the leader of the ruling Liberal Democratic Party on September 20 and formally installed as prime minister on September 26, he is the youngest man (fifty-two) to occupy the office since the Second World War. Indeed, he only entered parliament thirteen years ago and got his first cabinet-level job just last year.

But Abe didn't really need to serve a long apprenticeship; he sort of inherited the job. Twenty years ago, his father was foreign minister, and widely tipped as a future prime minister until he was sidetracked by a corruption scandal and then died relatively young. His grandfather, Nobosuke Kishi, was prime minister in the late 1950s, despite having been identified (but not tried) as a war criminal by the American occupation authorities. And this is not just a political lineage; it's a clearly defined ideological group within the Japanese ruling elite.

The people around Abe are uncompromising nationalists who insist that Japan must become a "normal" country. By this, they mean that it should stop apologizing for the Second World War; start rewriting school textbooks omitting all the material about war guilt and Japanese atrocities; and start rewriting the "peace" constitution so that Japan's euphemistically titled "Self-Defence Forces" can legally become ordinary armed forces, able to be deployed overseas.

Prime Minster Abe has even said that it is "not necessarily unconstitutional" for Japan to develop a nuclear deterrent. He advocates even closer military ties with the United States, and worries aloud about the intentions of a stronger China. Abe not only irritates the Chinese, whose relations with Japan are at the lowest point in decades after five years of his predecessor, Junichiro Koizumi; he actually frightens them.

No sane Japanese wants to turn the country's giant neighbour and biggest trading partner into an active enemy, and Abe isn't mad. But it wouldn't be the first time that a government has talked itself into a needless military confrontation.

Symbolism matters. If Abe continues Koizumi's habit of making annual visits to the Yasukuni Shrine in Tokyo—which is devoted to the souls of Japan's millions of war dead, including fourteen leaders who were hanged as war criminals after the country's defeat in 1945—then many Chinese will conclude that he is a real threat. Koizumi's official visits to the shrine as prime minister outraged people all over Asia whose countries were occupied by Japan during the war, but the Chinese in particular went ballistic.

Shinzō Abe visited the Yasukuni Shrine privately as recently as last spring. If he visits again as prime minister, Sino-Japanese relations will get even worse, and it will get still harder and harder for sensible people in Beijing to ignore the rhetoric of the American hawks and the warnings and pleas of their own hawks. With a little bad luck, we could be as little as a couple of years away from the start of a new Cold War in Asia.

We had good luck instead, and Abe was quickly gone from the scene: four of his ministers were forced to resign by scandals and a fifth committed suicide within ten months. His successor, Yasuo Fukuda, the son of a former prime minister, also lasted less than a year. Scraping the bottom of the barrel, the Liberal Democrats then chose Taro Aso, the grandson of a former prime minister but a man so prone to blunders and malapropisms that his name "Taro" has become a schoolyard synonym for "stupid." He lasted as prime minister not quite a year, and by mid-2009 the Liberal Democrats were gone from power.

August 25, 2009
JAPAN: NOT AN ELECTION, A REVOLUTION

Some years ago, a political-science professor at a Japanese university told me that he reckoned you could fit everybody who counted in Japan into one room. There are about four hundred such people, so it would have to be a ballroom. All but a couple would be men, of course—and at least half of them would be there because their fathers and grandfathers were in the same ballroom twenty-five and fifty years ago.

The Democratic Party of Japan (DPJ) is headed for a landslide victory in the election on August 30, sweeping the Liberal Democratic Party (LDP) out after an almost unbroken fifty-four years in power, but that is the system it must break if it is really going to change Japan. It won't be easy, especially since Yukio Hatoyama, the DPJ leader who will soon be prime minister, is also part of that system. He is the grandson of the prime minister who defeated Taro Aso's grandfather.

Recent polls by Japan's biggest papers predict that the DPJ should end up with between 300 and 320 members in the 480-seat House of Representatives. That should be a majority big enough to crush all opposition, but it's a bit more complicated than that in Japan. Not everybody in that small ballroom filled with the four hundred people who matter is a politician.

Most of them are the businessmen who run the giant corporations that used to be called *zaibatsu* (the pre–Second World War industrial conglomerates) and the top layer of senior civil servants—all of whom have been in bed with the LDP their entire working lives. In Japan they call it the "iron triangle": LDP faction leaders, senior civil servants and industrial bosses, all working together to stifle change and keep themselves in power. It's a hard combination to beat.

The one previous time in living memory when the LDP lost power, to a fragile coalition of opposition parties in 1993, the iron triangle immediately set to work to undermine and discredit the new government, and the LDP was back in power in eleven months. That isn't going to happen this time.

The Liberal Democratic Party has presided over fifteen years of economic stagnation since, and people no longer link it with the boom years. Moreover, this time it faces a single opposition party, ready to take over the government. Nevertheless, it will be a miracle if the Democratic Party of Japan can really change the country even with four undisturbed years in power.

About fifteen years ago, when I was young and foolish, I spent a couple of months in Japan pursuing a single question: why was Japan the only developed country outside the Communist world that didn't have a "Sixties"? (I had just finished a television series, which is the moral equivalent of living in a cave for two years, so I needed to get out a bit.)

Was there something unique in Japanese culture that insulated it from social and political trends elsewhere in the industrialized world? Why were Japanese people still so deferential, so hierarchical, so docile in the face of arrogant power and insolent corruption? Why was Japan, to all intents and purposes, a one-party state?

That was the question I went with, in my ignorance. But everybody in Japan knows the answer: Japan's equivalent of the Sixties actually began in the 1950s, but it was ruthlessly crushed.

By the 1950s, the Cold War was going full blast in Asia, and the United States was afraid that the youth revolution getting underway in Japan was the prelude to a Communist takeover. It probably wasn't anything of the sort, but the U.S. was occupying Japan and so took action to stop it.

The old *zaibatsu* were allowed to rebuild because that was the quickest way to get Japan back on its feet economically, and conservative politicians (including some war criminals) were encouraged to form a political party that received full American support, the LDP. The government that emerged from this, with considerable help from its yakuza (gangster) allies, beat the kids' revolt into the ground.

By the time the rest of the developed world had its Sixties the battle had been fought and lost in Japan. During the half-century that followed most people just kept their heads down and stayed out of trouble, and it is still rare for ordinary people to discuss politics in Japan, even though the active repression ended a generation ago.

That is the system and the mindset that the DPJ must start to dismantle if Japan is to become a normal democratic country. The iron triangle will fight until the very last ditch to preserve the present system, however badly it has served the country. So the key question becomes: can the Democratic Party of Japan reach and take the last ditch in only four years?

31.

THE INTERNATIONAL RULE OF LAW

In the past decade, the United Nations has virtually vanished from the public view. The world's greatest power invaded another country in open defiance of the UN Charter in 2003 (and went unpunished, of course). All efforts to "reform" the UN, mainly by giving emerging great powers like India and Brazil permanent seats on the Security Council, failed miserably. Even the departure of George W. Bush from the White House did little to rebuild the UN's credibility, although Barack Obama speaks more politely about the institution than his predecessor. Yet this is not just an important international institution; it is the indispensable one. It is our main safeguard against another war between the great powers.

June 22, 2005
UNITED NATIONS ANNIVERSARY

"The great force on which we must rely is the hatred of the cruelty and waste of war which now exists. As soon as the war is over the process of oblivion sets in . . . ," Lord Robert Cecil wrote as the First World War drew to an end. "It is only, therefore, while the recollection of all we have been through is burning fresh that we can hope to overcome the inevitable opposition and establish . . . a new and better organization of the nations of the world."

The organization that Cecil, a member of Britain's Imperial War Cabinet, hoped could prevent another such war was the League of Nations. It failed, of course, and so we got the Second World War, which killed five times as many people. By the end of that one, nuclear weapons were being dropped on cities—so the victors had no choice but to clone the League, making some significant improvements, and try again. Sixty years ago this Sunday (June 26), the Charter of the United Nations was signed by fifty nations in San Francisco.

There was not a single idealist among the men and women who signed the Charter. They were badly frightened people who had lived through the worst war in human history and who feared that an even worse one lay in wait for their children. They were so frightened that they were even willing to give up the most important aspect of national sovereignty: the right to wage war against other countries. Six decades later, how is their organization doing?

Two things cannot be denied: the UN has already survived three times longer than its ill-starred predecessor, and the great war that it was meant to prevent has not happened. In the various crises that might have ended with the superpowers sliding into a nuclear war—the Cuban Missile Crisis of 1962, the Middle East War of 1973, and so on—the UN Security Council was an essential forum for negotiations, and the Charter provided a new kind of international law that the rivals could defer to without losing face when they wanted to back away from a major crisis.

So, why is the United Nations so widely disdained today? One reason is that Lord Robert Cecil was right: "the process of oblivion sets in" quickly, and later generations cannot remember why it was so supremely important to create an organization to prevent future great-power wars. But actually, the UN isn't really all that widely disdained.

It gets a bad press in the United States, but that is mainly because it acts as a brake on the untrammelled exercise of American military power. In fact, it is still quite popular in most of the world, although it continues to annoy nationalists in all the great powers—and at the other extreme, it frustrates and infuriates all the idealists who want it to be about justice and democracy and maybe even brotherly love.

It's not. As Henry Cabot Lodge, a Republican senator and ambassador to the United Nations, said in 1955: "This organization is created to keep you from going to Hell. It isn't created to take you to Heaven." For all the fine words of the Charter, the UN is still mainly about preventing another major war between the great powers (and as many other wars as possible).

Does the UN need to be "reformed"? Certainly. It has acquired some bad habits, and its structures have not kept up with the realities of a rapidly changing world. The current main focus of reformers concerns the Security Council, whose permanent, veto-wielding members are still the five victorious great powers of 1945. Three-quarters of the countries that now comprise the UN were not even independent then, so clearly some adjustment is overdue.

However, the only imaginable solution is an expansion of the number of permanent members, because demoting any of the existing permanent members is unthinkable (and would simply be vetoed). But then come the questions—how many new members, which ones, and do they get veto powers, too?—so reform will not happen soon.

The United Nations is an attempt to change the way that international politics works because the only alternative is to accept perpetual war, and since 1945 this has no longer been an acceptable option. Not even the optimists imagined that it could succeed in less than a century or so, and, sixty years on, it may not yet be even halfway to its goal. No need to despair. As its most influential secretary-general, Dag Hammarskjöld, said: "None of us are ever going to see the world order we dream of appear in our lifetime. Nevertheless, the effort to build that order is the difference between anarchy and a tolerable degree of chaos."

Let us be quite clear about this. The United Nations Charter, signed by (and largely ghost-written by) the United States and the United Kingdom, makes the invasion and occupation of another country a crime, unless for some reason it is authorized by the UN *Security Council. The invasion of Iraq was not so authorized, and the heads of government who ordered it are therefore war criminals. That is the law.*

December 15, 2009
THE TRAVAILS OF THE YOUNG WAR CRIMINAL

Alan Watkins is my favourite British journalist. Well into his seventies now, each week he still produces an elegant and knowing column, usually about British politics. And with a casual understatement that you might easily mistake for irony, he has for the past six years regularly referred to former prime minister Tony Blair as "the young war criminal."

That may seem a bit harsh, for never has an alleged war criminal sounded more sincere, more open, even more innocent. As he said about his 2003 decision to involve Britain in the American invasion of Iraq in his resignation speech four years later: "Hand on heart, I did what I thought was right." But *everybody* does what they think is right.

They may mean pragmatically right, or morally right, or even ideologically right, but one way or another people will find ways to justify their actions to themselves: even Pol Pot believed that his actions were justified. When people's choices lead to the deaths of others, they must eventually be judged by more objective criteria than mere sincerity. That is now happening to Tony Blair.

On December 13 Blair admitted that he would have invaded Iraq even if he had known at the time that the "intelligence" about weapons of mass destruction in Iraq was wrong. "I would still have thought it was right to remove [Saddam Hussein]," he told BBC interviewer Fern Britton. "Obviously, you would have had to use and deploy different arguments about the nature of the threat."

Blair seemed completely unaware that he was throwing away the only plausible defence for his actions that might stand up if he were brought before the International Criminal Court. Since 1945, it has been a crime to invade another country: that was the main charge brought against the Nazi leaders at Nuremberg. The new rule was written into the United

Nations Charter, principally at the behest of the United States, and there are virtually no exceptions to it.

You have the right to defend yourself if another country attacks you, but you are not allowed to attack another country on the grounds that it has a wicked ruler, or follows policies you disapprove of, or even because you think it might attack you one of these days. No unilateral military action is permitted, and even joint action against a genuinely threatening country is only permissible with the authorization of the UN Security Council.

The United States is a very different country now than it was in 1945, and under the junior Bush administration, it announced a "national security" doctrine that directly contradicts this international law, arrogating to the U.S. government the right to attack any country it suspects of harbouring evil intentions towards the United States.

It's just the sort of thing that Britain might have declared when it was top dog in the nineteenth century, had there been any international law against aggression back then. But this is the twenty-first century, and Britain is no longer top dog, and there is a law now. There is even an International Criminal Court to enforce the law, although in practice it never takes action against the leaders of rich and powerful countries.

Tony Blair will never face the International Criminal Court, but he started a war on false pretenses—there were no weapons of mass destruction—and at least one hundred thousand people died as a result. He has now admitted that he would have started the war even if he knew that the weapons didn't exist (as he probably did). And he started the war without the authorization of the UN Security Council. He is a war criminal. And so is George W. Bush.

The leaders of the great powers all still have "get out of jail free" cards, but war criminals from less powerful countries do occasionally find themselves facing international tribunals that are empowered to enforce the law. The biggest fish to face such a tribunal so far was the man who led Serbia during the Balkan wars of the 1990s, Slobodan Milošević.

March 14, 2006
WHY TRY WAR CRIMINALS?

I never met Adolf Hitler before he became famous. (I never met him afterwards, either, due to the accidents of nationality and birth date.) But I did meet the "Butcher of the Balkans" before he became famous—and I promptly forgot him again.

Slobodan Milošević, the former Serbian leader who was found dead in his prison cell in The Hague last Saturday at the age of sixty-four, was famous because the wars he unleashed in former Yugoslavia killed at least a quarter-million people. He was nothing compared to Hitler, who was responsible for over twenty-five million deaths, but you'd think that he would at least leave a lasting impression. He didn't.

I first interviewed Milošević during some forgotten conference in Belgrade in 1982, having been refused interviews with all the more important politicians I had requested. All I really remember is his impressive hairstyle and the fact that he was a total apparatchik. He didn't come across as a rabid Serbian nationalist, or indeed as a man who truly believed in anything at all; just another run-of-the-mill sociopath. I didn't write the interview up. I didn't even save the tape.

So imagine my surprise when this bland nonentity resurfaced at the end of the 1980s as the charismatic ultra-nationalist leader who was going to carve a Greater Serbia out of Yugoslavia, even if it required "cleansing" this fantasy homeland of its many non-Serb inhabitants. But then, if I had met the young Hitler in Vienna before the First World War, I probably would not have spotted him as a future war criminal either. Sulky would-be artists can be trying but most of them don't turn into mass murderers.

Many potential monsters are born for everyone who actually grows up to become a mass murderer: they are creatures of circumstance. And this has some bearing on the controversy that now engulfs the international court that was trying Milošević on sixty-six charges of genocide, of crimes against humanity and of war crimes in connection with the wars he sponsored in Croatia, Bosnia and Kosovo.

I don't mean the "controversy" about how he died. Chief United Nations prosecutor Carla Del Ponte got it exactly right when she told reporters: "You have the choice between normal, natural death and suicide."

Milošević had long suffered from heart problems and high blood pressure, so a heart attack makes sense. He had been in prison for five years already and faced the certainty of spending the rest of his life behind bars, so suicide would also have made sense. What does not make sense is the allegation that he was poisoned by the international court's henchmen because otherwise it would soon have had to admit that the charges were false and release him.

"My husband has been killed by the Hague tribunal," his widow, Mirjana Markovic, told Belgrade's *Večernje Novosti* newspaper. "They did it because they were in trouble. Only thirty-seven hours remained, and they did not have anything to convict him." But those "thirty-seven hours" only mean that Milošević had already used up most of the 360 hours allotted to him to present his defence. That doesn't seem an unreasonably brief amount of time.

The court had no motive to want him dead, for it had already heard enough evidence from his former colleagues to ensure a conviction. The real controversy is about the inordinate length of the trial. Five years was a very long time—and, in the end, Milošević died before he could be convicted.

The mills of international justice grind exceedingly slowly because the trials of senior political figures for crimes like genocide involve huge numbers of charges and mountains of evidence. In Milošević's case, the delays were compounded because the court let him conduct his own defence. But what was the alternative? Force him to accept court-appointed lawyers, pick a few of the simplest charges, and push the case through in six months?

That would have given the court no more credibility than the one now trying Saddam Hussein in Iraq. The obscure charge on which Saddam is being tried was chosen not for efficiency's sake, but because to try him for any of his really big crimes, like the wars of aggression against Iran and Kuwait and the massacres that accompanied them, would have implicated the United States in one way or another. The point of that trial is to kill Saddam without delving into his complex relationship with Washington over the years.

The goal of genuine international courts like the one in The Hague is not to save us from mythical monsters by stringing them up: by the time they reach court, they are no longer dangerous. It is to expose in slow and painful detail how amoral political opportunism can lead quite ordinary people like Slobodan Milošević to commit appalling crimes in the name of the state.

In Milošević's case, 95 percent of that job had been completed before he died. A conviction would have been nice, but it would not have changed the minds of his diehard supporters, and the rest of us already knew he was guilty of monstrous crimes. The point of the trial was to document and record the detailed evidence of those crimes, and it had already succeeded.

Building the international rule of law has been the most important political enterprise of the past century, but the diplomats and lawyers who do that work don't always grasp the reality of what they are trying to regulate. The Law of the Sea, for example . . .

November 21, 2008
PIRATES OF THE HORN

On one side are eight navies, the world's largest shipping companies, the rich Gulf states that need to get their oil to market, and the great powers, whose commerce depends heavily on the shipping lanes around the Horn of Africa. On the other side are a few thousand Somali pirates in small boats with light weapons. So why are the pirates winning?

Not only are they winning, but the forces of law and order are almost completely paralyzed. The pirates have seized dozen of ships, extracting ransoms that total about thirty million dollars this year alone. Fourteen ships, including a Saudi Arabian supertanker carrying two million barrels of oil, are still anchored off the Somali coast awaiting ransom.

Yet with the honourable exception of the Indians and the French, nobody has used force against the pirates of the Horn. The Danish navy arrested ten of them in September, but turned them loose again because the government believed that it did not have jurisdiction to prosecute them. The British Foreign Office has advised the Royal Navy not to detain pirates of certain nationalities (including Somali) as they might claim asylum in Britain under human-rights laws.

As the boldness of the pirate attacks increases, the international response is to retreat. Major shipping companies that transport oil out of the Gulf have ordered their tankers to stop using the Suez Canal route, which takes them past the northern Somali coast. Instead, they are going all the way around southern Africa, adding two weeks to the voyage at a cost of twenty to thirty thousand dollars a day.

What to do? Most pundits declare that this problem cannot be solved at sea. Instead, it will only end when order has been restored in Somalia, the pirates' base. Since Somalia is currently divided between three different governments, only one of which (Somaliland) exercises even a modest degree of control over its territory, this seems a tall order.

The last major international attempt to take Somalia out of the hands of the warlords and their militias was in 1992–93. It ended with the hasty retreat of American troops from the country, followed by all the United Nations forces as well. If a call for volunteers to repeat that effort were to be sent out to UN member states today, an epidemic of diplomatic deafness would sweep the world.

If we must wait for a central government with real authority to take charge in Somalia before the pirate threat in the seas around the Horn of Africa is brought under control, we will be waiting a long time. Why not solve the problem at sea, where clan militias and suicide bombers are not a problem? Why not just capture or kill enough of the pirates to persuade the others to choose a different career?

Don't believe the nonsense about how it's too big an ocean area to monitor and control effectively. This is one of the tasks that great-power navies are designed to perform, and they have the right equipment to do it: satellite surveillance, maritime patrol aircraft and warships with powerful radars and lethal weapons. Moreover, the navies are usually looking for work, since there is not that much call for their services in peacetime.

The problem is the whole body of international law and human-rights legislation that has emerged in recent decades which has made the traditional remedies for piracy very hard to apply. The United Nations Convention on the Law of the Sea, for example, requires a warship to send a boarding party onto any suspected pirate vessel to confirm its criminal intent. Until that has been done, the warship may not open fire.

The colloquial term for the members of any such boarding party is "hostages." Back in the early eighteenth century, when the pirates of the Caribbean—the *real* pirates of the Caribbean, not Johnny Depp and Keith Richards—were finally being eliminated by the navies of the big European powers, there was no such foolishness. Pirates were defined as "enemies of all mankind," and there was a right of "universal jurisdiction" against them.

Any country could arrest pirates from any other country (or countries) and try them for their crimes. If they were captured in battle, they were even liable to summary execution. We don't need to do that, but killing them if they resist arrest? It shouldn't be a problem.

There was a reason why pirates were defined as "enemies of all mankind." The sea is an alien environment, a place where people die very quickly if things go wrong. Those who prey on other people in this environment have very little call on our sympathy. So while it is not the eighteenth century anymore, a UN Security Council resolution decreeing universal jurisdiction would certainly help.

Suppose that such a resolution were passed, declaring that any non-military vessels carrying armed men within five hundred kilometres of the Somali coast would be subject to arrest. If they did not submit when challenged, they would be sunk without further discussion. Do that a couple of times—as the Indian warship INS *Tabar* did last week—and the pirate threat drops away very fast.

Has the UN got the spine to declare those rules for the Gulf of Aden and the oceans bordering East Africa? Perhaps. It has just given the Indian navy the right of "hot pursuit" of suspected pirate vessels into Somali territorial waters, but it needs to go a good deal further. This thing can be stopped, with very little loss of life, if we just change the rules of engagement.

The law cannot get too far ahead of public opinion in any country, but public opinion is not static. It has changed on issues of sovereignty and international law, and it is also changing on questions related to human rights. Get past the legalese, and the basic assumption is that everybody in the world has equal rights, at every level from the local to the global.

July 3, 2009
DEAD IMPERIALISTS AND SECTION 377

It is forty-two years since homosexual acts were legalized in Britain (by a Labour government, of course), and things have moved on a lot since then. The current Conservative leader, David Cameron, who will almost certainly be prime minister within a year, declared this week that just as his party gave Britain its first woman prime minister (Margaret Thatcher), so "we are bound to have the first black prime minister and the first gay prime minister."

That remains to be seen, but things are moving on in the rest of the world, too. In India, they have finally done what the British did in 1967 and legalized homosexuality. But then, it was the British who criminalized same-sex relations in India in the first place.

For a century and a half, Section 377 of the Indian penal code, originally imposed by the country's British rulers, prohibited "carnal intercourse against the order of nature with any man, woman or animal." Nobody had gone to jail for breaking that law for years, but it made life a nightmare for Indian gays and lesbians. Corrupt police all over the country regularly used it as a pretext to shake them down for bribes, beat them up, and even rape them.

Now Section 377 is gone. On July 2, the Delhi High Court handed down a 105-page decision that said: "The inclusiveness that Indian society traditionally displayed, literally in every aspect of life, is manifest in recognizing a role in society for everyone . . . Those perceived by the majority as 'deviants' or 'different' are not on that score excluded or ostracized."

It is no longer against the law to be gay in the world's second biggest country, and the best thing about the ruling was the reason the judges gave for their decision. They didn't let themselves be drawn into any foolish arguments about whether this or that kind of sexual behaviour was good or bad. They simply said that Section 377 was at odds with the equal-opportunity provisions in the Indian constitution.

It's a useful reminder of what the politics of the past two centuries has really been about: the ever-widening application of the principle of equality until it includes every citizen of a particular country, even all of the people in the world. The very first people in the Western world to abolish discrimination against homosexuals were the French revolutionaries in 1791, and wherever the revolutionary armies went, the new policy went with them.

But the French Revolution was ultimately crushed, and during the nineteenth century, when European empires ruled almost the entire world, Europe's own anti-gay laws were extended to most of the imperial possessions in Asia and Africa. Even a country like India, with its long tradition of tolerance for a wide variety of sexual preferences and practices, was forced into the same anti-gay legal regime.

Now it is emerging from that long darkness, only a few decades after Europe itself did. Moreover, the Delhi High Court has shown a clear understanding of what is at stake: not just sexual practices but human rights in general. It would have made precisely the same decision, on exactly the same legal principles, if it were dealing with caste, gender or racial discrimination.

Creating legal systems that genuinely respect human rights is a huge undertaking, and it may be another century before all people everywhere live under such legal regimes. It may take even longer before the police everywhere respect the law, and private citizens everywhere have really accepted the notion of equal rights for people who are different. But the lives of millions of people are changing for the better, and that matters.

Half a century after the collapse of the European empires, almost all the former colonial territories in Asia, apart from the Muslim countries, have revoked the laws that discriminated against homosexuals. Indeed, the only remaining bastions of discrimination are the ex-imperial territories of Africa (with the shining exception of South Africa), most of the smaller Caribbean islands, and most Muslim countries (with the shining exception of Turkey).

Since China also legalized homosexuality twelve years ago, we have now arrived at a situation where at least three-quarters of the world's people live in places where the law no longer criminalizes gays. It shouldn't have taken so long, and it should have been less of a cause for wonderment when it finally arrived, but this qualifies as real progress on human rights.

It's not over yet in India. The High Court judgment only applies to Delhi, strictly speaking, although other jurisdictions will find it hard to ignore the precedent created by this decision. Various hard-line religious leaders in India are condemning the judgment and are demanding legislation to reverse it.

"We are totally against such a practice as it is not our tradition or culture," said Puroshattam Narain Singh, an official of the Vishwa Hindu Parishad, or World Hindu Council. "This Western culture cannot be permitted in our country," said Maulana Khalid Rashid Farangi Mahali, a leading Muslim cleric in the northern city of Lucknow. Neither of them, presumably, has ever seen the Khajuraho paintings, or learned anything about India's pre-colonial history.

But they will not win. Already, the newly re-elected Congress government is talking about rewriting the law so that all discrimination against minority sexual orientations becomes illegal. The clock will not be turned back.

We are trying to invent a better future, but we make progress by very small steps. Tennyson got the technology right, but he didn't realize how hard the politics would be.

April 27, 2007
THE PARLIAMENT OF MAN

> For I dipt into the future, far as human eye could see;
> Saw the Vision of the world, and all the wonder that would be,
>
> Saw the heavens fill with commerce, argosies of magic sails,
> Pilots of the purple twilight, dropping down with costly bales . . .
>
> Till the war-drum throbb'd no longer, and the battle-flags were furl'd
> In the Parliament of man, the Federation of the world.

—from "Locksley Hall" by Alfred Lord Tennyson, 1842

One hundred and sixty-five years later after the publication of his poem, Tennyson would be impressed by the amount of air travel, and he would be encouraged by the steep decline in wars among the great powers. (They still attack small countries from time to time, but at least they don't fight each other, which is when the mass deaths happen.) He would, however, be astonished that nothing has yet been done to make international society democratic.

There is already a world administration of sorts, in the form of the United Nations, the International Monetary Fund, the World Trade Organization and so on, but it is all in the hands of governments—and some governments are much more equal than others, so none of the global institutions ever acts against the will of the powerful. (Occasionally they refuse to approve some lawless deed of the powerful, as the United Nations did briefly over the American invasion of Iraq, but that is all.) And nowhere in all the layers of bureaucrats and diplomats is there any direct representation of ordinary people.

And so, only sixty-two years after the foundation of the UN, the Campaign for the Establishment of a United Nations Parliamentary Assembly (UNPA) launches this week in five continents. It has the signatures of 377 members of national parliaments from seventy countries, six former foreign ministers/secretaries, and various other international luminaries like Václav Havel, Günter Grass and former UN secretary-general Boutros Boutros-Ghali. But it also has a few little problems.

One is a distinct lack of Americans: only nine of the signatories are from the U.S. The well-known American allergy to international institutions that might infringe on the absolute sovereignty of the United States extends, in this case, to a body that could have no such impact because it would have no legislative or executive power. And that is precisely the problem: what is the point of this hypothetical world parliament, given that it would have no power over the UN Security Council, the International Monetary Fund, the World Bank, or any of the other real decision-making centres?

The Campaign, whose headquarters is in Germany, explains that the UNPA "is envisaged as a first practical step towards the long-term goal of a world parliament," but it would not even be elected in the first phase of its existence. Members from various national parliaments would be chosen, by whatever means each country saw fit, to sit together at the UN for a few weeks a year. It is the feeblest of symbolic gestures, and you wonder why they even bother.

European enthusiasts point out that, when the European Parliament was first set up in 1958, its members were chosen by the national parliaments of member states, and it had little control over the decisions of the European Union. As at the UN, decisions remained in the hands of national governments and of the international institutions that they directly controlled. But in 1979, they started electing members of the European Parliament directly, which gave it real democratic legitimacy and, little by little, it has gained some degree of control over what happens in Brussels.

It would take a very long time indeed for the same sort of evolution to occur at the UN level, where even the number of members each country gets would be the subject of fierce disputes. Would China really have as many members as the hundred smallest countries combined, which is what its population entitles it to? Would the United States settle for one-third as many members as India (assuming it agreed to be represented at all)? Obviously not, but what would be the right numbers?

At best, the supporters of the UNPA would have to work their way through all those problems and accept that, for the next twenty or fifty years, what they have created will be a debating chamber and nothing more. Is it worth all the effort for that damp squib of a result?

Yes, certainly. It would be open to individual countries to start electing their own members of the UNPA from the start, so that it had more democratic legitimacy. And although real power might take generations to arrive, from the very start a parliament of this sort would provide a very different perspective on the world—and a more realistic one—than the pious debates of the UN General Assembly and the hard-ball great-power politics of the UN Security Council. It would be very interesting at least, and maybe quite instructive.

So, tell Lord Tennyson to come back in another hundred years, and maybe we'll have something to show him.

32.

CRAWLING FROM THE WRECKAGE

My hope that we may be escaping from the miserable decade just past rests, to a worrisome extent, on the slim shoulders of Barack Obama. If he can change the way the United States behaves in the world, a great deal else will change for the better as well. So I wrote about him quite a lot during his first year in office, trying to figure out whether he was up to the challenges he faced. But I was well aware that he had already given one big hostage to fortune.

January 27, 2009
OBAMA'S VIETNAM?

You aren't really the U.S. president until you've ordered an air strike on somebody, so Barack Obama is certainly president now: two air strikes on Afghanistan in his first week in office. But now that he has been blooded, can we talk a little about this expanded war he's planning to fight in Afghanistan?

Does that sound harsh? Well, so is killing people, and all the more so because Obama must know that these remote-controlled Predator strikes usually kill not just the "bad guy," whoever he is, but also the entire family he has taken shelter with. They also annoy Pakistan, whose territory the United States violated in order to carry out the killings.

It's not a question of whether the intelligence on which the attacks were based was accurate (although sometimes it isn't). The question is: do these killings actually serve any useful purpose? And the same question applies to the entire U.S. war in Afghanistan.

President Obama may be planning to shut Guantanamo, but the broader concept of a "war on terror" is still alive and well in Washington. Most of the people he has appointed to run his defence and foreign policies believe in it, and there is no sign that he himself questions it. And yet, even fifteen years ago, the notion would have been treated with contempt in every military staff college in the country.

That generation of American officers learned two things from their miserable experience in Vietnam. One was that going halfway around the world to fight a conventional military campaign against an ideology (Communism then, Islamism now) was a truly stupid idea. The other was that no matter how strenuously the other side insists that it is motivated by a world-spanning ideology, its real motives are mostly political and quite local (Vietnamese nationalism then, Iraqi and Afghan nationalism now).

Alas, that generation of officers has now retired, and the new generation of strategists, civilian as well as military, has to learn these lessons all over again. They are proving to be slow students, and if Obama follows their advice Afghanistan may well prove to be his Vietnam.

The parallel with Vietnam is not all that far-fetched. Modest numbers of American troops have now been in Afghanistan for seven years, mostly in training roles quite similar to those of the U.S. military "advisers," whom Presidents Eisenhower and Kennedy sent to South Vietnam between 1956 and 1963. The political job of creating a pro-Western, anti-Communist state was entrusted to America's man in Saigon, Ngo Dinh Diem, and the South Vietnamese army had the job of fighting the Communist rebels, the Viet Cong.

Unfortunately, neither Diem nor the South Vietnamese army had much success, and by the early 1960s, the Viet Cong were clearly on the road to victory. So, Kennedy authorized a group of South Vietnamese generals to overthrow Diem (although he seemed shocked when they killed him). And Lyndon Johnson, who succeeded Kennedy soon afterwards, authorized a rapid expansion of the American troop commitment in Vietnam, first to two hundred thousand by the end of 1965, ultimately to half a million by 1968. The United States took over the war. And then it lost it.

If all this sounds eerily familiar, it's because we are now at a similar juncture in America's war in Afghanistan. Washington's man in Kabul, President Hamid Karzai, and the Afghan army he theoretically commands, have failed to quell the insurrection, and are visibly losing ground.

So, the talk in Washington now is all of replacing Karzai (although it will probably be done via elections, which are easily manipulated in Afghanistan), and the American troop commitment in the country is going up to sixty thousand. Various American allies also have troops in Afghanistan, just as they did in Vietnam, but it is the United States that is taking over the war.

We already know how this story ends. There is not a lot in common between President John F. Kennedy and President George W. Bush, but they were both ideological crusaders who got the United States mired in foreign wars it could not win *and did not need to win*. They then bequeathed those wars to presidents who had ambitious reform agendas in domestic politics and little interest or experience in foreign affairs.

That bequest destroyed Lyndon Johnson, who took the rotten advice of the military and civilian advisers he inherited from Kennedy because there wasn't much else on offer in Washington at the time. He still had time to get Medicare and Medicaid, the Voting Rights Act and the Civil Rights Act, federal aid to schools, and Head Start and food stamps through Congress before Vietnam brought him down, but he could have accomplished much more if he had not been brought down by the stupid war.

Obama is drifting into the same dangerous waters, and the rotten advice he is getting from strategists who believe in the war on terror could destroy him, too. He has figured out that Iraq was a foolish and unnecessary war, but he has not yet applied the same analysis to Afghanistan.

There are two questions he needs to ask himself. First, did Osama bin Laden want the U.S. to invade Afghanistan in response to 9/11? The answer to that one is: yes, of course he did. Second: of the tens of thousands of people whom the United States has killed in Afghanistan and Iraq, would a single one of them have turned up in America to do harm if left unkilled? Answer: probably not. *Other* people might have turned up in the U.S. with evil intent, but not those guys.

So, turning Afghanistan into a second Vietnam is probably the wrong strategy, isn't it?

I had particularly high hopes of Obama on the climate front, and the appointments he made to the key science and energy jobs in his administration confirmed my feeling. I never actually drew up a short list of the ideal five people to put in those posts, but he chose exactly the people I would have put there. I know what those people think because I have interviewed most of them. If he chose them, then he presumably agreed with them. So he really does get it.

But if he gets it, why hasn't he acted on it?

November 12, 2009
OBAMA AND CLIMATE

It is taking much longer than the Obama administration thought to get legislation on climate change through Congress. Even if the health-care legislation finally passes in a form that more or less fulfills Obama's hopes for it, that will mean that he only got two major pieces of new legislation out of the Congress in 2009. (The other was the $787 billion stimulus package to fight the recession.)

Congress will not pass legislation imposing cuts on greenhouse-gas emissions in the United States this year, so Obama goes to Beijing empty-handed. The Chinese will not deliver on their part of the deal until they are sure that Obama can deliver on his part. So the world's two largest emitters will arrive in Copenhagen next month without having made any official commitment to curb their emissions.

With no bilateral U.S.-Chinese deal to serve as a framework for a wider agreement, the Copenhagen conference is very unlikely to succeed. How upset should we be about that?

If failure this December means permanent failure, then we should be very upset indeed, but the problem is one of scheduling, not of bad intentions. Given another six months or so, Obama will probably succeed in getting Congress to agree to significant cuts in U.S. greenhouse-gas emissions.

The cuts will not be as deep as he wants: only a 4 percent reduction in U.S. greenhouse gas emissions by 2020 compared to the 1990 baseline used in the Kyoto treaty. They are certainly not as much as the other developed nations are willing to make: the European Union countries are committed to 20 percent cuts in emissions by 2020, and the Japanese to even more. But everybody understands that Obama is dealing with an electorate largely still in denial about global warming, and that as a matter of practical politics he simply cannot make the same kind of commitments others have made. They will be glad if he can just sign the U.S. up to the principle of cutting its emissions.

In particular, the Chinese will be very grateful if he does that, because they are very frightened about the probable impacts of climate change on their own country. They badly want a global deal that keeps warming under control, but it is politically impossible for them to make any kind of firm commitment so long as the United States had made none.

The best thing to do now, therefore, would be to postpone the Copenhagen meeting for a year, but it has become a diplomatic juggernaut that cannot be stopped. The next-best thing is to ensure that it fails now, leaving the way open for a follow-on conference that revisits the issue in twelve or eighteen months' time with a much better chance of success.

The best is often the enemy of the good, but patching together an inadequate climate treaty at Copenhagen just to avoid the stigma of failure would repeat the mistake of 1997, when the botched Kyoto accord locked the world into an unambitious climate policy for fifteen years. If the problem lies mainly in the political timetable in the United States—and it does—then just change the international schedule to deal with that reality.

In the end, Obama's health-care bill didn't make it through Congress until March 2010, and it's still unclear when or even if his (very unambitious) climate change bill will be passed.

But I begin to hope that he might actually be learning about Afghanistan.

December 1, 2009
OBAMA: IN SEARCH OF A "DECENT INTERVAL"?

It can't have taken three months to write the speech that President Barack Obama gave at West Point on Tuesday, but clearly much thought went into his decision to send thirty thousand more American troops to Afghanistan. Some aspects of his strategy even suggest that he understands how little is really at stake there for the United States.

This is despite the fact that his speech is full of assertions that al-Qaeda needs Afghanistan as a base. That is a fundamental misunderstanding of the nature of terrorist operations but it permeates American thinking on the subject. Even if Obama knows better himself, he cannot hope to disabuse his fellow Americans of that delusion in the time available.

Instead, he goes along with it, even saying that Afghanistan and Pakistan are "the epicenter of the violent extremism practiced by al-Qaeda . . . Since 9/11, al-Qaeda's safe-havens have been the source of attacks against London and Amman and Bali." This is utter nonsense, but, even if he knows it is nonsense, he cannot say so publicly.

Al-Qaeda doesn't run training camps anymore; it leaves that to the various local groups that spring up and try to follow its example both in the Muslim world and in the West. The template for Islamist terrorism is now available everywhere, so al-Qaeda no longer needs a specific territorial base. For the purpose of planning actual terrorist attacks, it never did.

The operational planning for the 9/11 attacks was done in Germany and the United States. The London attacks were planned in Yorkshire, the Amman attack probably in Syria, and the Bali attacks in Jakarta.

If the Taliban conquered all of Afghanistan and then invited al-Qaeda to set up camps there—neither of which is a necessary consequence of an American withdrawal—what additional advantages would al-Qaeda enjoy? Well, it could then fly its people in and out through Kabul in addition to using Karachi and Lahore, but they'd face even stiffer security checks at the far end of the flight. It hardly seems worth it.

The leaders of al-Qaeda would certainly like to see the Taliban regain power in Kabul, since it was al-Qaeda's attacks on the United States—specifically intended to provoke a U.S. invasion of Afghanistan—that brought the Taliban regime down in the first place. But al-Qaeda takes no part in the Taliban's war in Afghanistan: it is strictly an Afghan operation.

Even if Obama does not believe the Washington orthodoxy, which insists that who controls Afghanistan is a question of great importance to American security, his short-term strategy must respect that orthodoxy. Hence the "surge." But the speed with which that surge is to be followed by an American withdrawal suggests that he may know better.

July 2011 is not a long time away: all the Taliban leaders have to do is wait eighteen months and then collect their winnings. If they are intelligent and pragmatic men—which they are—they may even let the foreign forces make some apparent progress in the meantime, so that the security situation looks promising when the time comes to start pulling the U.S. troops out.

In fact, the Taliban might not even try to collect their winnings right away after the foreigners leave. There's no point in risking a backlash in the United States that might bring the American troops back.

This is actually how the Vietnam War ended. The United States went through a major exercise in "Vietnamization" in the early 1970s, and the last American combat troops left South Vietnam in 1973. At that point, the security situation in the south seemed fairly good—and the North Vietnamese politely waited until 1975 to collect their winnings.

In doing so, they granted Henry Kissinger, national security adviser to President Richard Nixon, the "decent interval" he had requested. A "decent interval," that is, between the departure of the American troops and the victory of the forces that they had been fighting, so that it did not look too much like an American defeat. In practical political terms, that is also the best outcome that Barack Obama can now hope for in Afghanistan.

If that is Obama's real strategy, then he can take consolation in the fact that nothing bad happened to American interests after the North Vietnamese victory in 1975. Nothing bad is likely to happen to American interests in the event of a Taliban victory, either. Nor is a Taliban victory even a foregone conclusion after an American withdrawal, since they would still have to overcome all the other ethnic forces in the country.

The biggest risk Obama runs with this strategy is that it gives al-Qaeda a motive to launch new attacks against the United States. The Taliban want the American troops out of Afghanistan, but al-Qaeda wants them to be stuck there indefinitely, taking casualties and killing Muslims. It's unlikely that al-Qaeda can just order a terrorist attack in the United States, but if it looks like the U.S. troops are really going home, then it may well try.

On the other hand, maybe all this analysis is too clever by half. Maybe Obama just thinks he can win the war in Afghanistan in the next eighteen months. In that case, his presidency is doomed.

Maybe I'm just grasping at straws but he certainly seems to be more intelligent than that.

INDEX

347

GWYNNE DYER has worked as a freelance journalist, columnist, broadcaster, filmmaker and lecturer on international affairs for more than twenty years but he was originally trained as an historian. Born in Newfoundland, he earned degrees from Canadian, American and British universities, finishing with a Ph.D. in Military and Middle Eastern History from the University of London. He went on to serve in three navies and to hold academic appointments at the Royal Military Academy Sandhurst and at Oxford University. Since 1973, he has written a twice-weekly column on current events that is published in more than 175 newspapers worldwide and translated into more than a dozen languages. Dyer is the author of the award-winning book *War* (1986), which was updated and reissued in 2004, *Ignorant Armies* (2003), *Future: Tense* (2004), *With Every Mistake* (2005) and *Climate Wars* (2008). He lives in London, England.